THE CONCRETE GOD

THE CONCRETE GOD

A New Beginning for Theology—
The Thought of Charles Hartshorne

by

Ralph E. James

THE BOBBS-MERRILL COMPANY, INC.
A Subsidiary of Howard W. Sams & Co., Inc.
*Publishers/*Indianapolis • Kansas City • New York

ACKNOWLEDGMENTS

The author wishes to thank the following publishers for permission to quote from the writings of Charles Hartshorne:

Beacon Press (Boston, Mass.)—*Whitehead and the Modern World* (Also by Victor Lowe and A. H. Johnson)
Harper & Row, Publishers, Inc. (New York, New York)—*Beyond Humanism* and *Man's Vision of God*
The Open Court Publishing Company (La Salle, Ill.)—*The Logic of Perfection* and *Anselm's Discovery*
The Philosophical Library (New York, New York)—From "Panentheism" in *An Encyclopedia of Religion*. ed. by Vergilius Ferm
The University of Chicago Press (Chicago, Ill.)—*The Philosophy and Psychology of Sensation* and *Philosophers Speak of God* (With William L. Reese)
Yale University Press (New Haven, Conn.)—*The Divine Relativity*
The Macmillan Company (New York, New York)—*Reality as Social Process*

To
Mary Lou,
Bradford,
Randall

Preface

The purpose of this book is to explore and to illuminate the philosophical and theological *method* of the American philosopher Charles Hartshorne (1897-   ). Hartshorne's method, consistently maintained in his work, is intelligible only if it is understood in a particular formulation. Further, he uses the *same* method in philosophy and theology with such regularity that implications, especially for Christian theology, can be readily drawn. In a larger perspective this method may well equip twentieth-century man with a fresh way to cope with the problem of the triumph of immanence over transcendence and subjectivity over objectivity.

Growing interest in Hartshorne's work dictates that serious study of his thought is in order. The present book certainly does not claim to be exhaustive. An important modern thinker of Hartshorne's stature deserves study from many perspectives, not just in terms of method. A study of Hartshorne's method, however, is especially needed because method is basic to any philosophical or theological program.

Hartshorne himself has been the chief inspiration for this book, the seeds of which were sown while I was his student at Emory University (1959-1961). Although the manuscript has undergone much subsequent revision, I should also state my indebtedness to my teacher, the late Carl Michalson of Drew University, who very carefully read and criticized the manuscript when it was in its dissertation stage. It was at Professor Michalson's insistence that the manuscript was submitted for publication. For various reasons my thanks are also due to Professors John D. Godsey, John F. Ollom, and Will Herberg of Drew. Also to Edwin Wilson of Wake Forest College, Theodore Runyon and William Mallard of Emory University, Ray Hart of Vanderbilt University, and John Dillenberger of the San Francisco Theological Union. Many helpful suggestions have also come from Thomas W. Ogletree of the Chicago Theological Seminary and Dr. Bradford Dunham, formerly of Duke University and now with I.B.M. Dr. Dunham, a symbolic logician, has been helpful not only in my struggling attempts to follow Hartshorne's use of formal logic, but as a long-time source of encouragement. I am also deeply grateful to Mrs. Charles Hartshorne for generously giving her time to a careful reading of the entire work in advanced form and offering many invaluable suggestions. Among my present colleagues at N. C. Wesleyan College special thanks are due to President Thomas A. Collins, Dean Jack W. Moore, Philip L. Elliott, Allen S. Johnson, and Fran and Mike Danoff, all of whom read parts of the manuscript. I must also mention the patient help of my good neighbor, Daisy Thorp. It is, of course, my wife, Mary Lou, who deserves greatest thanks for her devoted help. It is to her and my two sons that this book is dedicated.

I wish to thank the Knapp Fund for generous assistance with expenses incurred during the preparation of the manuscript. Also Mrs. Sylvia Parker, who typed the manuscript. Any young author is blessed if he can add the name of a first-rate editor to his appreciations. I have had just such good fortune with my editor, Lawrence Grow of the Bobbs-Merrill Company.

RALPH JAMES
March 15, 1967   Rocky Mount, N.C.

Contents

Abbreviations of
Titles of Charles Hartshorne's Books

AD   *Anselm's Discovery*. LaSalle, Ill.: Open Court Publishing Co., 1965, pp. 333.

BH   *Beyond Humanism: Essays in the New Philosophy of Nature*. Chicago: Willett, Clark & Company, 1937, pp. 324.

DR   *The Divine Relativity: A Social Conception of God*. The Terry Lectures, 1947. New Haven: Yale University Press, 1948, pp. 164.

LP   *The Logic of Perfection and Other Essays in Neoclassical Metaphysics*. LaSalle, Ill.: Open Court Publishing Co., 1962, pp. 335.

MVG   *Man's Vision of God and the Logic of Theism*. Chicago: Willett, Clark & Company, 1941, pp. 360. (After 1948 published by Harper & Brothers Publishers, New York.)

PPS   *The Philosophy and Psychology of Sensation*. Chicago: The University of Chicago Press, 1934, pp. 288.

PSG   *Philosophers Speak of God*. (With William L. Reese) Chicago: The University of Chicago Press, 1953, pp. 535.

RSP   *Reality as Social Process: Studies in Metaphysics and Reli-*

gion. Glencoe: The Free Press and Boston: The Beacon Press, 1953, pp. 223.

WMW   *Whitehead and the Modern World: Science, Metaphysics, and Civilization, Three Essays on the Thought of Alfred North Whitehead.* By Victor Lowe, Charles Hartshorne, A. H. Johnson. "Whitehead's Metaphysics" by Charles Hartshorne, pp. 25-41. Boston: The Beacon Press, 1950.

Introduction

There is a crisis in Western theology. Recent theological movements such as ecumenicity, secularization, and the death of God are not the cause of this crisis; they are symptoms of it. These theological efforts have actually prolonged the life of an orthodoxy that is itself the problem. Remodeling Western theology is not enough, because the problem is in the very structure of the building. We must now explore the structure of the concepts of God, of Jesus Christ, of Church. If these concepts are failing—and many believe they are—they must be reexamined with urgency, because these concepts undergird many of our basic institutions. A way of life, a civilization, is at stake in the examination of its theoretical base.

The theology of the death of God provides an unusually good way to illuminate this theological crisis because it is a response to the "core problem." The God who has failed is the abstract, unchanging Being of classical theology. Classical theologians always worshiped more than a merely abstract immutability, but they failed to show how the unchanging God could live in changing history. It is no accident that the theology of the death of God is an affirmation of history's life because it witnesses to God's death. Is it any wonder that men feel free because of the death of an unchanging being whose very immutability rendered freedom impossible?

The abstract God, the unchanging, eternal being of classical thought, is dead. Theology, dressed in black, is moving sadly away from God's grave toward a new horizon in the space age. Space-age man cannot live with an empty abstraction; so, acknowledging

God's death, he has begun the search anew. Groping in the darkness of modern relativism, he is now forced to feel his way through the stars with shaken confidence. Writing about the concrete God in the time of an abstract God's death is not easy, because there is no assurance that new shapes and forms *can* be satisfactory. It may be that the concrete God will turn out to be as implausible as His abstract predecessor.

In *The Brothers Karamazov* Dostoevski's Grand Inquisitor is questioning Jesus, who has appeared amid the flames of the heretics being burned in His name. The Inquisitor says to Jesus, ". . . You have no right to add anything to what you have already said in the days of old. Why, then, did you come to meddle with us?"[1] In this one, poignant question Dostoevski portrays the problem that seems to result from the presupposition that God is immutable. The immutability of God precludes relatedness to the mutability of history. God cannot escape His own static being expressed as that to which ". . . You have no right to add." The theological ground for unethical human activity is firmly encased in the Inquisitor's frozen metaphysical concept. His mind about God is made up; he is not to be confused by anything inconsistent with his presuppositions; he is using this concept as a basis for burning people. The abstract God readily supports an unchanging, static world-view. Conservative men cling to the abstract God not only because they need Him emotionally but because He provides an excellent basis upon which to oppose social change when the status quo is advantageous to their selfish ends. It is just this kind of problem, the abstract, frozen, static immutability of metaphysical and theological concepts, to which this book is addressed.

One of the realities that are influencing a sense of the loss of the abstract God is the unfolding drama of the space age. The space age is increasing awareness of man's "place" in the universe. A "cosmic consciousness" of the earth as a tiny dot in the universe is appearing. There are stars too large to pass between the earth and the sun, a

[1] Fyodor Dostoevski, *The Brothers Karamazov*, trans. and introduced by David Magarshack (Baltimore: Penguin Books, 1958), I. p. 293.

distance of ninety-three million miles. Betelgeuse, for example, is reported to have a diameter of approximately two hundred million miles. Man is discovering himself as a creature of the Milky Way, a galaxy containing millions of stars and probably thousands of planets with high probabilities for life. It would be a miracle if there were not other civilizations, even more developed ones. Estimates of the number of galaxies is climbing with each breakthrough in astronomical observation. Sir Bernard Lovell of the Jodrell Bank Observatory in England has estimated that within the 22nd–23rd magnitude of the largest telescope must be a million trillion galaxies!

The desk before me seems at rest physically. Actually, it is moving at blinding speeds in at least four ways: (1) the earth is rotating; (2) the earth is moving in orbit around the sun; (3) the sun is "orbiting" through its cycle around the core of the Milky Way (one sun year being 225 million earth years); and finally (4) the Milky Way is apparently moving through space as part of an over-all expansion in the universe. Strangely enough, in order to say that the desk is moving I do need some kind of abstract measure such as "at rest." In terms of size this can be illustrated by thinking how we could know if everything in the universe were suddenly to become one thousand times larger. Would not such concrete change be detectable only by comparing it with that which concretely did not change: could it be that knowledge is impossible without both concrete reality and abstraction? Knowledge of motion seems to suggest that we come up with some doctrine of the abstract in relation to the concrete, but not that outworn abstractions be maintained. The most valuable single contribution of space science may be the sense of concrete relativity it gives to the *abstract* absolutes of religion, race, and nation on earth.

Theology enters the whirl of the space age on shaky legs. Already the rise of the power of reason has battered the once sacrosanct walls of theological constructions, even from within. The development of technology has displaced many of the traditional functions of Deity. When the simple believer lived on the farm, he needed God's blessings for good crop weather, but when he moved to what Harvey Cox calls "technopolis" and began work in a factory, he became a casual observer of the weather. To the extent that God was to the simple believer the God of weather, he therefore became a casual observer of God. Urban man has abandoned his rural gods because he no longer feels a need for them. Theology can no longer count upon the foundation of a rural Olympus; it must now take its chances in the rush of the city where only merit, not ancient authority, can be counted upon.

Urbanization fragmented rural faith, but now there are signs that space-age theology may outlive urban fragmentation. Marshall McLuhan vividly describes the transcendence of fragmentation through electronics in his *Understanding Media*.[2] If McLuhan is correct, if modern life is "imploding" back into coherent unity through extended media, theology based upon abstractions (such as written and perhaps even spoken words) is finished. Abstraction itself and the fragmentation it supports may be disappearing into concrete unity. Television may after all be the greatest enemy of every nationalism, racism, and sectarianism. Television may be demonstrating the sham, not only of rural superstitions but of urban sophistications, of the abstract gods of the city. By the time the "Christian" faith comes to terms with the "secular city," both abstractions (Christianity and the city) may have evaporated.

Charles Hartshorne is one of the significant modern thinkers especially worthy of study in this theological and cultural crisis. Educated at Haverford College, Harvard, Freiburg and Marburg universities, he has taught at Harvard (1925-28), The University of Chicago (1928-55), Emory University (1955-62) and The University of Texas, 1962 till the present. He has also been visiting associate professor at Stanford University, 1937; New School for Social Research, 1941-42; visiting professor at Johann Wolfgang Goethe University, Frankfurt, 1948-49; University of Washington, 1958; Terry Lecturer, Yale University, 1947; Fulbright Lecturer, Melbourne, 1952; and Kyoto, Japan in 1958 and 1966.

The present book obviously cannot treat all of Hartshorne's writings. Its strategy will therefore be to organize Hartshorne's work around the one problem of the abstract God and Hartshorne's concrete solution. This does not eliminate consideration of his philosophical work, since it is crucial to an understanding of

---

[2] Marshall McLuhan, *Understanding Media* (New York: McGraw Hill Book Co., 1964).

Hartshorne's concrete God. In fact, Hartshorne's dialogues with major philosophers and philosophies illuminate his understanding of "concrete." This approach is designed to do more than simply state Hartshorne's philosophy: it aims at "engaging" major movements in contemporary thought in active philosophical discussion. Part I of this book views Hartshorne at work in his philosophical workshop; Part II sees him in his theological workshop.

A wide cross section of Hartshorne's writings has been treated in the hope that claims about his method will not seem forced upon him. To this end I have usually reserved critical judgment in the fond hope for "more objectivity." Any claim for a completely unbiased presentation is of course suspect. It is no accident that this is a sympathetic study; I am persuaded that Hartshorne's process thought is the most promising philosophical and theological work in the twentieth century. For the time being I am willing to associate myself with Hartshorne's *process* thought in a general sense with one particular reservation; namely, I am not sure how long it will remain practical to use theological language to describe the reality in which we stand. My own confidence in theological language has been profoundly shaken by a growing cosmic consciousness in the space age. Whether theological language remains practical will not greatly affect Hartshorne's relevance, however; his description of the world is worthy of consideration in purely philosophical terms.

There are three nominative questions that should be asked of any theological system: (1) Can it *really embrace the universe* with all its relativities, contingencies and changes, with all its real needs for unity and diversity? (2) Can it account for the logical situation that knowledge of the relative, the contingent, the changing, and the diverse seems to require *some kind of necessity* that is noncontingent? (3) Finally, can it show how the contingency of the world *is related to* logical necessity without effectively destroying either? I am persuaded that classical theology failed to answer adequately (1) and (3). Modern theology has failed (2) and (3). Classical theology could not account for contingency, change, etc. Modern theology has not been able to escape relativism, or, conversely, has failed to come up with an adequate understanding of necessity. Hartshorne has finally been able to achieve an adequate theology according to these criteria because he can account for the changing world, for necessity, and he can relate them without destroying either.

Because one of the criteria of adequate theology is logical necessity, I have certain misgivings about labeling either my own position or Hartshorne's "process theology." There is no contradiction between process and logical necessity; it is process that is logically necessary, but the reality of necessity means that process is not the whole story. Failure to note this, even by professional philosophers, may be a major reason why process thought is only now achieving the prominence it deserves. Hartshorne often calls himself a neoclassicist. This term, however, has the disadvantage of suggesting necessity at the expense of contingency and change. Perhaps some new term is required to describe the position. "Process-neo-classicist" would capture both dimensions but in an awkward manner. If a label would be helpful, and I am not sure it would, I would venture to call my own position "neo-process" thought. I intentionally avoid saying whether my position is philosophical or theological because "neo-process" thought would apply the three criteria of adequacy without regard to the old distinction between philosophy and theology. This distinction seems less and less convincing in the electronic age.

In analysis of the problem of the abstract in theology, Hartshorne is well aware that rejection of the abstract God has a long history. In his address at Athens, Paul declared, "The God who made the world and everything in it, being Lord of heaven and earth, does not live in shrines made by man, nor is he served by human hands, as though he needed anything, since he himself gives to all men life and breath and everything" (Acts 17:24-25 RSV). Paul was telling the Athenians that *their* understanding of God was a misunderstanding. Speaking from the basis of *his* faith in Christ, Paul was proclaiming the death of this Athenian God. In this sense Paul was one of the first Christian atheists. Standing in Christ he believed himself liberated from the "unknown" God of the Athenians; hence, he witnessed to his freedom from the unknown God *because* he believed he was freed by Jesus Christ. Paul's declaration of the death of the "unknown" God should be understood as a logical expression of his faith. The proclamation of the death of God by contemporary theologians Thomas J. J. Altizer and William Hamilton must first of all be seen in the light of Paul's faith. It is faith in the liberating power of Jesus that leads Altizer to witness to the death of the "mysterious" transcendental God. It is faith in Jesus that inspires Hamilton to ask for acknowledgment of the experience of the death of God in order to become "a Christ to your neighbor."[3] With varying degrees of emphasis, contemporary theologians are Christian atheists for the same reason Paul was. That is, they are able to say No to the "unknown" God *because they are Christian*. They stand in Christ.

The death of God always refers to a particular God. Paul was referring to the God of the Athenians. Friedrich Nietzsche, who proclaimed the death of God in the nineteenth century, was referring to the God of Christendom. Nietzsche felt the equalitarian nature of the God of the Church to be an enemy of the development of excellence, the excellence of "the higher men," the supermen. One must distinguish, however, between the God of Christendom or the Church and the moving Spirit of Christ. This distinction becomes especially important in the work of Altizer.

An underlying reason for Altizer's confession of the death of God is the notion that God is unchanging. When the Church appropriated from Greek philosophy the classical notions of God's unchanging nature, bare eternality, and lofty noninvolvement with the world, the stage was set for theological difficulty. If God is merely a static, unchanging, transcendental being, how could He relate to the world? It is just *this* God who could not be "in" the dynamics of history; hence, the death of *this* God. In Altizer's view this God's death can be declared only by Christians: " 'God is dead' are words that may only truly be spoken by the Christian, not by the religious Christian who is bound to an eternal and unmoving Word, but by the radical Christian who speaks in re-

[3] William Hamilton and Thomas J. J. Altizer, *Radical Theology and the Death of God* (New York and Indianapolis: The Bobbs-Merrill Company, 1966), p. 50.

sponse to an Incarnate Word that empties itself of Spirit so as to appear and exist as flesh."[4] Entering the flesh means that the death-of-God theology may be understod as *an attempt to bring God and the world together,* to solve the problem of noninvolvement.

In *The Secular Meaning of the Gospel,* Paul van Buren emphasizes the way in which the Incarnation "expresses the believer's deep concern with history, the world of men, and the world which man investigates, it indicates that his attitude toward men and their activities is related to his particular piece of history."[5] Christians have wished to understand the Incarnation as God actually coming into the history of the world. This was clear in Augustine's opposition to the Docetic heresy, which would have reduced Jesus to bare physical *appearance,* a nonhistorical being. The point that makes the death-of-God theology radical, as in Altizer's case, is the attempt to take the Incarnation *literally.* Saying God actually died when He came into the world swings the pendulum completely away from Docetism. Altizer's theology produces a radical doctrine of the Incarnation *because* it takes the Incarnation seriously. Not only did God actually come into the world, in this theology; He remains here as the "incarnate Word." The unchanging God is dead: the living Word is a Word of expression in the world, even if God remains somehow hidden there. The hidden God is similar to Hamilton's suggestion that "Jesus may be concealed in the world, in the neighbor, in this struggle for justice, in that struggle for beauty, clarity, order."[6]

Hamilton's mention of "this struggle for justice" underscores the ethical dimension of the death-of-God theology. Man is no longer a slave to the unknown God; he is now free to work for the known. There is obedience in this world, not to a transcendental, unchanging God, but to Christ. In Hamilton's words, ". . . we even dare to call men into the worldly arena where men are in need and where Jesus is to be found and served."[7] This seems to have implications for Church life. Namely, it calls the Christian away from

[4] *Ibid.,* p. 154.
[5] Paul van Buren, *The Secular Meaning of the Gospel* (New York: The Macmillan Co., 1963), p. 160.
[6] Hamilton, *op. cit.,* p. 49.
[7] *Ibid.,* p. 50.

his altars into the streets and byways where men are in need. Service has always played some role in Christian life; now it is made directly worldly or secular (cf. Harvey Cox, *The Secular City*). Concern for personal salvation gives way to ethical life *in this world*. Hamilton stands in the tradition of Walter Rauschenbusch, who said, "The Christian Church in the past has taught us to do our work with our eyes fixed on another world and a life to come. But the business before us is concerned with refashioning this present world. . . ."[8]

If ethical movement from otherworldliness to world seems to put religion aside, this may well be intended. Hamilton cites Dietrich Bonhoeffer's "religionless Christianity" in a "world come of age," where Christian man may cease to be religious man. To grasp this idea we need only think of the space-age mind as one that may no longer be convinced by *any* of the institutions of the earth. Religion is being relativized by our dawning consciousness of the earth as *one* of the places of existence in the universe. Being religious, to the extent that this means the systematic practice of man's ancient religious traditions, may become less central as the history of man becomes one of many universal "histories." Even the ecumenical movement may not be "in time" to save present religious cultural patterns.

Hartshorne's work is a path worth exploring in the time of "the death of God" precisely because Hartshorne and death-of-God theologians have addressed the same problem. The problem is *how to relate the abstractness of an unchanging God to the concreteness of a changing world.*

The particular relevance of Hartshorne's process theology to Altizer's understanding of the death of God is clarified when Altizer's assertion is understood as a metaphysical assertion about God. This is an ironical claim because Altizer stands in a long tradition of existential distaste for metaphysics as the science of first principles, principles that state what is universally real. Disenchantment with this kind of metaphysics is partly a result of the

[8] Walter Rauschenbusch, *Christianizing the Social Order* (New York: The Macmillan Co., 1962), pp. 40-44.

identification of metaphysics with Hegelian metaphysics, and reaction to *this* kind of metaphysics might well be called the "Kierkegaardian syndrome." Søren Kierkegaard was reacting to Hegel's "objectivity" by insisting that "truth is subjectivity."[9] The difficulty is that even Kierkegaard maintained to the end that God was unchangeable—the key characteristic of abstract objectivity. One of his last discourses, written in 1851, is entitled, "The Unchangeableness of God."[10]

Following Alfred North Whitehead, Hartshorne uses the term "metaphysics" in a different sense from Hegel or Kierkegaard, a sense indicated by his understanding of reality as social process, as becoming. From Hartshorne's perspective Altizer's doctrine of God is metaphysical because it is a *description* of an actual occurrence—God's death. Speaking of God's death means speaking of the nature of God. This does not mean that Altizer is speaking about the death of a concept; it means that the reality toward which Altizer's statement of reality is pointed, in his view, is an actual happening. Describing what happens is the task of the metaphysician, and this understanding of metaphysics acknowledges the problem of abstract principles that troubled Kierkegaard. It is unfortunate that Kierkegaard and his followers have rejected metaphysical language out of hand, because it blinds them to Hartshorne's very different kind of metaphysics. Like their brothers, the early logical positivists, existentialists have been dogmatic about the rejection of "metaphysical dogmas." The Hegelianism and neo-Hegelianism against which they have thrown their poison darts have long been dead—yet they continue to attack the corpse. Oddly enough, the relevance of Hartshorne will hardly be seen until Hegel's funeral is really over.

Is not the celebration of God's death remarkably similar to escape from abstract metaphysics? If it is true, as Hartshorne believes, that all reality stands together in a dynamic whole, would not structures restricting such a whole be opposed? Metaphysical

[9] See Kierkegaard, *Concluding Unscientific Postscript to the "Philosophical Fragments,"* trans. David F. Swenson; completed and edited by Walter Lowrie (Princeton: Princeton University Press, 1941).

[10] See Kierkegaard, *For Self-Examination and Judge for Yourselves!* (and *Three Discourses,* 1851), trans. by Walter Lowrie, except the final discourse, "God's Unchangeableness," trans. David F. Swenson. (Princeton: Princeton University Press, 1944).

language as abstract language surely had to die if life were to enjoy its freedom. Modern communications are joyful and dynamic because they do not force people into static containers. As McLuhan has seen, immediate participation is a cause for celebration that bypasses literary abstraction. Words in themselves are a form of abstract metaphysics.

So far, modern thinkers from Kierkegaard to Altizer have tended to solve the problem of abstraction by assuming an inherently negative stance. One of the reasons for Hartshorne's current relevance is his ability to present a constructive metaphysical program without falling into traditional abstraction. Though he may sound very abstract, very metaphysical in the old sense, he actually is embarked on a new enterprise. Hartshornian metaphysics describe the concrete with abstractions which are really abstractions; they are ontologically inferior to concrete togetherness. The world of immediate feeling in which men participate is described by metaphysics, but described in abstract words acknowledged as abstract. Hartshorne has helped to make metaphysics possible again for both philosophers and theologians because metaphysics is now understood as being abstract description of concrete reality.

In agreement with a large body of scholarly opinion, Altizer remarks that "the Christian idea of God is obviously a product of the fusion of the Bible with Greek ontology. . . ."[11] This fusion clothed the Christian God in Greek metaphysics; God became eternal, unchanging, little more than an abstract necessity standing above the turmoil of the world. Ever since, Christian thinkers have been trying to devise schemes to bring together such an abstraction and the concrete, changing world. These abstract concepts interfere with the Christian confession that God came into the world. Traditionally, solutions have ranged through the suggestions that (1) God only "appeared" to enter the world; (2) He paradoxically did and did not enter the world; (3) the world is God. The first assertion tends to deny the humanity of Christ and the reality of the world; the second creates a holy mystery; the third denies the transcendence of God. Altizer's theology of the death of God is intended to solve the problem of the Incarnation of God into the

[11] Thomas J. J. Altizer, "America and the Future of Theology," in Hamilton and Altizer, *Radical Theology and the Death of God,* p. 12.

world by saying that God died when He became incarnate. This is similar to the third solution, the pantheistic one, because to Altizer, as to Hegel, the Spirit is that which is working itself out in the world; but there is an important difference. To the pantheist the reality of God is usually a present reality, but to Altizer it is both a present, or "realized," reality and a future hope (eschatological). Altizer is more of a Hegelian than a pantheist in that his theology is above all designed to take the Incarnation of the Spirit with radical seriousness. A God or Spirit conceived in a way that would make incarnation impossible would be precisely the abstract God of Greek metaphysics. How could an unchanging God change in order to enter the world? Would He not be frozen in His own abstract definition? Altizer sees this problem when he remarks, "To the extent that faith or vision knows an eternal and unmoving sacred it can never know the reality of the Incarnation."[12] Hence, the God who is dead in Altizer's theology is the abstract God.

To be abstract is to be empty, withdrawn from everyday life, indeterminate, but above all to be *changeless*. The polar opposite of abstract is therefore full immersion in everyday life, namely, the concrete. Unlike the abstract, the concrete abides with rich diversity, real particularity; above all, *the concrete is changing*. Since knowledge seems to depend upon contrast (How would black be recognizable as black without white?), abstract and concrete must always be somehow "together" if knowledge is possible, particularly in the everyday world. When I call my friend by his name, "William," the name itself is an unchanging abstraction that is the same throughout his life. This habit, at least implicitly, assumes a concrete person who is changing all the time. I am not joking when I say that my friend seems a little dead when he does not change, because living and changing go hand in hand. Nor is it a joke to note that failure to remember that people change is the root of much of the mistreatment of human beings in the world, because overclassification (an abstract tendency) restricts creative growth. Concretely, my friend William is changing all the time; abstractly, he remains the same; he is still "William." Metaphysics

[12] "The Sacred and the Profane," *Radical Theology and the Death of God,* p. 149.

which describe can recognize him without forcing him into a static abstract category.

In his own way Hegel was attempting to formulate a metaphysic of the concrete. In 1807 he published his now classical *Phenomenology of Mind* in which the concrete takes on a new spiritual significance as life of the *Geist*. Much has been made of the fact that *Geist* can be translated either "mind" or "spirit," but a new work on Hegel by J. Loewenberg, *Hegel's Phenomenology: Dialogues on the Life of Mind*,[13] has thrown fresh light on this difficult and important subject. Loewenberg combines the question of the relationship between spirit and mind with the terms of the present discussion:

> . . . mind becoming progressively conscious of itself as spirit— this in a word is the subject of Hegel's diagnostic inquiry. More specifically, the inquiry is into man's typical persuasions for the purpose of discovering their dialectical order and connection. Although all persuasions have their source in mind (and in what else than mind can they originate?), the series they exhibit is one which is marked by increasing growth in spirituality, a quality characteristic of the concrete universal. Varying in their objects, the persuasions so far examined, from sense-certainty on, fail to grasp and enunciate the particular focus of their awareness or aspiration, and thus find themselves in the end enmeshed in abstract universals. If the previous stages of mind presuppose or imply a concrete content from which they are abstractions, the stages subsumed under spirit reverse the process and move towards their ultimate and explicit concretion. Yes, the movement from abstraction to concretion is the move of the dialectic throughout the *Phenomenology*. Transition to spirit is simply transition to mind comprehending as internally related the aspects of mind that hitherto appeared as if separable. Let us agree then to speak of mind as the generic subject the *Phenomenology* purports to be the biography of, spirit being the name of mind's culminating phase.[14]

Loewenberg's description of the life of spirit can be compared with Altizer's view of Hegel; but first, what of Hegel's use of the

[13] J. Loewenberg, *Hegel's Phenomenology* (LaSalle, Ill.: Open Court Publishing Co., 1965).
[14] *Ibid.*, pp. 186-187.

term "concrete universal"? That concrete particulars are subjective existents was the basis of Kierkegaard's objection to the loss of the self in an objective universal. Could it be that Kierkegaard confused abstract and concrete universals so that it is the abstract universal and not the concrete universal that results in the loss of the self? Could it be that modern existentialism was founded upon a misreading of Hegel? At least, existentialists should now hear the story of the concrete universal in and beyond Hegel. The concrete universal was Hegel's way of *preserving* the self as a social being, and the ground of social being is the community of spirit that may be dialectically seen when one puts aside abstractions. This sounds strangely like the New Testament idea of a community of the spirit. Hegel even sees the concrete universal in terms reminiscent of a future kingdom of God: "If the stages of the mind presuppose or imply a concrete content from which they are abstractions, the stages subsumed under spirit reverse the process and move towards their ultimate and explicit concretion."

Second, in Hegel's *Phenomenology* movement toward the concrete is a *process*, a process of going beyond life in the abstract in order to realize participation in spirit. The manner in which this process moves, i.e., dialectically (thesis, antithesis, and synthesis), is not as important as the fact that spirit does move. Failure to see this has contributed to "absolutistic" interpretations of Hegel, not the least damaging of which has been the Marxist inversion of the dialectic into an abstract system of economics. Hegel turned philosophy toward the concrete, but it must be admitted that he failed to provide a satisfactory solution to the problem of what happens to absolute abstractions. Again, the classical absolute is the crux of the problem. Kierkegaard was right in thinking that Hegel had submerged the self (as have the Marxists), but it should be remembered that in the doctrine of the concrete universal the question of the abstract being of a self is ontologically secondary. Perhaps Kierkegaard was actually looking for an abstraction.

With these points in mind, compare a passage from Altizer's interpretation of Hegel.

> If Spirit truly empties itself in entering the world, then its own essential or original Being must be left behind in an empty and lifeless form. Now, Spirit can exist and be real

only in a kenotic or incarnate mode that is the very opposite
of its original Being. Hegel and the radical Christian would
teach us that finally Spirit is this eternal movement of absolute
self-negation. Apart from what Hegel called the process of
absolute negativity, there lies no way of apprehending the
ontological reality of the Incarnation, and unless the Incarnation is known as effecting an absolute negation of the primordial or essential Being of God, there can be no knowledge
that God *is* love. A Christian proclamation of the love of God
is a proclamation that God has negated himself in becoming
flesh, his Word is now the opposite or the intrinsic otherness of
his primordial Being, and God himself has ceased to exist in
his original mode as transcendent or disincarnate Spirit: God
is Jesus.[15]

What else is the essential, empty, primordial, lifeless form of
original being than the abstract God of classical metaphysics?
How else could an unchanging abstraction become actually incarnate in the world than by negating its abstract quality? Docetists
reject the Incarnation, and Altizer rejects God; both are quite
logical on the presuppositions of classical metaphysics. Hartshorne's metaphysics, on the other hand, provides a way to accept
both the Incarnation and God, since abstract presuppositions are
deleted.

Having noted Altizer's proper rejection of the abstract God,
with whom no one could live anyway, let us mention one criticism
of Altizer's proclamation of the concrete God. In saying "God *is*
Jesus" and in making this the basis for his "Christian atheism"
Altizer says that *only* through Christ can persons be freed from the
abstract God. Is this necessarily the case? Could we not imagine
that the experience of love in everyday life also frees us from the
abstract? In fact, is it not true that Altizer ends in a kind of "religious exclusivism" in a world in need of radical tolerance? Is
defense of the theology of the "death of God" leading Altizer away
from the more open position of his earlier book, *Oriental Mysticism
and Biblical Eschatology?*[16] If this trend continues in Altizer's

[15] Thomas J. J. Altizer, *The Gospel of Christian Atheism* (Philadelphia: Westminster Press, 1966), p. 69.
[16] Thomas J. J. Altizer, *Oriental Mysticism and Biblical Eschatology*
(Philadelphia: Westminster Press, 1961).

thought will it not end in what Hegel would have called an abstraction? By turning to Hartshorne's treatment of the problem on the abstract God, one finds a way to avoid both religious exclusivism and the negativity of the death of God. This does not mean Altizer's proclamation is entirely negative—he advances his own eschatological concreteness; it means that Hartshorne's analysis in terms of the classical problem, the unchanging God, provides a better way to focus a constructive alternative to the problem of the abstract God.

Huston Smith says, ". . . the conviction to which Professor Hartshorne has devoted his intellectual life—that metaphysics is philosophy's central concern—will before long again be widespread in the philosophical community."[17] If metaphysical language really is to be reborn, it surely must begin afresh with the concrete world beyond abstract fragmentariness. If philosophy is to speak to the crisis in theology caused by classical metaphysics, it must follow Hartshorne's lead in discovering new possibilities in neoclassical metaphysics which describe the concrete.

[17] "The Death and Rebirth of Metaphysics," *The Hartshorne Festschrift,* ed. Reese and Freeman (LaSalle, Ill.: Open Court Publishing Co., 1964), p. 47.

I
Toward the Concrete

1

Husserl and the Age of Time

Phenomenology and process philosophy are two products of the twentieth century's penchant for the temporal. Hartshorne's critique of Edmund Husserl proceeds, then, within the bounds of large areas of agreement about the nature of the philosophical quest. Within their general agreement that reality is temporal, one can discern, however, several differences which illuminate dimensions of the Hartshornian concrete.

ONE OF THE MEN who has helped to usher in "the age of time," the age in which we live, is the father of modern phenomenology, Edmund Husserl.[1] Charles Hartshorne studied with Husserl between 1923 and 1925, and his critique of Husserl illuminates several fundamental characteristics of the concrete. These are time, intuition, and sociality. It is too much to compare the whole of process philosophy with all phenomenology. Hartshorne's critique of Husserl is more manageable. Focusing upon limited topics does not mean, however, that the process and phenomenological positions in general are not clarified. On the contrary, Hartshorne's critique of Husserl engages two of the major philosophical movements in the twentieth century at three vital points.

To see why Hartshorne applauds the temporality of Husserl's philosophy one must look beyond the bounds of phenomenology.

[1] For a bibliography of Edmund Husserl's works and works on Husserl, see E. Paul Welch, *The Philosophy of Edmund Husserl: The Origin and Development of His Phenomenology* (New York: Columbia University Press, 1941).

Indeed, Hartshorne is thinking of Husserl as a modern figure because he illustrates the "age of time." Time is to modern philosophy as eternal being was to the classical age and the eternal God was to medieval man. Unlike Thomas Aquinas or even a modern rationalist like René Descartes, Husserl explains the nature of human consciousness without use of God as a guarantee that knowledge of the world is real. To Husserl time was to be found in human consciousness "where the action is"; not as a mysterious gift from a benevolent or provincial Deity. One of the steps Jean-Paul Sartre *did not* have to take to develop his atheism within his teacher Husserl's phenomenology was to reject Husserl's God; Husserl had already ignored God. Sartre grounds his atheism in man's freedom as a temporal being,[2] and Husserl had already directed attention to a human consciousness in the realm of man's time, implicitly free from an abstract, eternal God.

If Husserl's approach to time is not theological, is it historical? The answer depends upon what one means by historical. Hegel's phenomenology was expressly a "historical" movement of the absolute *Geist* (Spirit or Mind). Temporal events were real because of their participation in the dialectical movement of the *Geist*. The absolute *Geist* included all particulars in its "objective march." But Hegel's objective idealism was a very different phenomenology of history from Husserl's. Husserl could not look to historical time in Hegel's "objective" sense, because this kind of history did not give sufficient consideration to the inward subjectivity of the self. A self participating in an objective *Geist* might "adopt" the historicity about him, but would it be his *own* time? Husserl turns to history, but history in the subjective, internal consciousness.

Husserl represents the non-Hegelian view that man does not live in time; rather time lives in him, time happens when he happens, time is a happening. Thinking of time as a happening is quite different from thinking of something as happening in time. Nevertheless, when one considers the essential, formal,

---

[2] Most basically Sartre's view of temporal freedom means "freedom to change," which is concrete freedom. *See* Sartre, *Being and Nothingness* (New York: Philosophical Library, 1956), p. 506. Also *see* William A. Luijpen, *Phenomenology and Atheism*, Duquesne Studies Philosophical Series, 17 (Pittsburgh: Duquesne University Press, 1964).

logical, and necessary core of Husserl's phenomenology, it is justifiable to ask why Husserl appears at all in a discussion of movement toward the temporal concrete.

Husserl was certainly not the first to reject outward time. His intellectual forebears Søren Kierkegaard and Franz Brentano had done considerable damage to "objective metaphysics." It was Kierkegaard who ushered in modern man's passion for the existential self, but Kierkegaard's "self" was a "self-before-God." Because Kierkegaard's existentialism was "theological existentialism," time was still theologically conceived. Abstract presuppositions had been more effectively challenged by Brentano when he described the uniqueness of inner perception: "Inner perception is not merely unique as perception; it is really unique as perception *(Wahrnehmung)* in the strict sense of the word. . . . The phenomena of so-called outer perception can in no way be demonstrated to be true and real, even by means of indirect reasoning."[3] The concreteness of Brentano's inward temporality is attested by Roderick Chisholm, who remarks, "Brentano repudiated all attempts to show that there *is* anything other than concrete individual things. . . ."[4] Brentano's inward reality and Kierkegaard's existential reaction to Hegelian objectivity prefigure the subjectivity of phenomenological time in Husserl.

To Husserl, as to Kierkegaard and Brentano before him, there were metaphysical reasons for describing reality subjectively. Chief among these was a burning desire to avoid abstract presuppositions. Husserl wanted to know reality in the mode of concrete immediacy, not "in" an objective reality outside consciousness. Bracketing out abstract otherness meant developing a rigorous method not unlike the method of Descartes. Descartes had sought certainty in the concrete self by cutting away false certainty with the razor of doubt. Husserl has described his method of cutting away the abstract as "transcendental reduction" in which "each of us, as Cartesian meditator, was led back to his transcendental ego

[3] Franz Brentano, "The Distinction Between Mental and Physical Phenomena," trans. D. B. Terrell, in *Realism and the Background of Phenomenology*, ed. Roderick M. Chisholm (Glencoe, Ill.: The Free Press, 1960), p. 53.
[4] *Realism and the Background of Phenomenology*, ed. Chisholm; editor's introduction, p. 5.

—naturally with its concrete-monadic contents as this de facto ego, the one and only absolute ego."[5] Whether it is called "doubting" or "being led back," the primary intention is to get to the concrete as the unique, inward, subjective, and transcendental self. To say that the individual, concrete self is transcendental means that it is the basis of perception or experience and has a sphere unto itself apart from participation in something like an objective *Geist.* Conversely, and contrary to rationalism, Husserl insists that ". . . the higher forms of such activities of 'reason' in a specific sense and, correlatively, the higher forms of *products* of reason, all of which have the character of *irreality* (that of 'ideal' objects), cannot be regarded forthwith as belonging to every concrete ego as such."[6] Concrete selves do not belong to something outside themselves, nor can that which has been considered universal, such as reason, belong necessarily to "every concrete ego as such." Rationalism smothered the uniqueness of subjectivity just because it "forced" each concrete self to "be" reasonable. It denied the uniqueness that Husserl was determined to preserve. It was the very universality of reason upheld during the Enlightenment with which Husserl was breaking, and it was the very universality of time that had to be rejected if the uniqueness of each subjective consciousness was to be preserved by phenomenology. Husserl's method for cutting away abstractions, his "transcendental reduction," was designed to remove objective outward cosmological time so that time could be properly described as a mode of the concrete inner consciousness. In Husserl's words, "Through the phenomenological reduction consciousness has forfeited . . . its setting in cosmical time."[7] The result is that concrete time "is not to be measured by any state of the sun, by any clock, by any physical means, and generally cannot be measured at all."[8] This distinction between concrete and cosmic time as it appears in Husserl's *Ideas* reflects his

[5] Edmund Husserl, *Cartesian Meditations: An Introduction to Phenomenology,* trans. Dorion Cairns (The Hague: Martinus Nijhoff, 1960), p. 69.
   [6] *Ibid.,* p. 78.
   [7] Husserl, *Ideas, General Introduction to Pure Phenomenology,* trans. W. R. Boyce Gibson (New York: Collier Books, 1962), par. 81. *Ideas* was originally published in 1913 under the title, *Ideen zu einer reinen Phänomenologie und Phänomenologischen Philosophie.*
   [8] *Ibid.*

prior work on time based upon lectures from the years 1904-1905 and 1905-1910, which were compiled and published by his student Martin Heidegger in 1928 as *The Phenomenology of Internal Time Consciousness.*[9] The problem of time in Husserl's earlier writings stems from the nature of phenomenology itself. How is the earlier phenomenology in conflict with Hartshorne's concrete temporality? This can be answered by first saying a word about the "essence" of phenomenology.

Phenomenology is fundamentally a method of knowing. The term "phenomenon" literally means "appearance," but not in the sense of appearance as opposed to reality. Phenomenological appearance is real in itself without reference to some other criterion. To know the essence of an appearance one must, however, reduce it to its ideal (eidetic) state; not in order to know hidden reality, but in order to know the phenomenon (appearance) itself. Husserl's transcendental reduction was a way of putting aside blinding presuppositions in order that essence might appear unencumbered. Grasping a phenomenon requires, however, that an actual phenomenon in full worldly dress first appear. Something must appear before being "reduced." This sounds like a truism, but it was important to Husserl, who feared outward world categories might hide real appearance. Given a phenomenon, the phenomenologist then cuts away toward its irreducible core. At the end of the removal process (transcendental phenomenological reduction), he discovers that which uniquely constitutes the being in question, namely, its *essence.* Each phenomenon has its own absolute essence instead of deriving its essence from something like an all-inclusive *Geist.*

The question remains whether the process of removing abstractions ends with an abstraction or with a concrete particular. This question is especially important in Husserl's earlier Cartesian period when he was more interested in *what* appearances were

[9] Husserl, *The Phenomenology of Internal Time Consciousness,* ed. M. Heidegger; trans. James S. Churchill with introduction by Calvin O. Schrag (Bloomington: Indiana University Press, 1964). Originally published as *Vorlesungen zur Phänomenologie des inneren Zeitbewusstseins.* Since Heidegger is another representative of movement toward the concrete (*see* Chap. 2) it is noteworthy that he was interested in Husserl's work on time.

than in how they were known. As the latter interest develops in his later work, he turns more to the human process of knowing. Now Husserl's phenomenology becomes a method of examining the consciousness of man. How does man have consciousness? To Husserl consciousness means consciousness "of" something. To have consciousness of something means to have an intention toward it; hence, the primary mode of consciousness, and indeed, the central theme of phenomenology, is *intentionality*. If we are to know the essence of things, we must therefore examine man's conscious intention of them. It turns out that not only must phenomenology begin with human consciousness; it must work (phenomenologically) to discover essences as ideal universals. Identification of ideal essences is the science of stating "eidetic" truths "about what is essentially necessary, possible, or impossible, in particular realms of being."[10] Ideal essences were Husserl's response to the need for a rigorous, if not mathematical, approach to philosophy (Husserl was a mathematician before becoming a philosopher). But how can ideal universal essences "participate" in the dynamic happenings of time? In looking for reality in the particularity of individual realms of being, and in focusing his phenomenological method upon the intentions of human consciousness, Husserl had taken a step toward concrete time; but his failure to "temporalize" ideal universals means that he has not yet reached the promised land beyond idealism.

From Hartshorne's perspective, ideal universals tend to be "absolute demarcations" or discrete interruptions of the flow of time. Concrete temporality is to Hartshorne "an ever-growing totality" [RSP, 200-201],* not in the static sense of a Hegelian *Geist*, but in the dynamic sense of real creativity. Hartshorne agrees with Henri Bergson and Alfred North Whitehead that "time . . . is creation or nothing" (RSP, 201). Presumably phenomenological deductions would leave a residual essence that would not be in the process of creation. The data of Husserl's essences seem to be

---

[10] Dorion Cairns, "Phenomenology," *A History of Philosophical Systems,* ed. Vergilius Ferm (New York: The Philosophical Library, 1950), p. 356. Cairns's article has the weakness of an approach that treats phenomenology almost entirely as a child of the twentieth century.

* Titles of books by Hartshorne most frequently cited herein are abbreviated. For the key to the abbreviations, see p. xi.

disruptive *whats* instead of temporally dynamic *hows*. Concentration upon *what* things are introduces an "intellectual" collection of necessary particular essences into the contingent world of time. Concrete time in Hartshorne's usage describes the *how* of ongoing process in which essences must be abstractions if the dynamic quality of the world is to be consistent. This means that Husserl's affirmation of concrete time is not sufficiently dynamic *because* ideal essences are in the concrete. To be compatible with process thought, phenomenological demarcations or essences would have to be *abstractions from* concrete time.

In 1939 Hartshorne wrote an article on Husserl's method entitled "The Method of Imaginative Variations."[11] This article provides clear evidence of the importance of a second dimension of the concrete, namely, intuition.

Like Husserl, Hartshorne understands abstractions to "have meaning in terms of concrete intuitions," but in Husserl's thought "intuitions . . . transcend the limitations of 'perception' in the ordinary sense. . . ."[12] Nevertheless, both men presuppose some kind of concrete intuition. The differences between Husserl and Hartshorne, therefore, develop after one observes a strong similarity in method. In other words, in Hartshorne's terminology, both refer abstractions to concrete intuition, and the debate resides in the differences that appear in that concrete reference. In describing the nature of the concrete, Hartshorne thinks ideal essences are less obviously available than does Husserl.[13] To Hartshorne the clarity implied in Husserl's ideal essences is reminiscent of the Cartesian

[11] Hartshorne, "The Method of Imaginative Variations." This article appears in "Notes Concerning Husserl," *Journal of Philosophy*, xxxvi, No. 9 (April 27, 1939), 233-234. This article is probably also based on conclusions reached during earlier studies.
[12] Hartshorne, "The Method of Imaginative Variations," p. 233.
[13] *Ibid.*, p. 234. In fairness to Husserl it should be pointed out that he thinks the availability of essences can be both adequate and inadequate. In addition to adequately given essences, which "we can easily procure," essential insight, "can also be more or less imperfect, inadequate, and not only in respect of its greater or lesser *clearness* and *distinctness*" (Husserl, *Ideas*, par. 3). Hartshorne's objection would properly be confined to that process in which essential insight is adequate or immediately clear.

notion that "the important and the clear, the fundamental and the readily discerned, coincide."[14]

Hartshorne's use of both temporality and immediate intuition in measuring the concreteness of Husserl's "readily discerned" ideal essences can be expressed in an analogy. Imagine a pond of slowly flowing water the surface of which is spotted with lily blossoms. It is a humid spring morning and a mist hangs over the pond, obscuring ready "discernment" of the lilies. The lilies represent ideal essences which become sharply distinguishable only if the mist is brushed away (transcendentally reduced), perhaps by a breeze. From Hartshorne's position the mist which obscures the sharp outlines of the "essential" lilies always remains; no matter how strong the breeze, more mist would arise out of concrete continuity of possibilities between water, mist, and lily blossoms. The reality of the water with its "wetness" is intuitable because the wet mist also touches the observer. Feeling at one with the continuity between mist and water, the observer "knows" intuitively that the blurred outlines of the lilies blend immediately into the whole (concrete) pond. Moreover, the observer can barely see the quiet currents beneath the water's surface. These are the currents of time which will some day absorb the lilies, although on that morning they look as if they would remain forever in their (abstract) clear essence.

In saying that ideal essences are disruptive of the temporally intuitable concrete, Hartshorne is concentrating on the ontological implications of Husserl's method, not emphasizing phenomenological method as method, as Husserl would understand it. Admittedly, ideal essences are discrete interruptions of concrete intuition, but they are in the concrete. Even if the lilies on the surface of the pond appear "clearly discerned," they are nevertheless in the pond as participants in that which constitutes the whole of the pond. It is just this wholeness that the observer of the pond intuitively enjoys with the touch of mist on his face. Hartshorne remarks, ". . . one may directly observe an esthetic unity of feeling between the self, and nature as immediately given. . . ."[15] All of our intellectual effort is based upon this intuitive feeling of the concrete

[14] Hartshorne, "The Method of Imaginative Variations," p. 233.
[15] Ibid., p. 234.

whole; a wholeness that no ideal essences can discretely interrupt because the concrete is immediately present in intuition. This means that to Hartshorne abstract thought is ontologically secondary to the concrete, and "since thought can only expand, generalize, extrapolate, and abstract, it follows that thought can arrive at no world other than a world of feelings, with their relations, aspects, varieties, and so forth. This is, in one respect, the social view of reality."[16]

Intuitive participation in the concrete leads to a third dimension, the social dimension. At this point Hartshorne's critique of Husserl shifts from the problem of discrete essences to the problem of how the subjective consciousness knows ideal essences. How are we to think of the objectivity of that which is beyond each subject? Hartshorne addresses the problem of subjectivism in Husserl in his contribution to the Husserl *Festschrift* entitled "Husserl and the Social Structure of Immediacy."[17]

It should be remembered that both Husserl and Hartshorne are men of "the age of time" in which time is a "happening." Both men oppose abstract superstructures (theologically, the abstract God) which smother the spontaneity of the self in social reality. But how does the self "intend" its objective social world? What is the relation of inward consciousness to its social context? Hartshorne admits that he and Husserl would be "verbally agreed that experience is immediately social, that is, immediately in relation to other minds, or that other minds are immediately given. . . ."[18] But, Hartshorne insists, they would not mean the same thing by this. The issue, as Hartshorne sees it, is expressed as follows:

. . . for Husserl other minds are directly given in, but not real constituents of, one's own stream of consciousness. Or again, that they are immediate but not immanent, rather "transcendent," factors of the stream, as indeed is one's own ego as a human personality. The alternative doctrine, there-

[16] *Ibid.*
[17] *Philosophical Essays in Memory of Edmund Husserl*, ed. Marvin Farber (Cambridge, Mass.: Harvard University Press, 1940), pp. 219-230.
[18] *Ibid.*, p. 219.

fore, is that one's own experience contains the actual experiences of others as real, immanent elements.[19]

Since intuitive participation in the concrete is the immanent mode, Hartshorne opposes Husserl's failure to include others in the constituency of the self. Hartshorne's question is: "How can I know others without their constituting part of my real knowing?" In Husserl's language this is the question of what "intention" of phenomena can mean without really (socially) including the intended phenomena.

Hartshorne is not alone in raising the problem of knowledge of the other in Husserl's method. Jean-Paul Sartre acknowledges that the other, the reality of fellow beings outside the self's stream of consciousness, is considered by Husserl to be necessary to the existence of the world.[20] Sartre maintains, however, that just because transcendental reduction goes beyond the concrete into the realm of ideal essences, it leaves the ground of social knowledge behind. To meet the difficulty of how to be both a transcendental self and a self-with-others, Husserl, Sartre thinks, was forced to define the other as *an absence.* In other words, to Sartre, Husserl's determination to proceed philosophically in the stream of an individual human consciousness created the problem of how to think of that transcendental ego as being-in-the-world. Sartre's criticism of Husserl's tendency toward solipsism arises out of a different set of philosophical presuppositions, but both Hartshorne and Sartre think Husserl's phenomenology produces an inadequate theory of sociality. In the case of Hartshorne, at least, this is a way of showing that the concrete must be social; it must include a method for relating beings in a real immanence, not leaving them in an isolated transcendence or, in a popular term, not leaving human selves as "rugged individuals."

The problem of sociality within Husserl's phenomenology has also been treated by another of Husserl's students, Alfred Schütz.[21] Schütz agrees with Sartre's criticism of Husserl and goes on to in-

[19] *Ibid.,* pp. 219-220.
[20] Sartre, *Being and Nothingness,* pp. 288 ff.
[21] *See* Alfred Schütz, *Collected Papers,* Vol. 1, *The Problem of Social Reality,* edited and introduced by Maurice Natanson (The Hague: Martinus Nijhoff, 1962).

sist that sociality is a problem in the existentialism of Sartre as well.[22] Schütz finds many reasons why Husserl is even more helpful in the attempt to account for social reality.[23] Not the least of these is Husserl's understanding of time: "Husserl's analysis of the consciousness of inner time with its interplay of pretentions and retentions makes it understandable that the I can partake in the other's stream of consciousness in a vivid present, whereas the I can grasp—and then only in the reflective attitude—merely past phases of its own stream of consciousness."[24] To Schütz, "partaking" in the reality of the other, i.e., getting out of the problem of the transcendental ego, is possible because the same phenomenological analysis that applies to the transcendental also applies to the natural.[25] This means that to Schütz, Husserl's distinctions, such as the one mentioned above between concrete time and cosmological time, are secondary, because what is valid in inward time is also valid in the "natural" outward attitude. If Schütz's argument is correct, Hartshorne's criticism of Husserl's doctrine of the transcendent ego loses its force. By the same token, Husserl must actually have a different understanding of the concrete, a natural understanding, which would be closer to Hartshorne's own insistence that the concrete is social.

If the concrete is objectively social in that the other is a constituent of the self's consciousness, is Hartshorne reintroducing something like Hegel's *Geist*? Does really immanent sociality interfere with particular concrete emergence? To this Hartshorne replies that the transcendent particular is the primary mode and that the immanence of real constituency, i.e., faint overlapping, is secondary.[26] In fact, "phenomenal evidence for the overlapping

22 *Ibid.*, pp. 197 ff. Existence and sociality are discussed by implication in Chap. 4.
23 *Ibid.*, pp. 145-149.
24 *Ibid.*, p. 147. Retentions and pretentions are connections in the stream of thought in inner time, connecting it "with what just now happened and with what may be expected to happen immediately, and refers to cognitions of the more distant past by recollection and to the future by anticipations" (*ibid.*, p. 109).
25 *Ibid.*, p. 149.
26 "Husserl and the Social Structure of Immediacy," *Philosophical Essays in Memory of Edmund Husserl* (Cambridge, Mass.: Harvard University Press, 1940), p. 224.

must be chiefly indirect, for instance, through analogy with the mind-body relation as social and given as such."[27] Hartshorne is saying, in effect, that the continuity between water (the intuitive ground) and mist (the extension of that ground past all ideal essences) is not itself apparent. Continuity between water and mist must be known indirectly, because the distinct appearance of the lilies encourages the observer to think of them as being essentially clear.

Apart from real immanence, socially conceived, Hartshorne thinks that human understanding is in constant danger. The danger arises because "the cards are stacked by nature to produce dualistic doctrines"; an example is Husserl's discussion of the "manipulation or exploitation of 'tools' or 'materials.' "[28] Hartshorne argues that the dualism involved in this discussion ". . . appears as secondary if we admit that fellow beings can be used as well as sympathized with, and that thus the social view includes and explains exploitation while exploitation cannot explain sympathy."[29] On the surface, this is an illustration grounded in its ability to make a doctrine more intelligible. It is better "explained" by the notion of sympathy, Hartshorne says, but notice that in this discussion Hartshorne gives an amplification which may be helpful to our attempt to understand why he thinks this or any dualism does not "explain."

> Every society involves order and interdependence, and the possibility of "mechanical" manipulation follows deductively, though somewhat intricately, from these ideas. Hence the manipulability of things is no proof of their non-social character, and adds nothing whatever to such character, while it abstracts from or neglects much of it. This abstraction seems to me to explain dualistic theories which it nevertheless is incapable of justifying.[30]

The striking thing is the fact that Husserl's "dualism" does not explain because it is an abstraction, an abstraction from the social whole. Not only is the surface problem of dualism that which is to

27 *Ibid.*
28 *Ibid.*, p. 226.
29 *Ibid.*
30 *Ibid.*

be opposed in Husserl, but underlying this, abstraction itself is here used by Hartshorne in a negative sense. In this case, to abstract is to neglect the whole realm of social interdependence. Abstractions are the forms of communication, but, as Fritz Buri puts it, "the realm of concepts through which we communicate with each other is not the world as it exists independently of us 'in itself' . . . rather a second world of our own creation, the created world of mental objects."[31] It appears, then, that abstraction leads away from the intuitable immediacy of social experience.

There are marked similarities between Hartshorne's critique of Husserlian abstraction and Marshall McLuhan's argument that Western man is passing through a literary stage. McLuhan believes that the fragmentation brought about by abstract thinking is now giving way to a sense of coherence.[32] Such coherence is expressed by modern communication media, like television, which are themselves a message of "cool" participation in the social whole. Who can doubt that the other *really is* being incorporated more fully into the self's consciousness through immanent participation (Hartshorne) and electric involvement (McLuhan)? Abstract (discrete essence) distance is overcome by immersion in concrete wholeness.

Because of immanent sociality we literally are our brother's keeper if we would "keep" ourselves. Conversely, we cannot look after ourselves without looking after our brothers. The concrete, the implied ground from which abstraction is abstracted, is the intuited social whole. By implication, intuition is the positive correlate of negative abstraction. That this is the case in Hartshorne's discussion of Husserl is further indicated by Hartshorne's understanding of the very nature of phenomenological method:

> Apart from the social issue there seems little that is fundamental dividing Husserl's philosophy from that of James, Peirce, Whitehead, or Bergson. The essential methodological element in phenomenology, broadly conceived, is common to these men. James had a radical empiricism, Peirce a formal

[31] Fritz Buri, *Christian Faith in Our Time*, trans. Edward Allen Kent (New York: The Macmillan Co., 1966), p. 63.
[32] *See* Marshall McLuhan, *Understanding Media* (New York: Mc-Graw-Hill Book Co., 1964).

doctrine of phenomenology (or "phaneroscopy" as he also called it), Whitehead perpetually emphasizes the appeal to immediate intuition, and Bergson's doctrine is also put forth as a description of the essential character of existence as directly intuited.[33]

Broadly speaking, Hartshorne considers the phenomenological method the intuitive method; social appearances are to be measured by immediate participation in concrete intuition.

When faced with Husserl's fully evident and clear ideal essences, it is the intuited concrete whole, the whole of creative time, the continuity of water and mist, to which Hartshorne appeals. When faced with the subjectivity of Husserl's phenomenological method, as it is exhibited in the question of sociality, Hartshorne insists others must really be included in the self.

In effect Hartshorne opposes what he takes to be a certain abstract intellectualism with his own concrete intuitionism. This serves to illuminate the presuppositions out of which both thinkers speak, especially as far as Hartshorne's understanding of the concrete is concerned. Husserl represents movement toward the concrete, but his rationalistic and idealistic heritage prevented his full realization of its possibilities.

[33] Hartshorne, "Husserl and the Social Structure of Immediacy," *Philosophical Essays in Memory of Edmund Husserl*, p. 228.

2

Heidegger: Existence and the Problem of Passivity

Hartshorne thinks Heidegger's existentialism is more concrete than Husserl's phenomenology, but he is eager to find categories that overcome weaknesses in existentialism. "Actuality" therefore becomes a way to emphasize the process character of the concrete, and aesthetic "objectivity" underscores concrete transcendence of existential subjectivity.

IN 1929 HARTSHORNE wrote one of the early reviews of Heidegger's now classic *Being and Time*. In this review Hartshorne summarizes how he sees movement toward the concrete from Husserl's phenomenology to Heidegger's existentialism.

> Phenomenology was itself from the outset a reform tending in the very direction we have been considering—the direction, as we conceive it, of ever greater concreteness. Still, phenomenologists hitherto have tended to a disappointing extent to interpret experience chiefly in terms of such traditional and relatively abstract conceptions as "consciousness," "object," "essence," "perception," and the like, to the neglect of the concreter ideas of feeling, willing, valuing, loving, and their kin.[1]

[1] Hartshorne, review of *Sein und Zeit* by Martin Heidegger and of *Mathematische Existenz* by Oskar Becker, from *Jahrbuch für Philosophie and Phänomenologische Forschung: Herausgegeben von Edmund Husserl*, Achter Band. *The Philosophical Review*, xxxviii, No. 3 (May, 1929), 284-293.

This comment not only concisely states how Hartshorne views the movement toward the concrete, but also indicates why Heidegger's brand of phenomenology, emphasizing feeling, willing, valuing, and loving, is attractive to Hartshorne. In Heidegger's existential phenomenology the metamorphosis is complete; existence breaks through its outer shell. The reason Heidegger's terminology is more appealing to Hartshorne becomes apparent when one recalls the immediacy of intuited concrete experience in the critique of Husserl. Also, in describing the movement from Husserl to Heidegger as a step in the direction of greater concreteness, Hartshorne is attempting to place Heidegger in the history of philosophy. To this end he applauds Heidegger's attack upon "abstract general ideas" after the fashion of George Berkeley, as "worthy of perpetual renewal."[2]

In his early work Heidegger bases his attack upon abstract ideas on the historicity of his fundamental metaphor, *Dasein* (being-there). The existential analysis of *Dasein* follows from the primacy of the question of Being. Heidegger says,

> . . . to work out the question of Being adequately, we must make an entity—the inquirer—transparent in its own Being. The very asking of this question is an entity's mode of Being; and as such it gets its essential character from what is inquired about—namely, Being. This entity which each of us is himself and which includes inquiring as one of the possibilities of its Being, we shall denote by the term "*Dasein*." If we are to formulate our question explicitly and transparently, we must first give a proper explication of an entity (*Dasein*), with regard to its Being.[3]

The abstract essential relations of the inquirer are secondary to the primacy of the question of being. Asking the question of being makes one aware of his own concrete existence.

As with Husserl, the radically concrete starting point of Heidegger's interrogation of *Dasein* is clearer against a larger background. It must be remembered that modern philosophy is still

[2] *Ibid.*, p. 286. The subjectivity of the positions of Berkeley and Heidegger provides the bases for a comparison of subjective idealism and existentialism that merits further study.
[3] Martin Heidegger, *Being and Time*, trans. John Macquarrie and Edward Robinson (New York: Harper & Row, 1962), p. 27.

casting off its medieval dress and that realization of the concrete self had been secondary to the supernatural home of the self. Even at the beginning of the modern period, Jean Jacques Rousseau, the romanticist, had developed the self in something "outside" existential, concrete, personal existence, namely, the self-in-nature. In his emphasis upon subjective feeling, Rousseau anticipated twentieth-century phenomenology and existentialism—but these movements rebelled against Rousseau's self-in-nature because nature took away something vital to personal existence.

Existentialists have generally taken the position that the romantic self-in-nature fails to realize authentic existence. Existentialists might reverse the saying, "You can't see the forest for the trees," to read, "You can't see the trees for the forest" (you miss the existential self if you look at the essential, or if you look at the whole you may not give proper attention to the particulars that comprise it). To existentialists the problem with Hegel's absolute *Geist* is that it submerges the self by making it a self-in-mind, or consciousness, a self that is itself through participation in a larger whole. William Kluback and Jean T. Wilde are correct in saying, "Hegel necessitated Heideggerian existentialism by his conclusion that existence is reconciled in consciousness."[4] Heidegger seeks concreteness *apart from* either nature or consciousness in order to avoid thinking of being-in-the-world as simply deducible from some aspect of the world. In this respect Heidegger is continuing Husserl's determination to cut away presuppositions that might prevent concreteness. The difference is in the manner of cutting or bracketing; Husserl proceeds by thinking back to ideal essences; Heidegger by thinking of concrete death, the self's own death, so that being-toward-death becomes the principle of individuation. Heidegger remarks, ". . . *death*, as the end of *Dasein*, is *Dasein's* ownmost possibility. . . ."[5]

Although Hartshorne is sympathetic to the goal of existential concreteness in Heidegger's analysis of *Dasein*, it is not accurate to call Hartshorne an existentialist. This is true because of Harts-

[4] From the introduction to Martin Heidegger, *The Question of Being*, trans. with an introduction by William Kluback and Jean T. Wilde (New York: Twayne Publishers, 1956), pp. 30-31.

[5] Heidegger, *The Question of Being*, p. 303.

horne's insistence upon the importance of *actuality* in addition to existentiality. This distinction becomes especially important in Hartshorne's later work on the ontological argument, but it also provides a way to distinguish Hartshorne's view of the concrete from Heideggerian existentialism. Existentialists have distinguished between essence and existence, giving priority to existence in order to preserve concrete independence from abstract presuppositions. Hartshorne goes a step further and insists upon actuality because it implies *an event or happening* that could never be interpreted classically as merely being-there [RSP, 22].[6] Of course, Heidegger's analysis of *Dasein* from the standpoint of its temporality gives evidence of a similar interest, but Hartshorne believes clarification results if some term other than existence is used. "Actuality" satisfies Hartshorne's intention, and we might venture to call him an "actualist" (whatever value such a label might have) because he goes beyond the existentialist's concern for the primacy of existence.

From the standpoint of Hartshorne's actualism, it is not difficult to project Heideggerian existentialism against the backdrop of romanticism or objective idealism. It is also possible to discover concern for concreteness even in Berkeley's subjective idealism. Berkeley wrote:

... another great source of errors and difficulties with regard to ideal knowledge is the doctrine of abstract ideas. ... The plainest things in the world, those we are most intimately acquainted with and perfectly know, when they are considered in an abstract way, appear strangely difficult and incomprehensible. Time, place, and motion, taken in particular or concrete, are what everybody knows; but, having passed through the hands of the metaphysician, they become too abstract and fine to be comprehended by men of ordinary sense.[7]

The tone and method of Berkeley's attack are certainly different from Heidegger's work, but even Berkeley's subjective idealism was a movement toward concreteness.

[6] Also see Hartshorne, *Anselm's Discovery, passim.*
[7] George Berkeley, *The Works of George Berkeley,* ed. Alexander Campbell Fraser (Oxford: Clarendon Press, 1901); Vol. I, *Philosophical Works* (1705-21), p. 311.

Hartshorne understands Heidegger's early program to be "the interpretation of the initially abstract, empty, and supposedly indefinable concept of Being in terms of 'phenomena,' i.e., immediate experiences."[8] This description is clarified by Hartshorne's statement of Heidegger's treatment of purpose and meaning. "Meaning, the more abstract (i.e., indeterminate), is here explained by purpose, the more concrete, determinate conception."[9] In terms of immediate concrete purpose "the person on the other side of the street to whom one calls is 'nearer' in the phenomenological sense, i.e., as appearance, than the pavement upon which one stands or the glasses on one's nose."[10] The appearance of the person on the other side of the street may, however, be obscured when the consciousness of the self is overlaid by an impersonal substitute—the "one" (*das Man*).[11] Hartshorne declares this, "the treatment of *conscience* as the central revelation of the self," and its inevitable tendency toward the obscurity of the "one," the more developed and original part of Heidegger.[12] The inauthentic obscurity of the neutral "one" in Heidegger's analysis appeals to Hartshorne because it is Heidegger's way of rejecting life in the abstract. Hartshorne joins Heidegger in this not only for philosophical but for theological reasons, and they in turn have been joined by contemporary theology. It is no accident that the theology of the death of God arose during a period of history saturated with the existential mood. The problem of the neutral "one" is illustrated theologically by the death of the abstract (neutral) God.

The concreteness of temporal existence and the concept of the "one" are attractive to Hartshorne, but more than the distinction between

[8] Hartshorne, review of *Being and Time*, p. 286.
[9] *Ibid*, p. 288.
[10] *Ibid*.
[11] *Ibid*. Hartshorne is in agreement with John Wild in translating *das Man* as "the one." Wild's translation is an alternative to the translation "the they" used by John Macquarrie and Edward Robinson in their translation of *Being and Time*. See John Wild, "An English Version of Martin Heidegger's *Being and Time*," *The Review of Metaphysics*, XVI, No. 2, Issue No. 62 (December, 1962).
[12] Hartshorne, review of *Being and Time*, p. 288.

existence and actuality separates him from Heidegger. Additional difference emerges in Hartshorne's chief criticism of Heidegger, which comes in the form of two wishes: "(1) that a more positive conception of the relation of philosophy to mathematics—*via* the concept of structure or logical form . . . and (2) that a greater interest in and sensitiveness to aesthetic phenomena, so obviously relevant to such a philosophical program, had contributed their quota to the concreteness of the results."[13]

Fulfillment of the first wish "would have brought the relationship of the new 'hermeneutic' phenomenology, on its logical side, to the logic of relations and kindred logical issues."[14] Apparently the wish for the logical side in Heidegger remains unfulfilled as far as Hartshorne is concerned. As late as 1963 he speaks of Heidegger's thought as an "antirationalistic rhapsody" [LP, 10]. If anything, Heidegger seems to move in the direction of poetry instead of mathematics or logic.

By the second wish, the wish for an aesthetic side, Hartshorne seeks "to correct the one-sided emphasis upon the practical accent in the description of physical objectivity."[15] Care should be taken here because of the common tendency to associate aesthetic feeling with subjective feeling. In calling for the aesthetic dimension, Hartshorne is requesting just the opposite of subjectivity. Heidegger, he thinks, conceives phenomena "too exclusively in terms of practical and subjectively emotional attitudes, and too little in terms of that objective participation which is aesthetic enjoyment."[16] Hartshorne is more sympathetic with something like the objectivity of Hegel's *concrete universal* than with the subjective stance of Heidegger. This does not mean that Hartshorne is willing to permit the self to be submerged in the "one," in that which is other than the self. It means that aesthetic appreciation of the self is impossible without some contrasting objectivity, without something in which the self is a self.

Hartshorne is saying in effect that we cannot enjoy our selfhood apart from being in a "neighborhood." The greater the diversity of

[13] *Ibid.*, p. 289.
[14] *Ibid.*
[15] *Ibid.*
[16] *Ibid.*, p. 290.

the "neighborhood" the greater our chances for unified aesthetic enjoyment, but there must be a neighborhood if the self is to enjoy its individuality. Heideggerian existentialism can be accommodated to almost any social position because of its dearth of objective criteria (neighborhoods).

This problem is correlative to Sartre's and Schütz's attempts to resolve the question of the other. Sartre, Schütz, and Heidegger have struggled to establish something like an effective understanding of social reality without reverting to the categories of classical being. They have generally seen the need for objectivity if freedom is to be real, but they tend to understand freedom as "freedom from," not "freedom in," the concrete neighborhood of social existence. Heidegger does move in the direction of an appreciation of the aesthetic in his later work, but instead of unifying objectivity, he offers mystical meditation.

When preparing his review of *Being and Time*, with a few modifications, for *Beyond Humanism*, Hartshorne gave a reason for Heidegger (and Croce) not ". . . seeing in our sensory contact with reality the blurred sympathetic intuition of the feelings of other individuals . . ." [BH, 304]. Hartshorne believes Heidegger fails to maintain the fully objective character of the feelings of other individuals because he belongs to "the tradition of subjective or anthropomorphic idealism, together with the notion, encouraged by that tradition, of science as tending to an abstract and materialistic view of nature" [BH, 304]. Vincent Vycinas thinks criticisms of this kind are not fair to Heidegger because they presuppose another philosophical position and quite naturally find Heidegger lacking. Vycinas' point is profound because it acknowledges the role of presuppositions in *all criticisms*. But this raises the question of how one can judge between Vycinas and Hartshorne as valid critics of Heidegger. Hartshorne would readily admit that Heidegger's position appears anthropomorphic *because* it is measured by a standard that is nonanthropomorphic. Hartshorne's understanding of the concrete man *in* a larger social context extends beyond mankind. Heideggerian concern for the individual would be included in Hartshorne's "concrete" because each man or temporal occasion realizes itself in terms of its potentialities, *one of which* is death.

It happens, then, that Heidegger's movement toward the concrete appears to Hartshorne to produce a problem. Certainly, the more concrete terms such as "loving" and "willing" which Heidegger provides are the core of subjective existence, temporally understood. Does this mean that from Hartshorne's point of view Heidegger is too concrete? In the critique of Husserl the concrete was not only intuited experience, but the social whole immanently real. Again, with his two wishes for *Being and Time* it is especially the *objectivity* of social reality that is required. Hence, to suggest that Heidegger's analysis is finally too much within the tradition "of subjective or anthropomorphic idealism" is not to say that it is too concrete. The concrete as a whole is real to Hartshorne in a way that would not permit subjectivism in this sense. Hartshorne believes Heidegger's analysis of *Dasein* depicts only a part of the concrete. From Hartshorne's point of view this means that Heidegger, like Husserl, falls into the difficulty of indefinite abstraction. Though Heidegger's terms are less abstract, they nevertheless are abstractions from what Hartshorne considers the concrete to be. Put in terms of the self, the difficulty with Heidegger's thought is not that it is not centered in the self, but that it is not definite enough with respect to the self's real relations. A possible reason for the problem of the self in Heidegger may be his active understanding of the disclosure of being, which seems to engulf the thinking self in a sweep of fate. This has been crucial to Hans Jonas' objections to the usefulness of Heidegger for theology.[17] It should be recognized, however, that by emphasizing continuity between the earlier and the later Heidegger a perspective develops that enables William Richardson to remark, "Reading from our present perspective, we can appreciate with what justice Heidegger could protest, in a letter to Jean Wahl (1937), that the anthropological interpretations given to the early work gravely misrepresented (with or without warrant) his own intentions."[18] Obviously, Hartshorne's judgment that the Heideggerian self is lacking in real relations is made from a perspective that is different from either Richardson's or Heidegger's.

[17] *See* Hans Jonas, "Heidegger and Theology," *The Phenomenon of Life* (New York: Harper & Row, Publishers, 1966), pp. 235-261.
[18] William J. Richardson, *Heidegger Through Phenomenology to Thought* (The Hague: Martinus Nijhoff, 1963), p. 259.

Hartshorne's perspective is clarified if one understands why Heidegger appears in Hartshorne's attack upon humanism. Placing Heidegger in humanism suggests, on the one hand, the problem of subjective anthropomorphism, and, on the other, the problem of God. "Subjective anthropomorphism" implies that Heidegger is representative of humanistic "disintegration." The notion of disintegration follows from Hartshorne's definition of humanism: "In the best sense, 'humanism' is simply the expression of an interest in man; in the worst sense, it is this interest become a monomania, excluding interest in anything else" [BH, 1]. Heidegger is depicted as one whose interest in man produces an inadequate treatment of the objective social whole. Whether Heidegger reaches the state of a monomania or not, to Hartshorne his work represents exclusion; hence, humanistic disintegration.

On the question of God, Hartshorne may correctly have placed Heidegger in the humanistic stream simply because of the latter's "silence" on the question. But it does seem that Hartshorne overstated the case with regard to Heidegger's "atheism." In *Being and Time* Heidegger does not advance an atheistic program; he is silent on the question. He does appear to approve movements in theology that give "a more primordial interpretation of man's Being towards God, prescribed by the meaning of faith itself and remaining within it."[19] The step in which the more primordial is sought is taken after the fashion of phenomenological bracketing to get back to that which is essential, the holy. The discussion of the holy which arises in later works seems to confirm that the work of *Being and Time* was not intended to be atheistic.[20] Vycinas maintains that after passing through two prior stages, being-in-the-world and openness to being, Heidegger moves finally into a stage of dwelling with the gods and silence toward God.[21]

With Max Müller, Vycinas thinks Heidegger did not publish a third part of *Being and Time*, which would have dealt with the question of God, because the question was speculative. This means that God is a supernatural problem to Heidegger, unlike the prob-

---

[19] Heidegger, *Being and Time,* p. 30.
[20] The question of God in Heidegger's later works is discussed in Vincent Vycinas, *Earth and Gods* (The Hague: Martinus Nijhoff, 1961).
[21] Vycinas, *op cit.,* p. 312.

lem of the natural discussion of gods.[22] Vycinas also remarks, "Heidegger thinks the truth of Being, but not that of *a* being and thus not of the Supreme Being."[23] The crucial point here is the easily overlooked problem of the particularity of God as a being. Hartshorne would be able to go beyond Vycinas and Müller and say that Heidegger not only is correct in not looking for a *supernatural* being, but also is correct in not looking for *a being among beings.* The latter point has, in Hartshorne's view, been grossly neglected by our philosophical heritage [*see* LP and AD]. In this sense Heidegger's failure to address the question of God may be the result of both his perception that God is not addressed as *a* supernatural being, and his failure to see the alternative way of putting the question. In other words, he has rightly ignored the abstract God; but what of concrete possibilities? At best he has reached the stage of the death of the abstract God as graphically pictured in *Holzwege*:

> We are today in the deep woods where the familiar trails to reality are swallowed up in thickets of confusion: the spoors are thickly overlaid, and what we seek is some fresh track, some footprint of the gods, which may lead us out of the darkness and out of our time of spiritual dearth.[24]

That Heidegger's declaration of our "spiritual dearth" does not come from his early period is also noteworthy because a strange thing happens to human thinking in the latter two periods, which Vycinas mentions: openness to being, and dwelling with the gods.

From Husserl's early idealism to Heidegger's emphasis upon the openness of being, the human self sinks into an increasingly passive role. Already in Husserl's rebellion against abstract metaphysical presuppositions, the aim of thought had been the restricted task of analysis of concrete phenomena. Heidegger's work in *Being and Time* is consciously a limiting of the role of thought to investigation

---

[22] *Ibid.*, p. 316.
[23] *Ibid.*, p. 315.
[24] Heidegger as quoted by Stanley Romaine Hopper in "On the Naming of the Gods in Hölderlin and Rilke," *Christianity and the Existentialists*, ed. Carl Michalson (New York: Charles Scribner's Sons, 1956), p. 156. This essay anticipates the current death of God theology.

of *Dasein* in the concrete world. In Husserl's phenomenological method—i.e., thought did something itself—it had a real effect issuing from the agency of the existential self. As Heidegger's philosophical career progresses, thinking becomes more and more passive.[25]

Richardson has charted the course of "thought" in his *Heidegger Through Phenomenology to Thought*. Being, which is prior to the being-of-thought, wishes thought to be itself as the arena for the revelation of Being. Richardson observes, "In hailing the thinker into Being, Being imparts itself to him as gift, and this gift is what constitutes the essence of the thinker, the endowment by which he is. What is more, Being not only bestows the gift but conserves, preserves, sustains it, remains the abiding sustenance of thought."[26] Bestowal of the gift of Being has striking religious overtones precisely because this is a traditional way of speaking of God's revelation to man; His conserving, His preserving, His sustaining of man. Traditionally, this has been discussed under the rubric of will, and the question has been, "How can man's will relate to God's will?" In the relationship between God's will and man's will, especially in the Augustinian-Calvinist-Barthian tradition, God's

[25] The problem of passivity in thinking is addressed in Heidegger's later work, *Discourse on Thinking*, a translation of *Gelassenheit* by John M. Anderson and E. Hans Freund with an introduction by John M. Anderson (New York: Harper & Row, 1966). Here Heidegger attempts to transcend the distinction between activity and passivity (p. 61) in favor of "meditative" thinking. Meditative thinking, "a higher kind of activity than is involved in the exercise of any subjective human power" (p. 25), leads to Being in a way impossible in "calculative" thinking in which "we deal with things in our terms for our advantage" (p. 24). Moving from activity and passivity, the mode of will, to "releasement" (pp. 61 ff.), the mode of meditative thinking, is an effort to put thinking on a new basis, a nonrepresenting basis. Moving along this path means that no active seizing of Being ("that which regions," p. 65) is possible if calculative thinking is to be avoided. Rather, the nature of thinking coming from that-which-regions is disclosed in openness made possible by waiting (p. 68). Heidegger wishes to "will nonwilling" (p. 79), but the question remains whether this is anything other than an attempt by the self not to be the self. How can the self will its nonwilling without willing its demise? Does pushing the issue beyond activity and passivity present a new ground for thinking or beg the question of thinking altogether? From Hartshorne's perspective Heidegger's meditative thinking appears to lose the meditator!

[26] Richardson, *Heidegger*, p. 599.

will tended to emerge triumphant. Now, just as God's will has over-whelmed man's will, Being takes the initiative away from a being-in-the-world.

Admittedly, Heidegger understands thinking more actively when he is speaking in "the strict sense as the achieving of authen-ticity by resolve,"[27] but his later usage stresses unfolding Being. To the extent that "passive thinking" means participation in some-thing beyond the self, Hartshorne has little ground for quarrel be-cause of his own notion of aesthetic participation. On the other hand, there is danger in thinking of thought as a gift from God, leaving the self as little more than a "shepherd" of Being. What can a passive thinker do except let someone else, even God, do his thinking for him? Since Hartshorne is convinced that man plays an active role in the ongoing creation of concrete reality, Heidegger may be asked the implicit question whether concrete man has been swallowed up by an abstraction or not. What happened to the ex-istential man? For Hartshorne, thinking can only develop what is given, but that development of the given is an active act, a "con-crete doing." In the later work of Heidegger, thought begins to re-semble "being done" or "being thought." Hartshorne is not opposed to some passivity, because he thinks one of the weaknesses of clas-sicism was failure to allow *any* passivity, especially in God. His point is that some activity is required in order for the concrete to maintain its valid existential constitution.

In sum, Hartshorne generally finds Heidegger moving in the right direction, i.e., toward the concrete. Heidegger's concepts rep-resent a more adequate expression of immediate experience than Husserl's ideal essences. For example, Heidegger's insight into the problem of the "one," the neutral inauthentic otherness in which existence is unaware of itself, is applauded. Implicitly, passivity in human thinking (developed in the later Heidegger) represents an answer to Hartshorne's criticism of insufficient attention to aesthet-ics. The value for theology of Heidegger's later program is limited from Hartshorne's perspective, however, because unfolding Being, like the traditional notion of the will of God, submerges human thinking and being. Although Hartshorne does not explicitly ad-

[27] *Ibid.*, p. 596.

dress this problem, it is helpful to note that Heidegger's early work in *Being and Time* is more compatible with human activity than passivity. Hartshorne's general understanding of concrete existence would require both real activity and passivity in the self. It is from this perspective that Heidegger seems to Hartshorne to be limited by subjective humanistic anthropomorphism. On the other hand, the temporality of Heideggerian existentialism remains important to Hartshorne. In fact, Hartshorne is even ready to characterize his study of Husserl and Heidegger as a reinforcement of "my belief in the ultimate reality of temporal process" [RSP, 19].

3

Peirce: The Continuum

Concreteness means that the actuality of the empirical world is real, but what makes particular actualization possible? To answer this question, Hartshorne invokes Peirce's continuum of real possibilities. Explanation of actuality in terms of a continuum of possibilities leads to a definition of the very nature of philosophy.

AFTER COMPLETING his European studies in 1925, Hartshorne returned to Harvard, where he was an assistant to Professor Whitehead. During this period he devoted considerable time to editing the manuscript writings of Charles Sanders Peirce. Studying Peirce amounted to shifting attention from phenomenology and existentialism to pragmatism, but this does not mean the theme of movement toward the concrete was disrupted. In fact, Hartshorne has declared phenomenology's reform to be similar to Peirce's "profound transformation of traditional empiricism."[1] The theme of movement toward concreteness is continued when "Peirce points out that the most general conceptions must either be dismissed as 'ultimate,' 'simple,' ideas, opaque to all rational interpretation and thus really without scientifically verifiable meaning, or else must be interpreted through those 'concrete and familiar conceptions of everyday life' which express modes of human behavior and purpose."[2] This does not mean, however, that Hartshorne's interest in

[1] "Whitehead and Contemporary Philosophy," *The Relevance of Whitehead*. ed. Ivor Leclerc (New York: The Macmillan Co., 1961), p. 21.
[2] Hartshorne, review of *Being and Time*, *The Philosophical Review*, XXXVIII, No. 3 (May, 1929), 285.

Peirce is primarily an interest in the similarity between phenomenological and pragmatic method.

What does "pragmatism" mean? The "American school of pragmatism," which Peirce originated, has a more formal conceptualization than Peirce's followers, such as William James,[3] took it to have. Behind the somewhat anti-intellectual stance of James's pragmatism one finds Peirce himself emphasizing both philosophical and scientific rigor. Peirce's pragmatism was first stated in his now well-known maxim: "Consider what effects, that might conceivably have practical bearings we conceive the object of conception to have. Then, our conception of these effects is the whole of our conception of the object."[4] An understanding of this maxim would have to take into account a more elaborate statement of his method found in his article of 1877, "The Fixation of Belief."[5] In the latter work Peirce develops his method in terms of the relationship between the one who holds a conception and the object of conception. The underlying structure is the real—that which remains. In Peirce's words:

> There are real things, whose characters are entirely independent of our opinions about them; those realities affect our senses according to regular laws, and, though our sensations are as different as our relations to the objects, yet, by taking advantage of the laws of perception, we can ascertain by reasoning how things really are, and any man, if he have sufficient experience and reason enough about it, will be led to the one true conclusion.[6]

This might be called scientific method, but Peirce's point is that this concept of the real can be believed because "the method and

[3] See especially William James, *Pragmatism, a New Name for Some Old Ways of Thinking* together with *Four Related Essays from the Meaning of Truth* (New York: Longmans, Green and Co., 1946).
[4] This was formulated in Peirce, "How to Make Our Ideas Clear," *Popular Science Monthly*, January, 1878.
[5] Peirce, "The Fixation of Belief," *Popular Science Monthly*, November, 1877. Reprinted in *Problems of Philosophy*, ed. John A. Mourant and E. Hans Freund (New York: The Macmillan Co., 1964). Page references below are to the reprint.
[6] Peirce, "The Fixation of Belief," p. 528.

the conception on which it is based remain ever in harmony."[7] The *real potentiality* upon which scientific method operates is the methodological basis of Peirce's philosophy. Thus, when we press back to the basis of Peirce's own pragmatic method, we discover that *real potentiality* is even more fundamental than the more practical dimension. As late as his 1963 paper on "Real Possibility,"[8] Hartshorne insists that logic is in harmony with real possibilities. Again, it is not Peirce's pragmatism as such that interests Hartshorne, because he is convinced that "what is valid in pragmatism is largely contained in Whitehead."[9] The aspect of Peirce's philosophy that does especially interest Hartshorne is the solution he finds to what is described as a slight compromise in Whitehead. Namely, Hartshorne thinks Whitehead's doctrine of "eternal objects" is a compromise of the dynamic temporal character of reality; hence, "In Peirce's theory that abstract forms evolve from a primordial continuum of indefinite potentiality, I have hoped one could see a corrective of Whitehead . . ." [RSP, 20].

Thus, it is the "primordial continuum of indefinite potentiality" (not "actuality," because the continuum does not refer to actuality) that most interests Hartshorne in the study of Peirce. Hartshorne, while attracted to Peirce's indefinite continuum, is nevertheless puzzled by one seemingly inconsistent remark by Peirce. Hartshorne notes that in the same essay "in which Peirce speaks of an evolution of specific qualities out of a primordial continuum which does not contain them, he refers to qualities as 'eternal possibilities,' and indicates that the evolution is prior to time (6.200)."[10] Hartshorne's question is clarified by returning to the analogy of the lily pond used to describe the intuition of temporal concrete wholeness in the

[7] *Ibid.*

[8] Hartshorne, "Real Possibility," *Journal of Philosophy*, LX, No. 21 (October 10, 1963).

[9] Hartshorne, review of *Being and Time*, p. 285.

[10] Hartshorne, "The Relativity of Nonrelativity: Some Reflections on Firstness," *Studies in the Philosophy of Charles Sanders Peirce*, ed. Philip P. Wiener and Frederic H. Young (Cambridge, Mass.: Harvard University Press, 1952), p. 351, n. 9. The number 6.200 refers to the numbering system used by Hartshorne and Paul Weiss in editing Peirce's *Collected Papers* (Cambridge, Mass.: Harvard University Press, 1931-1935).

problem of Husserl's ideal essences (*see* p. 10). Substitute "eternal possibilities" for "ideal essences," and the question becomes how that which is discretely eternal can "flow" in the currents of time. Moreover, if the pond, the concrete whole that illustrates continuity, *is* continuously itself (a temporal continuum), how can its continuity be interrupted by discrete lilies? "Eternal possibilities" (lilies) must float above concrete continuity precisely because their eternality is foreign to the temporal flow. Eternal possibilities would have to stand abstractly above time in order to be eternal, because time is a series of happenings that do not exist until they happen. If concrete possibilities were eternal, they would not have to wait upon the flow of time in order to come into being.

In his 1929 article, "Continuity, the Form of Forms, in Charles Peirce," Hartshorne clarifies his interpretation of Peirce in his own definition of philosophy: "The descriptive science of the most general characters of experience, and the explanatory science of the total universe of actuality and possibility. . . ."[11] Hartshorne maintains that the development of this definition "will exhibit the centrality of the conception of continuity for all philosophical inquiry." Discussion of continuity or the continuum is at least one way of discussing what Hartshorne understands the nature of philosophy itself to be. Each point in this 1929 article is an elucidation of Hartshorne's definition of philosophy and is designed to demonstrate the centrality of the continuum.[12]

1. "*Description as comparison.* All descriptive science begins by comparison or classification, by positing relations of likeness and difference." Hartshorne illustrates the necessity for positing a continuum of likeness and difference in terms of color. "Red and orange are both alike and different, and the likeness, together with difference, involves, and seems almost to consist in, a continuous series of possible intermediaries between the two."[13] In Hartshorne's book *The Philosophy and Psychology of Sensation* (1934), the continuum is developed not only as the ground for intermediaries between colors, but also as the ground for mediation between color

[11] Hartshorne, "Continuity, the Form of Forms, in Charles Peirce," *The Monist*, XXXIX, No. 4 (October, 1929), 521-534.
[12] *Ibid.* The subsequent seven points are from pp. 522 ff.
[13] *Ibid.*

and other aspects of experience, such as sound.[14] This is sharpened by a familiar theme: "Aesthetic experience is not the mere undergoing of an effect; it is the direct intuition of relationships embodied in what is immediately presented." For example:

> The feeling that sounds are not comparable to colors is partly due to our habit of thinking chiefly, in this connection, of "surface" colors. If "light" colors, "shine," and atmospheric or "depth" colors, are taken into account, together with the subjective or pre-sensational qualities . . . it will be more readily seen that the characteristic difference between sound and color, as well as that between both and the more subjective aspects of experience, admits of degrees.

That comparison is a matter of degrees is to be taken quite seriously. Against the notion of discontinuity that would make the difference between red and orange or color and sound a "difference of kind," Hartshorne contends: "But the idea of separate kinds has a merely relative validity, is itself a matter of degrees; ultimately there is but one kind of thing, namely, the kind of thing which in the broadest sense of the word is a thing, or is a something."

Does such a monistic stance mean that Hartshorne's concrete continuum is ruling out pluralism? No; monism applies to the *ultimate* continuum of real possibilities. Pluralism refers to the actualization of some of those possibilities. Actual colors and actual sounds are relative differences in kind within *the* concrete continuum of possibilities, which is "one kind of thing." For example, man is one of the actualizations of general potentiality, but his difference from lower animals is a matter of degree. Even more obvious is the lack of *ultimate* difference between races of men. On Hartshorne's terms ultimate differences cannot appear among concrete particulars in the world.

[14] Hartshorne, *The Philosophy and Psychology of Sensation* (Chicago: The University of Chicago Press, 1934), p. 226. In this book Hartshorne calls his theory of sensory qualities the doctrine of the "affective continuum" (p. vii). "The designation 'affective' for the whole continuum of experiences indicates that all qualitative contrasts, in whatever dimension, repeat recognizably the contrast characteristic of affection in its typical cases, so that these contrasts may be said to generate the continuum. Such polarities are joy and sorrow, self and not-self, liking and disliking, etc." (p. 9).

2. "*Science*. The definition of philosophy as a science suggests that we should consider what may be the logic of comparison employed by the recognized or 'successful' sciences, such as physics." Here, Hartshorne finds continuity evident in the "blending of space and time, of matter and energy, of law and freedom." Special attention is given to the latter pair throughout Hartshorne's works.[15] His general thesis is that the relationship between law and freedom has been often misunderstood because it has been put in terms of an either/or question. Law has been thought to be conceivable only in strictly deterministic terms, and freedom has been discussed as if it were absolute. Indeterminism does not mean that no results will follow from a given set of causal conditions, but rather, that the results are not strictly predictable as to details (cf. quantum mechanics). For example: "Given dry TNT, a confined space, and a lighted fuse, there will inevitably, or with practically infinite probability, be an explosion; but it does not follow, and indeterminism denies, that the exact details of the explosion, the behavior of each atom and particle, will be the only possible ones . . . under the circumstances" [LP, 163]. In this case a deterministic either/or would reflect discontinuity; the probability of the explosion with respect to exact details would reflect the degrees of a continuum.

3. "*Generality*. Philosophy, like any science, deals with general characters or universals." Hartshorne sees the great scope of the problem of universals in the history of philosophy, but he adds, ". . . the definition of the universal as a continuum of possibilities, a view first proposed by Kant and developed by Peirce, seems without a rival as an analysis of the formal characteristics of the universal." In this analysis the more metaphysical universals, such as "reality," "essence," and "experience," remain obscure "unless . . . continua are posited for them." In other words, "the remedy for this obscurity is to see in such universals references to an *all-comprehensive* continuum of possibilities, of which the narrower universals [here, Hartshorne is referring to universals such as "triangle, dog, goodness, humanity . . ."] represent limited portions. The realm of essences or possibilities is then to be regarded as a single *n*-di-

[15] Cf., for example, Hartshorne, "Efficient Causality in Aristotle and St. Thomas," *Journal of Religion*, xxv, No. 1 (January, 1945), 25-32.

mensional continuum in the sense of pure, that is nonspatial, geometry."[16]

In a nuclear age one cannot fail to observe the political possibility of this notion of generality. The political possibilities of universality as a topic for philosophical generality have been developed by Rulon Wells, who notes "Peirce's great hope that, just as the several states united themselves into a nation, the entire world will be united through knowledge and through love into a single community."[17] Wells thinks Peirce "generalizes unification into a universal norm. . . ."[18] In saying that "the narrower universals" do not mean radical discontinuity, Hartshorne does not disagree with the idea that Peirce provides a point that should especially be remembered, not only as a political but as a theological possibility.

4. *"Possibility.* The power of the conception of continuity as an instrument of philosophical analysis depends further upon the definition of this conception . . . as a unity transcending all discrete multitude." It is at this point, the transcendence of multitude by the continuum, that we can focus on the problem of the "slight compromise," which Hartshorne sees in Whitehead but not, for the most part, in Peirce. That is, in adopting the transcendental unity of Peirce's continuum, Hartshorne establishes the basis upon which he is to do battle with Whitehead's "eternal objects."

> . . . If one defines the universal as the continuum of its possible instances, this does not mean that it is the instances which as a multitude make up the continuum, for the latter is defined as a principle inexhaustibly generative of multitude rather than identical with any distinct multitude. It follows that possibilities or qualities apart from actualization do not subsist as a plurality of self-identical entities ("they have no identity"); there is no set or multitude, finite or infinite, of "eternal objects," but there is an eternal creative source of qualities such that, given any two actualized qualities, there is an inexhaustible possibility of intermediaries between them.

[16] Hartshorne, "Continuity, the Form of Forms, in Charles Peirce," p. 526.
[17] Rulon Wells, "Peirce as an American," *Perspective on Peirce,* ed. Richard J. Bernstein (New Haven: Yale University Press, 1965), p. 17.
[18] *Ibid.*

The problem with "eternal objects" is that they interrupt the continuum with their discrete identity, an identity not in process. (Recall Hartshorne's criticism of Husserl's ideal essences.)

Does this imply Hartshorne is a realist instead of a nominalist? As far as the traditional argument between realists and nominalists is concerned, Hartshorne maintains that his view is neither nominalistic nor realistic in the usual way.[19] He does insist, however, that this "mathematical analysis of the problem" remains "inseparable from a recognition of the objective significance of the ideas of vagueness, possibility, potentiality, creativity, free becoming" [BH, 306]. And, recognition of objective significance, especially with regard to logical possibility, is the mark of the realist, not the nominalist. As Hartshorne elsewhere remarks, "logical possibility" without a function in reality is the nominalist point of view. Eternal objects are nominalistic from Hartshorne's point of view because, being eternal, they seem disruptive of dynamic concrete continuity.

5. *"Experience: The Problem of the Datum.* There is a crying scandal in philosophy. This is the paradox of an extreme diversity of opinion in regard to the immediately given as such (that is to say, apparently, in regard to the obvious in its very obviousness)." Hartshorne resolves the "crying scandal" by reference to the continuum which is at once affective, aesthetic, and social. In this way, "Realistic idealism as social animism or direct affective community will be established by the data themselves as the sole descriptively accurate account of experience."

Acknowledging that his "realistic idealism" account of experience is only generally outlined by Peirce, Hartshorne calls for a more detailed development [*see* PPS]. Hartshorne's willingness to designate his position as "an idealistic one" does not mean, however, that he is formally an idealist. Hartshorne writes: "If, indeed, 'idealism' means that reality is essentially spiritual, and if 'spiritual' means, as I think it should, irreducibly socio-emotional, or having to do with 'love,' then the most general conclusion which I feel war-

---

[19] Hartshorne, "Continuity, the Form of Forms, in Charles Peirce," p. 527. A study of the relationship between Peirce and at least one type of Scholastic Realism is found in John Boler, *Charles Peirce and Scholastic Realism: A Study of Peirce's Relation to John Duns Scotus* (Seattle: University of Washington Press, 1963).

ranted in drawing from the evidence supporting the chief historical suggestions of the word 'idealism,' I should as little wish to defend as the 'realists.'" Another response to Hartshorne's call for a more detailed development appears in his article of 1949, "A Synthesis of Idealism and Realism" [see RSP, 69 ff.]. Here "realistic idealism" is developed through four theses which Hartshorne holds are complementary:

1. An "object," or that of which a particular subject is aware, in no degree depends upon that subject.
      Principle of Objective Independence.
      Common sense, Aristotle, Whitehead, Perry, Moore.

2. A "subject," or whatever is aware of anything, always depends upon the entities of which it is aware, its objects.
      Principle of Subjective Dependence.
      Common sense, Aristotle, Whitehead.
      (1) and (2) constitute "realism."

3. Any entity must be (or at least be destined to become) object for *some* subject or other.
      Principle of Universal Objectivity. "Idealism."
      Berkeley, Whitehead.

4. Any concrete entity is a subject, or set of subjects; hence, any other concrete entity of which a subject, S1, is aware, is another subject or subjects (S2; or S2, S3, etc.)
      Principle of Universal Subjectivity. "Panpsychism."
      Leibniz, Peirce, Whitehead. [RSP, 70]

The basic congruity of these four theses is captured in the term "panpsychism," "the view that all things, in all their aspects, consist exclusively of 'souls,' that is, of various kinds of subjects, or units of experiencing, with their qualifications, relations, and groupings or communities.[20] In panpsychism the immediately given of experience is treated from the standpoint of all four theses. Mentioning Peirce only under "Universal Subjectivity" does not limit his position to one aspect of the synthesis; for, as a synthesis, each part plays into the other. Universal subjectivity does suggest, however, how Peirce's continuum differs from the concreteness of phenomenologi-

[20] "Panpsychism," Chapter 35, *A History of Philosophical Systems,* ed. Vergilius Ferm (New York: The Philosophical Library, 1950), p. 442.

cal and existential subjectivity. Phenomenological and existential subjectivity tend to remain in the tradition of anthropomorphic idealism, while full concreteness requires that subjectivity go beyond man, that it be objectively extended from insects[21] to birds[22] through man to the stars; that concrete continuity is truly universal and not enclosed in personal subjectivity.

6. *"Explanation and contingency.* . . . The universe as a whole is logically contingent with respect to the realm of possibility. Explanation in metaphysics cannot then be in terms of causal necessity. The alternative to necessity is chance." As we noted in the discussion of law and freedom above, Hartshorne is a philosopher of freedom in that freedom is real in the universe. He finds an especially vivid expression of freedom in Peirce's "tychism"[23]—"An important contribution involved in Peirce's view is his uniquely vivid sense of the spontaneous, creative, or chance-character of the life of feeling; the radical absurdity of looking for a reason for blue or green or sour or any other quality of feeling."[24] Inclusion of a "chance-character" in concrete reality gives metaphysical explanation a new direction. This direction may lead to God.

> The actual is explicable as the progressive creation by fiat of logically contingent discontinuities out of that necessary continuum of possibilities whose being consists in the eternal unity of the creative power. This power may, according to Peirce, best be conceived through the admittedly vague conception or experience of God.[25]

7. *"The Universe.* The law of continuity is a formal principle, a principle of analysis, or a *regulative* principle. Its constitutive cor-

---

[21] See Hartshorne, "Is God's Existence a State of Affairs?" *Faith and the Philosophers,* ed. John Hick (New York: St. Martin's Press, 1964), p. 30.

[22] Hartshorne expresses his feeling for small creatures in his ornithological writings, for example, "The Phenomenon of Bird Song," *Emory University Quarterly* (U.S.A.), XII, No. 3 (October, 1956), 139-147.

[23] See especially Peirce's *Collected Papers,* VII, Book I.

[24] "Panpsychism," Chapter 35, *A History of Philosophical Systems,* p. 449.

[25] The coincidence of God and the continuum in metaphysical explanation is a topic for Part II. Note, however, such coincidence arises in Hartshorne's discussion of Peirce's understanding of continuity and contingency.

relate in the concrete, its metaphysical basis and final meaning . . .
is the principle of *social community*." Social community as correlate
of concrete continuity returns us to the foundation upon which
Hartshorne based his critique of Husserl and Heidegger. Although
the descriptive terms change, we can also discover why Hartshorne
sees in the continuum a basis for the intuitively known real immanence of social reality. And here, as in the following passage, the
universal character of actual experience emerges.

> The universe is the synthesis of the possible and the actual.
> The actual, in turn, is that which can be reached solely through
> its dynamical contact with present experience. Not otherwise
> can it be defined. But this implies that all actuality is organi-
> cally contained in the individual present experience. The result-
> ing organic or dynamical relativity is continuity in its existen-
> tial mode. According to this, even numerical difference, indi-
> vidual being, is a matter of degree, as may be illustrated by
> the phenomena of multiple personality, and in a thousand ways.

Scientists are now finding it necessary to abandon the old classifi-
cations—animal, vegetable, mineral, etc. The problem of classifying animals and plants in the continuum is not unrelated to the
problem of saying what a "man" is. Recent studies have destroyed
the old definitions of man, such as "toolmaker"; at the same time
the space age has lifted visions of the universe out of anthropocen-
tric categories, causing even more uncertainty in the use of the
abstract concept "man." Facing the problem of a definition of man,
Hartshorne has recently suggested that "instead of 'man' we could
say, 'rational being, other than God.' . . ."[26] Microcosmically and
macrocosmically, Hartshorne's principle of degrees in continuity is
illustrated on every hand.

In summary, Hartshorne's study of Peirce reveals a movement toward the concrete that parallels the historical direction
of Husserl and Heidegger. Earlier presuppositions are now given
sharper expression through Peirce's continuum. In the 1929 article,

[26] Hartshorne, "Real Possibility," p. 594. For a systematic development of the theology of Peirce see John E. Smith, "Religion and Theology in Peirce," *Studies in the Philosophy of Charles Sanders Peirce*,
pp. 251 ff. Peirce's published writings on religion appear in *Collected
Papers*, vi, Book ii.

Hartshorne's discussion of the centrality of the continuum takes on larger significance because it is developed as an "exegesis" of Hartshorne's own definition of philosophy, namely, "The descriptive science of the most general characters of experience, and the explanatory science of the total universe of actuality and possibility." Out of the development of this definition, Hartshorne elucidates several of the more important dimensions of his philosophy, each of which underscores concrete continuity.

4

Whitehead: Actual Occasions

Hartshorne is sometimes called a Whiteheadian. Their extensive agreement on metaphysical issues gives solid reasons for the truth of this claim. They are both committed to concrete actuality, constitutive memory, aesthetic evaluation, descriptive metaphysics, real creativity, the reality of change, freedom and social becoming. Their disagreement on the question of eternal objects is, in Hartshorne's view, secondary. Perhaps their greatest difference will be found in Hartshorne's development of Whiteheadian theology and not within the present philosophical discussions at all. In any case, no elucidation of the Hartshornian understanding of the concrete is complete without attending to Whitehead's philosophy of actual occasions.

FROM THE STANDPOINT of classical metaphysics, one can see why Hartshorne thinks phenomenological and existential emphases upon particular experiences are *more* concrete. Certainly concreteness also requires some sort of explanatory principle like Peirce's continuum to account for concrete actualization. But from Hartshorne's perspective it is only in Whitehead that the concrete is adequately described. From a Whiteheadian point of view, Hartshorne is prepared to say exactly why other philosophies, for example phenomenology, fail to achieve full concreteness.

As Professor Whitehead would phrase it, they have committed the "fallacy of misplaced concreteness": that is to say, since by abstract we mean indeterminate in respects which a more concrete mode of representation would "fill in" or render determinate, they have tended to take as the most fundamental and all-explanatory ideas those which are the least determinate

43

in their meaning. In other words they have sought to explain the definite by the indefinite.[1]

In describing phenomenology's shortcoming by using Whitehead's notion of the "fallacy of misplaced concreteness," Hartshorne equates concreteness with definiteness. How is this equation to be understood in the light of Hartshorne's over-all thought and his discussion of Whitehead in general? *What* is definite?

To Whitehead the definite is the actual occasion or actual entity. Just as Heidegger's "definite" appears in the analysis of *Dasein* in *Being and Time*, Whitehead's "definite" is described in the analysis of the "actual entity" in his major work, *Process and Reality*. Here Whitehead says,

> "Actual entities"—also termed "actual occasions"—are the final real things of which the world is made up. There is no going behind actual entities to find anything more real. They differ among themselves; God is an actual entity, and so is the most trivial puff of existence in far-off empty space. But, though there are gradations of importance, and diversities of function, yet in the principles which actuality exemplifies all are on the same level. The final facts are, all alike, actual entities; and these actual entities are drops of experience, complex and interdependent.[2]

Generally, that mode of analysis which expresses the interdependence of actual entities or actual occasions is the concrete mode: that mode of analysis which expresses the independence of an actual entity is the more abstract mode. The fact that there are different types of analysis, however, does not indicate that there are two realities, because Whitehead's philosophy is a thoroughgoing monism. How abstraction and concretion are "held together" becomes *the* question of philosophy: "The explanatory purpose of philosophy is often misunderstood. Its business is to explain the emergence of the more abstract things from the more concrete things."[3]

A Whiteheadian answer to this question must begin with the analysis of the most definite concrete reality, the actual entity. How

---

[1] Hartshorne, Review of *Sein und Zeit*, p. 285.
[2] Alfred North Whitehead, *Process and Reality, An Essay in Cosmology* (New York: Harper & Row, 1960), pp. 27-28.
[3] *Ibid.*, p. 30.

do actual entities become what they are? Actual entities become actual entities by virtue of the selections which individual subjective aims (wills) make from the range of concrete possibilities presented to them individually. In human terms, a man becomes what he is partly through the decisions he makes. Once a decision has been made, it is actual and thus immediately a participant in the realm of possibilities out of which future actualizations emerge. When the subjective aim chooses (concrete thinking) on the basis of its freedom, it becomes in that immediate situation something novel; an actual entity is born.

Even this brief sketch reveals many differences between Whitehead's method and phenomenology. If nothing else, their concerns lead in different directions. For example, Whitehead is willing to give *Process and Reality* the subtitle "An Essay in Cosmology." To Whitehead this means that the analysis of the actual entity should be sufficiently fundamental to the whole of reality or the cosmos to permit no exceptions. (In other words, phenomenologists, and existentialists, focus upon essence somewhat subjectively.) Unafraid of metaphysics, Whitehead attempts to analyze generally exhibited characteristics in the objective cosmos. To Whitehead philosophical analysis is abstraction from the concrete experience of the cosmos, but this does not mean that *what* is analyzed is any less definite.

Abstract philosophical descriptions are descriptive of definite concrete entities. When phenomenology describes less definite "ideal essences," the "fallacy of misplaced concreteness" occurs. This "principle" can be clarified by examination of some of Hartshorne's praise of Whitehead in *Science, Metaphysics, and Civilization, Three Essays on the Thought of Alfred North Whitehead*.[4]

[4] Hartshorne, "Whitehead's Metaphysics," in *Whitehead and the Modern World: Science, Metaphysics, and Civilization, Three Essays on the Thought of Alfred North Whitehead*, by Victor Lowe, Charles Hartshorne, and A. H. Johnson (Boston: Beacon Press, 1950), pp. 25 ff. The twelve points of praise of Whitehead are: (1) rationalism; (2) empiricism; (3) realism; (4) idealism; (5) belief in the God of religion; (6) doctrine of causality; (7) embodiment of relational logic in a metaphysical system; (8) notion of character as product; (9) generalization of biological cell theory; (10) reason for temporal atomicity; (11) universalization of societies; (12) "generalization of comparative psychology and sociology downwards to include physiology, biology, chemistry, and physics as studies of the more elementary types of sentient individuals and societies." Numbers (6), (7), (8), and (11) will be discussed here.

Such an examination will provide a foundation for what Hartshorne considers Whitehead's truly novel contribution. Since this discussion is designed not only to illuminate dimensions of the Hartshornian concrete, but to engage traditional questions, it will be appropriate to conclude with a statement of the relationship between being and becoming.

In his first point of praise, Hartshorne claims that "Whitehead, more than any other, has really 'answered Hume'!" Here, the reference is to Hume's skepticism concerning causality. Hartshorne thinks that in Whitehead's "account of memory and physical purpose, generalized in his 'reformed subjectivism,' by his explanation of order in terms of aesthetic drives, focused in God," causality is given a new basis. "Reformed subjectivism" is equated with Hartshorne's own "realistic idealism" [RSP, 70]; but what of memory and aesthetic drives? Memory and aesthetic drives are key concepts, not only in understanding causality, but as definite dimensions of concrete experience.

With Whitehead,[5] Hartshorne understands memory as constituent of being. "A man *is* a bundle of memories that are relatively vague and general" [BH, 136]. Because it is ontologically grounded, memory requires no epistemological mechanism for its operation upon its objects. Memory "simply *is* the experience of these objects. . . . Past experiences, since they have actually occurred, are available for experiencing, and present experience enjoys them as its objects" [LP, 227]. The function of the brain is to add new harmonious content. Hartshorne gives the example of looking at green grass. Where does the greenness that we see when we look at green grass come from? Since we can have vivid experience of greenness with our eyes closed, it seems that the greenness must be coming from the brain or nerve cells. Following Whitehead, Hartshorne maintains that these cells cause experience such as greenness by being the immediate content of the experience itself. Ontologically overlapping, influence between cells, moreover, is reciprocal; hence,

[5] In addition to memory as constituent of being, Whitehead mentions that "memory is a disengagement of mind from the mere passage of nature" (*The Concept of Nature* [Ann Arbor: University of Michigan Press, 1957]). Cf. this doctrine of memory as disengagement with being as abstraction below.

"cells can influence our human experiences because they have feelings that we can feel" [LP, 229].

Time also depends upon memory in that past experiences (the content of memory) are potential for future actualizations. This means that when we look back from effect to cause, "we find a certain definite past to be implicated as furnishing the 'real possibility' of the sort of effect which has taken place; looking toward the future, the effect is implicated only as a kind, or class, of really possible effects, some instances or other of which must occur."[6] For example, if the effect is greenness, then greenness is a class that stands open to the future in memory. It should be recalled that memory is not merely something the self has—it is what the self is. However, the self is not limited to memory; having a subjective aim or will implies a transcendental self. The self can be its past experiences as memory and at the same time transcend them because the future is really future.

In Hartshorne's example: "If . . . I am seeing green grass, this will inhibit some memories and favor others, partly for reasons of aesthetic harmony and discord" [LP, 288]. Inhibition is the negative side of positive selection among real possibilities.[7] In his essay "Harmony in Life and Nature," Hartshorne maintains there must be both likeness and difference if harmony among possibilities is to be intelligible [RSP, 44 ff.]. Aesthetic harmony entails unification of likeness and difference, unity in contrast.[8] This means that "there are only two ways of failing to achieve harmony—by too little contrast ('insipidity,' 'monotony'), and too little similarity ('discord,' 'incoherence,' and 'chaos')."[9]

[6] Hartshorne, "Whitehead and Contemporary Philosophy," *The Relevance of Whitehead: Philosophical Essays in Commemoration of the Centenary of the Birth of Alfred North Whitehead*, ed. Ivor Leclerc (London: Allen and Unwin, 1961), p. 40.

[7] It is interesting to compare this notion of inhibition with Heidegger's understanding of truth as nonconcealment. Cf., for example, Heidegger's *Holzwege* (2nd ed., Frankfurt: Klostermann, 1952), p. 245.

[8] Hartshorne elsewhere remarks that "the more an artistic unity can permit rich individuation of its members the higher the unity (thus drama is superior to an oriental rug) . . ." [DR, 115].

[9] Hartshorne, *The Divine Relativity, A Social Conception of God* (New Haven: Yale University Press), p. 46.

At first glance there appears to be a conflict between the "law" of aesthetics and the desire to avoid prescriptive abstractions. The conflict is resolved, however, when it is recalled that a law or character must be a product. Hence, aesthetic characterization is derivative description; otherwise, it would have the effect of committing the "fallacy of misplaced concreteness" by implying that the law itself has concrete priority.

This does not mean that no aesthetic experience can occur until it is abstractly described. In fact, Hartshorne is convinced that

> . . . all abstract knowledge presupposes intuitive awareness. Hence, esthetics establishes data that all abstract knowledge must take into account if its basis in immediacy is to be understood. And unless this basis is understood, we cannot know what the abstractness of the knowledge consists in, what it is of concrete reality that is omitted.[10]

Following Whitehead, Hartshorne presupposes intuitive aesthetic experience as the concrete reality from which abstractions are made. The "fallacy of misplaced concreteness" occurs when the situation is reversed. Because "intuitive awareness," concrete immediacy, is the experience of the whole, any concreteness claimed for an abstraction from that whole is a "fallacy." The definite is intuitively experienced, the indefinite is abstraction from that experience. This "aesthetic" scheme is clearly more than a theory of art. The synthesis of likeness and difference involved in selection among possible alternatives amounts to aesthetic enjoyment of the universe. Hartshorne agrees with Whitehead in making aesthetics fundamental to metaphysics and cosmology. The Whiteheadian-Hartshornian notion of aesthetic harmony can be found in Hegel, but in Hegel, as in many others, classical absolutization nullifies its force. Is it only chance that reactions to Hegel's formulation of unity-in-contrast have tended toward too much unity (communism) or too much diversity (existentialism)?

Hartshorne's second reason for praising Whitehead is his opinion that "Whitehead is the first to embody modern relational logic in a

[10] *Ibid.*, p. 44. This should also be remembered in understanding Hartshorne's version of the ontological argument for God's existence. (*See* Chapter 7.)

fairly complete metaphysical system. (Peirce perhaps came nearest to anticipating this achievement.)" In drawing out the importance of Peirce's continuum, something of the nature of relational logic has already been seen. Now Hartshorne views Whitehead as the one who has put Peircian logic into an adequate metaphysical system. Hartshorne here understands *logic* to be "the study of relational structures as involved in meaning."[11] *Metaphysics*, he thinks, "ought to be the study of relational structures as embodied in reality as such, or taken generally."[12] It is this metaphysical embodiment of logic which accounts for the "systematic clarity and comprehensiveness" that Hartshorne thinks Whitehead has achieved.

Hartshorne's third point of praise presents a setting in which to see the problem of the "eternal objects," the major point of disagreement between Hartshorne and Whitehead.

> Whitehead is among the first to see the philosophical generality inherent in the principle of evolution, the principle that the characters of things, as expressed in their ways of acting, are products of change; and to see that this enables us to dispense with the mythical notions of laws as eternally fixed, yet quantitatively definite, aspects of behavior. . . .

In contrast to generality, Hartshorne thinks Whitehead's "eternal objects" are incompatible with the notion that characters are products of change. Like Platonic forms,[13] eternal objects unnecessarily control temporal change. Instead of being products of change, eternal objects "must be distinct from and independent of any given individuals, since they infinitely antedate the latter."[14] Also, characters or universals must remain vague. Eternal objects, Hartshorne

[11] Hartshorne, "Whitehead's Metaphysics," p. 34.
[12] *Ibid.*
[13] In his essay, "Santayana's Doctrine of Essence," Hartshorne remarks, "Whitehead's eternal objects seem to me to involve excessive concessions to a Platonism of Santayana's type" (*The Philosophy of George Santayana*, ed. Paul Arthur Schilpp [Evanston: Northwestern University, 1940]). A corrective to Whitehead's Platonism is also suggested from an explicitly nominalist standpoint. Cf. Hartshorne, "Whitehead and Contemporary Philosophy," p. 35.
[14] Hartshorne, "The Compound Individual," *Philosophical Essays for Alfred North Whitehead* (New York: Longmans, Green and Co., 1936), p. 217.

maintains, "are not specific qualities, as Whitehead (perhaps even Peirce) seems to think, but only vague directions of determinability or specificability."[15] Hartshorne thinks, ". . . since by Whitehead's own method of extensive abstraction continuity is treated as the possibility of endless division. . . . Eternally there is just the unitary vague field of quality, not a set of pointlike determinate qualities."[16] Hartshorne admits actualities are "everlasting," not eternal, but he is not speaking of actualities, because continuity represents the continuum of *possibilities*, not actualities, of possible forms.

Again, he says, "I have here been greatly influenced by Peirce's conception of the 'evolution of . . . the very Platonic forms themselves.'"[17] This focuses the problem of eternal objects for Hartshorne, because "eternal" objects cannot participate in the temporal flow. This makes it clear why Hartshorne was attracted by Peirce's continuum of possibility, and why Peirce presents a "slight corrective" to Whitehead.[18] Hartshorne is willing, however, to defend Whitehead's system as a whole against the charge of Platonism.[19] Such an approach, he thinks, overestimates the extent to which Whitehead is committed to eternal objects.[20] Further, the charge of Platonism cannot be maintained along with the very key to Whitehead's system, "creative synthesis."[21] This key "is not merely *a* Whiteheadian principle, but *the* principle—'the category of the ultimate.'"[22] Hartshorne fears that creativity is damped by eternality. If reality were eternal, what sense could creativity have?

[15] Hartshorne, "The Relativity of Non-Relativity," *Studies in the Philosophy of Charles Sanders Peirce*, p. 224.

[16] *Ibid.*

[17] *Philosophical Interrogations,* ed. with an introduction by Sydney and Beatrice Rome (New York: Holt, Rinehart and Winston, 1964), p. 329. Hartshorne cites Peirce's *Collected Papers*, vi, Sections 194, 185-212.

[18] In attacking Whitehead's "eternal objects," Hartshorne views the issue very differently from, say, Ivor Leclerc. *See* Ivor Leclerc, "Whitehead and the Theory of Form," *Process and Divinity, The Hartshorne Festschrift,* ed. by William L. Reese and Eugene Freeman (LaSalle, Ill.: Open Court Publishing Co., 1964), pp. 127-137. Leclerc thinks eternal objects are necessary to Whitehead's system.

[19] Hartshorne, "Whitehead and Contemporary Philosophy," p. 35.

[20] *Ibid.*

[21] *Ibid.*

[22] *Ibid.*

Of course, this argument could be reversed and put: "Why create since nothing is eternal?" The latter question does not bother Hartshorne because of his conviction that everything is everlastingly in the memory of God (not eternally). This is a plausible solution, and it maintains the primacy of temporal events, since nothing *is* until it has happened in time. The question may be: Can we live with time? More than asking that we live without Whitehead's eternal objects, Hartshorne is asking us to live without eternity altogether!

The principle of Hartshorne's thought might be explained as "reality is social process."[23] In his final point of praise, Hartshorne finds himself in basic agreement with Whitehead on this principle.

> Whitehead seems to be the only philosopher to note the universality of societies in the cosmos, at all levels; also, and best of all, he is the first to see that what is called an individual in common life (and much philosophy) can only be understood as a *form of sequence* of particular actualities socially inheriting common quality from antecedent members; and that personality itself is a special temporally linear case of such social— that is, sympathetic—inheritance.

The first basis of this social view is the universality of sympathy, "though it is sometimes very rudimentary, and sometimes qualified strongly by antipathy" [RSP, 21]. A man knows others and himself because of concrete social togetherness, sympathetic sociality. Although there are many possible interpretations of Whitehead's philosophy, most agree it is social in this sense. Hartshorne emphasizes the social instead of, for example, the organic. The latter emphasis can be found in Dorothy M. Emmet's *Whitehead's Philosophy of Organism*.[24] Hartshorne, as he remarked before the American Catholic Philosophical Association in 1961, prefers "a more

---

[23] The theme of reality as social process appears, as we have already seen, in earlier writings and continues throughout his work. In a graduate seminar at Emory University in 1961, at which Hartshorne was present, Hartshorne did not object to Harry Cannon's suggestion that this theme "sums up" Hartshorne's philosophy.

[24] Dorothy M. Emmet, *Whitehead's Philosophy of Organism* (London: Macmillan and Co., 1932).

central technical term than 'organism.' "[25] In addition to being more "technical," the social, or "societism," "amounts to a social theory of reality."[26]

Second, the theory of individual personality as a *form of sequence* means that abstract forms are products of temporal actualities of events.[27] The form "of" a sequence is not prior to that sequence, but the product of that sequence. This means that character is a cross section of man's temporal growth at any given moment [BH, 153]. This is what is meant when personality is described as a "linear case."

How forms are in actual sequences is clarified in our second over-all point concerning Hartshorne's view of Whitehead and the "fallacy of misplaced concreteness." In the above four points of praise much of Hartshorne's view of Whitehead has emerged; but what single aspect of this system is considered to be both new and central? In his 1963 essay, "Whitehead's Novel Intuition,"[28] Hartshorne says, "Whitehead . . . wrote one phrase which comes as close as any to capturing the novel insight which his philosophy expresses: 'The many become one and are increased by one' [PR, 32]."[29] This statement is not in conflict with the above-mentioned "key," but is rather an expression of how the key works. Hartshorne develops Whitehead's novel intuition, insisting that there is a new insight in the notion that the pluralism of the "many" enters into an additional unity. Each event is a potentiality for subsequent be-

[25] Hartshorne, "Whitehead, The Anglo-American Philosopher-Scientist," *Proceedings of the American Catholic Philosophical Association* (Washington, D.C.: The Catholic University of America), p. 165.
[26] *Ibid.*
[27] Hartshorne uses the term "events" interchangeably with Whitehead's "actualities," and "events" have the same characteristic as Whitehead's "actual occasions." For example, they are immortal in the same way. Hartshorne says, "Western neoclassical philosophy has produced a synthetic-conservative theory of events in which the 'immortality of the past' is provided for, without any relapse from the standpoint of becoming. . . . Events endure—but in later events, not in any mere being. Fechner, Bergson, and Peirce adumbrate this doctrine; Whitehead is perhaps the first clear expositor of it" [LP, 18].
[28] In *Alfred North Whitehead: Essays on His Philosophy*, ed. George L. Kline (Englewood Cliffs, N.J.: Prentice-Hall, Inc., 1963), pp. 18-26.
[29] *Ibid.*, p. 18. PR is Whitehead's *Process and Reality, An Essay in Cosmology.*

coming, and when it is actualized it moves from the externality of being a possibility to the internality of being realized. This means that the actual events themselves do not change; *change is merely their successive becoming.*[30] This may be illustrated by counting. In the series, 1, 2, 3, 4, each number changes its antecedent (in this case 1's antecedent is any fraction) by being *an addition* to the total series of which that number is a part. Each new number adds, and is not simply derived; hence, looking from 3 to 4 the relation is external; from 4 to 3, internal. The number 3 may be said to be a possibility for 4, and 4 an actuality after 3; but when an actuality "becomes," it becomes a unity through novel addition.

When Hartshorne adds to his discussion of Whitehead's "intuition" the argument that indeterminism is implied, the problem of the abstract reappears.

> Whitehead's indeterminism is implicit in what has been said. If the new unity were deducible from the old, it would logically be no addition at all, and the degree of multiplicity would not be "increased." Any causal laws used for the deduction must be viewed as mere abstract aspects of the previous multiplicity; and in any case, how can a law prescribe just how a set of items is to be embraced in a new equally unitary item?[31]

Hartshorne and Whitehead may justly be called philosophers of freedom. Both think of novel happenings as free because the future is open and the unifying intuition can actualize from more than one possibility. Concrete freedom is real just because the possibilities remain possibilities and not actualities. Hartshorne is fond of describing what he calls the "Harvard Law of Indeterminacy," in which a Harvard scientist tries to control every response of an animal under laboratory conditions. The frustrated scientist finally deduces the following axiom: "A given animal under carefully controlled conditions—will do whatever it damn well pleases!" We might say the scientist is legalistically trying to force a "concrete"

[30] *Ibid.*, p. 19 (italics added).
[31] *Ibid.*, p. 20.

being into prescribed conditions, and freedom is illustrated by the practical conclusion that its alternative, strict determinism, does not work (as quantum mechanics confirms). Whitehead's "novel intuition," it seems, pushes abstract law in the direction of a negative. Perhaps our third area of discussion, the relationship between being and becoming, will clarify this.

What happens to being? Is not "being" the "whole," and consequently immune to Whitehead's "fallacy"? Hartshorne answers this question on the grounds of his study of both Peirce and Whitehead.

> Peirce and Whitehead, it was pleasant to learn, both taught that the structure of reality is social through and through; but Whitehead had the fuller, sharper conception of this structure, in relation to facts of direct experience and scientific inference. And Whitehead had, what no other man had ever had, as it seems: a complete, all-sided, explicit conception of social *process* as the concrete ultimate mode of reality, of which mere "being" is always an abstract element, or, in the less abstract cases, a deposit or fixed resultant. [RSP, 20]

Because the concrete whole of social process is becoming and not being, concrete being would reintroduce the "fallacy of misplaced concreteness." In the same way that character is a "cross section" of a man's temporal sequence, being is an abstract "cross section" of a becoming. The definite is concrete becoming; the indefinite is abstract being.

Although Husserl and Heidegger represent a movement toward the concrete, and Peirce adequately describes its nature as a continuum, Whitehead provides the "fuller, sharper conception." In accomplishing this, Whitehead is praised for his solution to the problem of causality, especially in terms of memory and aesthetics; for his embodiment of relational logic in a "fairly complete metaphysical system"; for his notion of characters as products, except for the problem of eternal objects; and for his realization of the universality of societies. Moreover, Whitehead's really new contribution is his notion that "The many become one and are increased by one." Successive becoming means change, change by addition. Finally, out of Hartshorne's discussion of Whitehead, the relationship between the abstract and the concrete emerges as being analogous to the fact that characters are abstract descriptions of concrete becoming. Hence, Whitehead's notion of the "fallacy of misplaced concreteness" clarifies both aesthetic experience and the nature of being. The "fallacy" is committed when any law, concept, or other abstraction such as "being" prescribes concrete becoming. What being will be depends upon what the concrete becomes. Concrete time is real and the future is really open.

5

Hartshorne:
The Inclusive Concrete

There is one methodological principle fundamental to Hartshorne's thought. This is his conviction that the concrete is greater than and includes all abstractions. An understanding of this principle is required if his treatment of theological topics is to be understood. The principle can be elucidated as an understanding of the nature of abstraction, identity, immortality, necessity, and thinking. It is based, however, upon all dimensions of concrete reality. As such it is clearly a way to describe just what metaphysical principles are intended to describe—the whole of reality inclusive of contingent particulars.

HARTSHORNE'S CRITIQUES of Husserl, Heidegger, Peirce, and Whitehead reveal much of what concrete means in his philosophy; a more systematic formulation will unify these elements.

In order to define Hartshorne's concrete, it is necessary to think of definition as a product of function, just as character is a product of a changing person: Hartshorne believes "a thing is what it does" [BH, 146]. During World War II when the United States government was having difficulty classifying physicists for military purposes, a panel of experts was called to Washington and charged with the task of defining a physicist. After hours of careful deliberation they concluded: "A physicist is—what a physicist does!" The problem they acknowledged is the problem recognized by Hartshorne when he says actual doing is concrete becoming, and what "is" after it has occurred is an abstraction. Because it is crucial that abstraction follow, and not precede, concrete occurrence, to describe and not prescribe actualization, a formula is required to ensure this relationship between the terms. Hartshorne's descriptive method of understanding may be symbolized:

C = the concrete
) = is greater than and includes
A = the abstract

A) C means that the inclusive concrete contains the abstract; is ontologically prior to the abstract; precedes the abstract temporally; and that the changing concrete is superior to abstractions which do not change.

For example, A) C may be applied to a hypothetical situation in jurisprudence. Imagine that several traffic accidents have occurred in a small town and the first traffic light has been installed. New town ordinances on traffic lights are written, but the city fathers forget to make exceptions for fire-fighting equipment. In other respects the new laws are good; they represent an assessment of the concrete situation of life and the formulation of abstract laws by which needed order is introduced. One day a fire develops, and as the fire truck rushes across town through the red light it injures a child in the crosswalk. Subsequently the child's family sues the firemen because they were breaking the law, which did not cover this situation. What is needed (and what many laws actually have) is a contingency factor so that the abstract law can be adjusted to the concrete need. Certainly, it would be good for the child's family to have compensation, but the firemen should have some protection, because they are required to rush to the aid of other citizens and the legal adjustment has clearly been an oversight. The problem of inflexible abstractions that result in harmful limitations upon the concrete is easily extended to other realms of concern; for example, members of some religious sects still oppose blood transfusions even for excellent medical reasons.

The relationship between the abstract and the concrete is significant in everyday life. What is its significance in Hartshorne's thought? For Hartshorne, characters are abstract descriptions, i.e., products of temporal change. He praises Whitehead as a philosopher who had "... a complete, all-sided, explicit conception of social *process* as the concrete ultimate mode of reality, of which mere 'being' is always an abstract element, or in the less abstract cases, a deposit or fixed resultant." Clearly, in general terms Hartshorne sees the relationship as A) C, but what does this mean specifically?

In the first place the formula A) C is itself an abstract theory. In Hartshorne's words:

> Any theory, even a theory that there can in a given sphere be no theory worthy of the name, is composed of abstractions. Now an abstraction in general is a way of dealing with a multiple of facts as constituting for certain purposes one fact. It is a mode of unification of experience. [PPS, 29]

Our formulation, A) C, is designed precisely to deal with "a multiple of facts," or "events," but by what method can it be tested? According to Hartshorne, there are "two dimensions along which the success of abstract formulations should be measured . . ." [PPS, 29].

One dimension is "the extent and variety of the facts so reduced to one fact . . ." [PPS, 29]. Immediately, the advantage of the distinction between the abstract and the concrete appears. If reduction to one fact were concrete reduction, reality as social process would not be described; it would be forced into an unreal abstraction. Taken in this way, metaphysics would be the mortal enemy of reality. Aesthetic enjoyment of the universe would be impossible because unity would erase contrast. A) C is clearly not concrete reduction, because it is an abstract theory that is being tested. Reduction of variety is abstract reduction. In A) C reduction as limitation is not negative; it implies a positive understanding of concrete reality through descriptive classification. The purpose of deduction is descriptive classification. The first point of Hartshorne's elucidation of his definition of philosophy and Peirce's continuum was just this kind of description. *Description as comparison* remains unintelligible apart from the distinction between the abstract and the concrete. The adequacy of a description is subject to test because in its status as an abstract theory it gives itself to more than one possible application. That is, an abstract philosophical expression may be tested in different concrete situations precisely because it is abstract. The greater the "extent and variety" of the concrete field tested, the more force an abstract explanation obtains. If A) C can be helpfully applied to the universe as a whole, it is ultimately more adequate than abstractions which take into account very limited data.

The other dimension in which abstract formulations should be measured follows closely upon the first. Namely, it should be tested for "completeness and thoroughness of unification." Aesthetic enjoyment does not collapse the diversity of concrete contrast, because the concrete itself remains diverse. The other extreme is also to be avoided. The abstract must be a unification or remain blind (cf. Kant). The self that does the abstracting must somehow intend concrete diversity (cf. Husserl) or lose its function. Either a human will unifies or it is useless. The test is how complete or thorough the unifying agency is. If will itself is disclaimed, nothing "is," because a thing or person "is what it (or he) does." The question, then, is not whether or not an agent abstracts, but whether abstraction is adequately accomplished. If one goes to a concert and hears only a succession of noises (when a symphony was intended), either the performance or the listener failed adequately to abstract. If the intended symphony is truly symphonic, truly unifies diverse sounds, the test of adequate abstraction (from a series of noises) has been successful. The question is: When the formula A) C is applied to reality, does reality, as we experience and know it, resemble a succession of unintelligible noises or a symphony? This is the test to which reality as a whole or any subclass may be put. This test of the formula shows that the formula itself is an abstraction that does not prescribe reality but, rather, describes it.

Second, the formula provides a way to maintain a doctrine of identity. Perhaps the greatest single difficulty that a casual observer has with a philosophy of becoming is the problem of identity. Identity appears to be swept away in a Heraclitean flux. In the notion of change as successive addition already discussed lies a clue to Hartshorne's approach to this problem. Change does not mean that the entity itself changes, except in its eternal relations to future occurrences or events. It follows that the changeless may be said to be self-identical. What then happens to this identity when it is seen as a part of a sequence or series of self-identical events? The answer lies in Hartshorne's adoption of a distinction between "strict" and "genetic" identity. For this formulation Hartshorne acknowledges his indebtedness to Heinrich Scholz (*Metaphysik als strenge Wissenschaft*).[1] Scholz contrasts *Identität* with *Gen-identität*. *Identität*, or strict identity, refers only to single occasions (Whitehead) themselves. Hartshorne thinks:

> No other *concrete* entity is immune to change, always simply and purely identical with itself. True, the occasion is not eternal or timeless. Being a unity of becoming, its actuality is essentially subsequent to the occasions prior to it in time. But for all future times, it will remain self-identical. Only references to it can change; the what referred to, if it is referred to, will be simply and wholly the same.[2]

Here, immunity to change means an occasion, as opposed to a series of occasions; it is complete in itself internally. When complete it can no longer change itself. It remains in concrete memory, however, as a potentiality for the future. "Potentiality is a part of the individual essence of an existent, and it varies from one unit of existence to another."[3] If the entity had no abstract possibility for subsequent events, even its self-identity would be lost. How could identification occur without comparison of different temporal events? Without *Identität* nothing could occur that would be recognizable as a something. But just as some realization does not exhaust

[1] Cf. Hartshorne, "Strict and Genetic Identity: An Illustration of the Relations of Logic to Metaphysics," *Structure, Method, and Meaning: Essays in Honor of Henry M. Sheffer* (New York: Liberal Arts Press, 1951), pp. 242-243. In *Anselm's Discovery* Hartshorne says of Scholz, "I sometimes think that Heinrich Scholz was the noblest human being that I have ever known (I met him in 1949), a theologian who turned from theological studies to formal logic because—and this is characteristic of the man—he thought that there was no other equally honest and effective way to further the clarification of theological questions. With Whitehead he is for me the most highminded and inspiring rationalist of our century" (pp. 278-279).

[2] Hartshorne, "Strict and Genetic Identity: An Illustration of the Relations of Logic to Metaphysics," p. 244.

[3] Hartshorne, "Santayana's Doctrine of Essence," *The Philosophy of George Santayana*, "The Library of Living Philosophers," II, ed. P. A. Schilpp (Evanston: Northwestern University, 1940), p. 143.

abstract possibility, *Identität,* or strict identity, does not exhaust the whole reality of a given substance. It only refers to identity through essential qualities.[4]

In *Man's Vision of God* Hartshorne places this distinction between actual and possible things first on his list of assumptions for the classification of doctrines [MVG, 24]. Possibility and actuality refer to concrete realities which are individually subject to description as strictly self-identical. Even the continuum is an abstract description of how relationship occurs. This can be stated in terms of generalization:

> Generalization has meaning only when we have accepted, as valid independently of generalization from particulars, the generic (not merely general) idea of the actual world as such, as distinguished from mere possibilities, implying that observed particulars belong to "realities," that is, are not just isolated disembodied qualities, but samples of a universe with some principle distinguishing it from all-possibility, some principle of "limited variety". . . . [MVG, 65]

The generic idea, grounded in variety distinguishable according to the principle of strict identity (*Identität*), is itself the ground of further abstract generalization. Strict identity obtains when an occasion occurs in itself; generic identity *(Gen-identität)* is abstract description of a sequence or group of occasions. Here again the reality of the description must be described retrospectively. That is, as a characterization of a series, the generic can be only a subsequent abstract product. The notion that events may be grouped generically underscores their real interrelatedness.

When Hartshorne speaks of interrelatedness he understands relations to occur asymmetrically as to time. Past events are actual; future events are potential [LP, 248]. Being actual, past events represent modes of possibility based on their own actuality, but future events have no actuality. To become actual, possibility is embodied internally in concrete relations. "It is, then, the meaning of the universal, the abstract, as such, that it is capable of external relations, that it can be identified without considering all the rela-

----

[4] Hartshorne, "Strict and Genetic Identity: An Illustration of the Relations of Logic to Metaphysics," p. 244.

tional contexts, the concrete cases, in which it might be embodied" [MVG, 237]. Both strict and genetic identity are abstract, but "the relations of abstractions are made possible by the fact that both universals and particulars are embraced in, are internal to, concrete experiences, or individual events, as wholes" [MVG, 238]. Looking back from a present event to a past one (from 4 to 3), relations are internal. Looking forward from a past to a future event (3 to 4), relations are external.

The series 1, 2, 3, 4 may be generically described as "numbers." Considered as events within a classification, each event has its own strict identity; i.e., event number 2 is strictly identifiable as 2 and not as 1 or 3. But even the number 2 is an abstract element, a designation which itself does not exhaust the concrete reality to which it points. All identity is abstract. "And only by means of an abstract or indeterminate aspect, contrasted to a concrete, determinate one, can an individual be conceived as identical through concrete changes" [MVG, 237]. Hence, "*Being* is intelligible as the abstract fixed aspect in *becoming*, and eternity as the identical element in all temporal diversity" [LP, 248].

Following the relationship expressed in A) C, nothing has to "be" what it already "is." Rather, everything "becomes" what it "is." Of course, the range of possibilities available to ordinary events is finite and limited by virtue of that finitude. Past occurrences give prediction a high probability, but identity must always await the completion of a given event. Jean Wahl, who also advocates concrete continuity,[5] fears that the distinction between potentiality and actuality bifurcates the wholeness of the concrete. Responding to Milic Capek's charge that this leads one away from openness to the future, Wahl counters that his alternative "merges all successive stages into one single event (which is the world) but not necessarily into one single present (*actualité*)."[6] A) C is a path between the contentions of Capek and Wahl because the concrete possibilities do not have necessary relations to actualities. In this

[5] See Jean Wahl, *Vers le concret*, the essay entitled "La philosophie spéculative de Whitehead" (Paris: J. Vrin, 1932).
[6] "Interrogation of Jean Wahl Conducted by Newton P. Stall-knecht," *Philosophical Interrogations*, ed. Sydney and Beatrice Rome (New York: Holt, Rinehart and Winston, 1964), p. 193.

way, the way of high probability, concrete continuity is maintained as Wahl wishes, and Capek's desire to maintain the distinction between possibility and actuality is satisfied. It would be a devastating blow to Hartshorne's view of the concrete, and even to Wahl's view, if this distinction were not at least implicit. Like Wahl, Hartshorne wishes to maintain concrete wholeness. Hence his praise of Whitehead as one who says "that what is called an individual in common life . . . can only be understood as a form of sequence of particular actualities socially inheriting common quality from antecedent members. . . ."

For Hartshorne, identification of concrete becoming does not require actual knowledge of the future. If future indeterminacy were "misplaced," A) C would collapse because the concrete would assume the role of the abstract. There would no longer be freedom as "open" possibility on Hartshorne's terms. The indeterminism implicit in A) C, on the other hand, provides a way to avoid both strict determinism and the failure of all causality. "Indeterminism enables us to explore a third possibility, which is that conditions logically imply not any particular subsequent event as their inevitable outcome, but only a class of 'really possible' outcomes . . ." [LP, 173].

Such a third possibility maintains the value of a conjunctive A and C relationship, but, especially with regard to time, it makes the relationship of the conjunctive terms much more precise. Herein, there is "sociality of selfhood which leaves personal identity and separate freedom intact." William Ernest Hocking thinks this is "a key which promises to unlock many a door, whether in theology or in the general world-view, or in the dilemmas of a distracted world-melange aspiring to become a world order" [RSP, 16]. The distance between a traffic law for a local community and "a world order" may be very great, but if our formula is adequate, it should be applicable irrespective of the degree of complexity involved.

Before we leave the discussion of identity and the nature of temporal events, we should give some attention to a third issue, namely, immortality. The question of immortality has already been broached under the notion of concrete memory, and will arise again in the theological discussion of Part II. It appears at this point because of its kinship to the question of identity.

When an event is completely actual its identity is strictly established and not subject to change in itself. (Recall that change occurs through addition.) Yet, being strictly established does not mean being lost. Hartshorne believes that "if process is conceived as cumulative change, the having occurred of previous events may become a fixed item in later events, and so the reality of the past as object of reference in the present can be accounted for" [LP, 249].[7] Past events are externally related to later events, because, being complete in themselves, they no longer internalize (they subjectively perish). Hartshorne is well aware that this view of immortality is radically unlike the popular concept.

> A popular idea of immortality is that after death the artist will paint new pictures in some finer medium; by the same principle, the statesman will have some finer mode of group leadership opened to him, and so on. I wonder. The chance to paint pictures or lead groups seems to be here and now, and there will not, I suspect, be another—for us. Our chance to do right and not wrong, to love God and in God all creatures, is here and now. Not only will there be "no marrying and giving in marriage" in the heavenly mansions, there will, I imagine, be no personal actions of yours and mine other than those we enact before we die. [LP, 254]

Hartshorne follows Whitehead's doctrine of "objective immortality"[8] in that only the subjective will,[9] the decision-making creative agency of an individual, perishes. Hence, Hartshorne argues, ". . .

---

[7] In Hartshorne's article, "The Reality of the Past and the Unreality of the Future," the reality of the past takes on a final significance. Hartshorne says, ". . . if, after the human adventure is done, it will be exactly as if it had never occurred, then indeed there is no rational value to living," *The Hibbert Journal*, XXXVIII, No. 2 (January, 1939), 249. Also *see* "Time, Death, and Everlasting Life," Chap. 10, LP, pp. 97-107, and "The Immortality of the Past: A Critique of a Prevalent Misinterpretation," *Review of Metaphysics*, VII, No. 1 (September, 1953), 98-112.

[8] Whitehead says, ". . . actual entities, 'perpetually perish' subjectively, but are immortal objectively. Actuality in perishing acquires objectivity, while it loses subjective immediacy" (*Process and Reality*, Harper Torchbook edition, 1960), p. 44.

[9] Whitehead terms this "subjective aim" (*ibid.*, p. 29).

death is not destruction of an individual's reality but merely the affixing of the quantum of that individual's reality" [LP, 255]. He continues, "Death only says to us: More than you already have been you will not be. For instance, the virtues you have failed to acquire, you will now never acquire. It is too late. You had your chance" [LP, 255]. As the affixation of a quantum, death also does not imply the destruction of future possibility. Becoming fully concrete does not destroy an occasion as a possibility for future actualization. This understanding of immortality requires the asymmetry of time. If the future were actual[10] instead of possible, time would lose its distinction between past and future. "What time requires is *not that the past be lost,* but that the future be *really unattained* so long as it is future . . ." [MVG, 130].[11] Instead of being lost, the past becomes a concrete possibility with abstract identity. The objective immortality of the affixed past is established by concrete actualization.

The point which most concerns an understanding of A) C is the fact that enduring abstract individuality is "relative to the momentary acts which are the final concrete individuals."[12] The longer the span of time in which an abstraction must endure as self-identical, the more abstract it becomes.[13] Yet, in the same way that the relations of the continuum are real, abstractions are real. "'Abstract' does not mean unreal, but does mean real within something richer in determinations than the factor said to be abstract."[14] Abstract identity, then, does not contain concrete occurrence, but is contained by it.

[10] The problem of symmetry in the notion of actualized future time was apparently one of the topics to be discussed in Hartshorne's *The Universal Orthodoxy,* which has not yet appeared. This work was originally planned as the third part of a trilogy of which BH and MVG were the first and second parts. However, the Dwight H. Terry Lectures at Yale University, which were published as *The Divine Relativity* in 1948, seem to carry out much of the original plan. Cf. MVG, pp. xviii, 133. The latter reference mentions that Chap. 7 of *The Universal Orthodoxy* would have dealt with the matter before us.

[11] Also *see* Hartshorne, "Hume's Metaphysics and Its Present-Day Influence," *The New Scholasticism,* xxv, No. 2 (April, 1961), 158; and LP, p. 250.

[12] "The Philosophy of Creative Synthesis," *Symposium: Creativity as a Philosophical Category,* in *Journal of Philosophy,* I, v, No. 22 (October 23, 1958), 949.

[13] *Ibid.,* pp. 949-950.

[14] *Ibid.,* p. 950.

John Wild has questioned Hartshorne on this understanding of identity because of its implications concerning moral responsibility for the past of the self.[15] How can a concrete occasion be accountable for that which it literally did not do? Hartshorne replies there is a qualitative continuity if no relevant repentance has occurred, and discontinuity ("born anew") where repentance and forgiveness are complete. With Rudolf Bultmann, he concludes that "innocence-and-guilt is a new issue every moment."[16] The latter claim makes sense because of Hartshorne's view of the concrete and his rejection of any attempt to view the cosmos in terms of a strict accounting in a reward-punishment scheme. "The world is not," he insists, "a cosmically extended police court."[17]

But does Hartshorne's claim for continuity on the condition of repentance and forgiveness answer the intent of Wild's question? As it stands Hartshorne's reply introduces a condition that is ontologically secondary, because concretely what has happened is fixed in history and can be changed only by additional attitudes. What are Hartshorne's grounds for maintaining continuity *if* repentance and forgiveness are present? According to A) C the continuity of a particular self is abstract with respect to character and there is always a new concreteness whether or not other conditions may be met. Hartshorne's ethics are "situation ethics"[18] with respect to the freedom of concrete duration. It is understandable that Wild is not aware of Hartshorne's distinction between strict and genetic identity, but why did Hartshorne not employ it in his reply? The terms that Hartshorne does employ, "repentance" and "forgiveness," are relevant to everyday attitudes, but Hartshorne has not sufficiently clarified how they really affect the continuity of the self. Of course, if Wild seeks either an Aristotelian or Cartesian substantial self, Hartshorne could consistently hold that there is no such reality. Because of concrete addition in which the self is always born anew, strict accounting must certainly require something like a substantial self. Hartshorne's situational ethics would not allow this kind of accountable self even before God: "I grant that God

[15] "Interrogation of Charles Hartshorne Conducted by William Alston," *Philosophical Interrogations*, p. 338.
[16] *Ibid.*, p. 339.
[17] *Ibid.*
[18] Cf. Joseph Fletcher, *Situation Ethics: The New Morality.* (Philadelphia: Westminster Press, 1966).

judges all acts, but on the understanding that the past self alone is judged for past acts, and the present self only for its present acts or intentions."[19]

Fourth, the formula A) C means that the concrete, reality as social process, is necessarily the inclusive category. Hartshorne is convinced that becoming includes being.[20] (In other terms, this is the all-inclusiveness of creative synthesis.[21]) Hartshorne maintains that the thing differentiating modern philosophy from most earlier philosophy is "the strength of its conviction that becoming is the more inclusive category" [PSG, 19]. This is not to say only that becoming is a better idea than being; it is to say that becoming includes all reality—including being. Being and becoming "must somehow form a single reality" [RSP, 19]. When we abstract from the various real common factors included in becoming, we have the "being" of a factor; but such an abstraction remains real by virtue of its participation in all-inclusive reality. Just as in the discussion of identity, the process of becoming as the inclusive category "is not the mere identities of 'being'; it is the identities with the differences, or rather it is the diverse states with abstract aspects of identity" [PSG, 19]. Hartshorne's meaning is clarified if the discussion of man as a Whiteheadian occasion is recalled. What a man *is* (his being) must always wait upon what he happens to become (his becoming). To get his being, one simply abstracts from what he has been. The problem would occur if this process were reversed, which would mean C) A. Deriving becoming from being is tantamount to seeking the concrete in the abstract—the classical mistake.

A similar argument can be put in terms of "creative synthesis."[22]

> Synthesis is . . . the solution of the problem of "the one and the many." Each synthesis is a single reality, not reducible to interrelated parts. But it includes such parts. . . . But the including reality is as much a unitary entity as is any one of the

[19] *Philosophical Interrogations*, p. 339.
[20] Cf. "The Philosophy of Creative Synthesis," p. 946.
[21] *Ibid.*, p. 944.
[22] *Ibid.*, p. 945. "Creative synthesis" is admissible for emphasis despite its redundancy. The words are treated at length in the Hartshorne paper. Here, Hartshorne puts Whitehead's "novel intuition" into practice.

parts. Unity in this view is always a unification, an integration, and what is unified is always a many.

. . . Synthesis, by its very meaning, must be emergent, a creative addition.[23]

Emergence through the creative addition of a new unity is the way becoming becomes. This makes the correlation of synthesis and becoming obvious, but also it places the abstract and the concrete in perspective. As an analysis of reality, the notion that synthetic becoming "contains" diversity can be seen only by making it *abstract in order to make the collection, as a definite multiplicity, an object of thought*."[24] When reality is becoming, there is no logical inference from the abstract unity to concrete particularity. For example: "From 'animal,' the more concrete term 'cat' is not inferrible; nor is 'animal' from 'something.' "[25]

What of John E. Smith's charge that the synthetic "togetherness" of becoming, the becoming of becoming, either is or is not— and if it is, "being" is finally the inclusive category?[26] Hartshorne's response is that Smith fails to see that he does not contrast becoming with being, but rather, with "fixed being."[27] Hartshorne agrees with Smith that being need not be taken as "fixed being"; but if it is not taken as "fixed," Hartshorne sees no difference between the terms "being" and "becoming," because in the latter case it is held that "being" is only another word for "becoming."[28]

An example of the correctness of the formula A) C appears in Hartshorne's response to Smith's understanding of the self.

Professor Smith finds that he experiences becoming as *in* something, namely himself. But this self, is it not in course of becoming or no? Surely we experience no human self which, as a whole, simply is without having had to become. Moreover,

[23] "The Philosophy of Creative Synthesis," p. 945.
[24] *Ibid.*, p. 946.
[25] *Ibid.*
[26] *See* Smith's review of *The Theology of Paul Tillich*, which appeared in *Journal of Philosophy*, I (1953), 644-645. The part in question is Smith's discussion of Hartshorne's contribution, "Tillich's Doctrine of God."
[27] Hartshorne, "Process as Inclusive Category: A Reply," *Journal of Philosophy*, I, ii, No. 4 (February, 1955), 95.
[28] *Ibid.*, p. 96.

it seems apparent that the whole or concrete self of the present becoming is only just now becoming. . . . The reason "I" escapes being completely token-reflexive[29] for each moment of use is that, as I have pointed out elsewhere, its normal meaning is more or less abstract, and one does not intend, in most cases, to refer to the *fully inclusive* personal reality of the given moment.[30]

If the self itself did not become, but remained the fixed container of becoming (as Smith suggests), the formula would be reversed: C) A. Here again, correctly understanding the relationship between the abstract and the concrete is central to Hartshorne and an understanding of his work. Not only would C) A throw the identity of "I" into confusion, even contradiction; it would effectively smother the fundamental character of becoming as the inclusive category. As inclusive, becoming, Hartshorne insists, "does include things which do not become."[31] This is clear in two ways.[32] The first follows from the objective fixed immortality of those objects which a given subject selects from the realm of possibility as he becomes. These objects are not eternal objects because they did not exist before they themselves became, but having completed their concrete becoming, having happened, they are everlastingly established. As such, they are one aspect of abstract being that a concrete event may include. The objective being of one object may thus be included by more than one event of concrete becoming. It is not destroyed by inclusion any more than a painting is destroyed by being viewed.[33] Second, becoming includes being through inclusion of something wholly abstract, such as "the generic nature of becoming as such."[34] Considered in this way, the abstract way, be-

---

[29] *Ibid.* Hartshorne uses "token-reflexive" to refer to that usage in which the reference is not "fixed," therefore having a partly new meaning in each moment of use. In itself the term functions as an abstraction such as a demonstrative pronoun.

[30] *Ibid.*, p. 97. At this point Hartshorne also appeals to the distinction between *Identität* and *Gen-Identität*.

[31] *Ibid.*, p. 96.

[32] *Ibid.*, pp. 95 ff.

[33] Hartshorne does not intend an objective relativism by this. That is, we are not discussing the question of whether or not things exist objectively before any viewing whatsoever. Cf. *Philosophy and Psychology of Sensation*, p. 18, n. 9.

[34] Hartshorne, "Process as Inclusive Category: A Reply," p. 96.

coming does not become. Generically, it has no reality apart from becoming because "nothing *is*, in any sense, except in conjunction with things that become, and this conjunction itself becomes in each new case."[35] Lest the word "conjunction" appear to support a "conjunctive" relationship between the abstract and the concrete, let it be noted that conjunction occurs within becoming—the inclusive concrete! In Hartshorne's words, "The inclusive category, to repeat, is the one which can contain the contrast which the category involves, while the noninclusive is the one which, if taken as inclusive, would contradict the contrast and so destroy the basis of its own meaning."[36]

In the first of these two ways in which becoming includes being, the point of view is the generic term "becoming." That is, reality is perceived from the abstract looking toward the concrete. As the inclusive concept, "becoming" designates. The objects included in the designation are relative to the event of becoming. In the second case "becoming" does not designate, but is itself designated. That is, as Hartshorne holds in his essay "Metaphysical Statements as Nonrestrictive and Existential," "an experience which is relative to its objects, may itself become an object and so something absolute,[37] though not in respect to the same relationship."[38]

The question of absoluteness points back to the beginning of the discussion of inclusive becoming as a "necessary" specification of the formula A) C.

On Hartshorne's terms, being as included in all-inclusive becoming necessarily obtains. "Becoming itself is necessary and eternal because it has nothing more general or ultimate above it. . . . Although particular becomings are contingent, that something or other becomes is necessary."[39] This illustrates Hartshorne's belief in the modality (or necessity) of metaphysical propositions. In fact, he defines metaphysical doctrines in terms of modality.

A metaphysical doctrine, in my usage, is a *modal state-*

[35] *Ibid.*
[36] *Ibid.*
[37] Here "absolute" means strictly identifiable in the sense of *Identität*.
[38] "Metaphysical Statements as Nonrestrictive and Existential," *Review of Metaphysics*, xii, No. 1 (September, 1958), 43.
[39] "Creativity as a Philosophical Category," p. 947.

ment about existence, saying what could, could not, or must exist. It is, as Aristotle said,[40] about being as such, or what could not be otherwise than is. To make this definition coincide with ours, we need only remark that (pure) possibilities themselves are, as such, necessary; for if something is logically possible or conceivable it could not have been inconceivable (though we might have lacked capacity to conceive it).... We are here speaking of possibility in the purely logical sense, not in the sense of "real possibility," possible here and now according to the causal laws which actually obtain.[41]

Movement from the realm of "pure possibilities" toward the necessity of "pure possibility" is movement from the concrete toward the abstract. "Thus, when we reach the most abstract and universal conceptions, we arrive at entities which are entailed by any statements whatever, and this is precisely what necessary means" (PPS, 14). Because becoming has "nothing more general or ultimate above it," we may correctly call it the ultimate abstraction.

The process of objectifying the term "becoming," which itself is a designation of concrete experience, raises the question of thought itself. Our formula has been examined as an abstraction, as a framework for identity, as a way to understand immortality, and as a statement that becoming is necessarily inclusive of being. The last issue is: What understanding of *thinking* itself resides in A) C? Addressing the question of thinking under a discussion of the relationship between the abstract and the concrete should immediately cause one to suspect that Hartshorne's A) C indicates a very definite relationship between A) C and thinking.

A passage from *The Philosophy and Psychology of Sensation* will be helpful here.

We do not first project emotional qualities intuited as our own into an external organism, but rather a considerable part of the emotional content of experience is intuited from the outset as something coming from and qualifying the world

---

[40] Cf. Aristotle, *Works,* trans. under editorship of W. D. Ross (Oxford: Clarendon Press), *Metaphysics,* Book IV, 1930.
[41] "Hume's Metaphysics and Its Present-Day Influence," p. 152.

in the first instance, and ourselves only derivatively or by participation. How far this intuition of objective feelings is an accurate awareness of the environment we need not here ask. (We pointed out above that the most immediate environment, the body, is a living one.) In any case, the general form of our imbeddedness in a social world—a form supposed to be a revelation exclusively of judgment or association or instinct operating upon sensory content is, in observable fashion, the very form of the contents themselves as contents, the form of their intuitive givenness. Thought and learning elaborate the details under this form, as in general the function of thought is not to produce the universal principles of experience, but to enhance the clear and effective grasp and control of the principles provided by the more primitive functions. [PPS, 97]

There is striking similarity between "intuited objective feelings" and Husserl's phenomenological essences. Compare the following from *Ideas*. Husserl says:

> The essential property which the term "temporality" expresses in relation to experiences generally indicates not only something that belongs in a general way to every single experience, but *a necessary form binding experiences with experiences*. Every real experience (we ratify this as self-evident on the ground of the clear intuition of an experimental reality) is necessarily one that endures; and with this duration it takes its place within an endless continuum of durations—a concretely filled continuum. [Par. 81]

The essential character of Hartshorne's intuited contents as contents is quite similar to Husserl's notion of "a necessary form binding experiences with experiences" ratified in intuition. Further, both presuppose a continuum. Husserl insists that this continuum is filled, i.e., is an endless series of durations. This parallels Hartshorne's notion (and Whitehead's) of immortally objective occurrences. These occurrences are necessary because they cannot change what they are. The purpose here is not to prove Husserl and Hartshorne have identical starting points for thinking, but only to indicate a striking similarity which throws light in both directions.

In the second place, then, thinking (in the passage from PPS) is enhancement. Following the principle that a thing is what it does, the essence of thinking comes from its "enhancement of"—"the clear and effective grasp and control of the principles provided by the more primitive functions." In Hartshorne's discussion of White-head, Hartshorne praises Whitehead for his "rational method." Hartshorne insists upon an intuitive method also (*see* p. 9). Now it is evident how seriously this is to be taken. To the extent that rationalism may be identified with the act of thinking,[42] reason here becomes something of a secondary factor. The "more primitive functions" of immediate intuitive experience have fairly usurped rationalism's place. Thinking is not the creator but the creature. Nevertheless, as creature, thinking plays an important role. En-hancement is not a trivial function; it is the all-important act of making a contribution. Hence:

> ... we human adults may, in higher degree than most creatures, contribute to the definiteness of the world. It is no mere question of liking our causally-appointed roles—finding our chains agreeable or imperceptible—but of making these roles in some degree. Either we have a hand in the authorship of the play, or we are mere actors, and even less than actors, for these in concrete fact always in some measure, and un-predictably, create the play as enacted. [LP, 23]

As enhancement, thinking is creaturely authorship of the play of life. To create definiteness is to make the contribution that thought makes.

Although the term "enhancement" correctly situates thinking after "more primitive functions," it is an unfortunate term in that

---

[42] Descartes also appeals to intuition. As Copleston points out, "It is true that intuition is required for deductive reasoning. For we must see the truth of each proposition clearly and distinctly before we proceed to the next step. At the same time deduction is distinguishable from intui-tion by the fact that to the former, though not the latter, there belongs 'a certain movement or succession'" (Frederick Copleston, *A History of Philosophy*, Vol. IV [Westminster, Md.; Newman Press, 1961]), p. 74. The reason that Descartes's method is rationalistic in a sense that Harts-horne does not accept is that the A) C relationship, when correlated with deduction and intuition, would be reversed. Hence, Descartes's intuition, devoid of "a certain movement or succession," assumes the place of the abstract on Hartshorne's terms. Cf. *Oeuvres de Descartes*, ed. C. Adam and P. Tannery (Paris, 1897-1913), Vol. x, p. 370.

it tends to signify a naïve optimism. Do not forget Hartshorne's call for the "tragic sense of life," especially since "we North Americans tend to see the opportunities for good, but not those for evil . . ." [LP, 320].[43]

In order better to understand the nature of thinking in the light of A) C, another of Hartshorne's early articles, "Four Principles of Method—with Applications"[44] is important. These four principles illuminate both the "situation" of abstractions and what Hartshorne intends by the notion of "more primitive functions." The four principles are as follows:

(1) The *empirical* principle. This is to be taken in a most exacting sense: the meaning of fundamental concepts is to be held capable of elucidation without residuum in terms of direct and concrete experience. No esoteric "intellectual intuition" is to be granted; abstractions are drawn in all cases from ordinary, sensory or emotional, perceptual or imaginative intuitions, and are to be traced to these concrete sources for their definitive meanings.

(2) The *rational* principle. Experience is, without residuum, illustrative of rational, i.e., logical, structure, and there is nothing whatsoever that must be left as mere isolated brute fact, mere ineffable quality, wholly inexplicable datum.

(3) The *biological* principle. The context of all ideas, by reference to which they must always be at least approximately definable, is the experience of man conceived as biology conceives him; namely, as a certain type of animal, differing in no absolute way from other animals, possessing no faculty with which they are not endowed, beyond an almost immeasurable extension of the powers of *memory* and *imagination*. Thought can never be other than some form of imaginatively *extended adjustment* to an environment in part instrumental or physical, and in part social; in short mechanical control or social understanding and sympathy, imaginatively or symbolically extended so as to embrace (at the limit) "all time and all

---

[43] Also *see* Hartshorne, "Tragic and Sublime Aspects of Christian Love," RSP, pp. 145-154.

[44] Hartshorne, "Four Principles of Method—with Applications," *The Monist*, XLIII, No. 1 (January, 1933), 40-72.

existence," are the key functions of the mind, even in its highest logical achievement.

(4) The *value* principle. Whatever else any thought is, it is surely the attempt to achieve value, it is a certain kind of purpose in act. It therefore comes under the more general study of purposes. Value is a category in the strict sense. The priority of value over other categories lies in its combining categorical generality with recognizable relevance, unique among categories to experience in its concrete fullness.[45]

Each principle refers abstractions or thoughts ("abstracting" roughly correlates with "thinking") to the concrete. The very nature of thinking appears to flow from the distinction expressed in A) C. The *empirical* principle traces abstractions to ordinary concrete intuitions. The *rational* principle implies the continuity of the concrete. Because abstractions have concrete continuity as their reference, even they "are subject to the law of connectedness. If they do not include each other contextually as determinate entities, they include a common field of potential determinations."[46]

The *biological* principle deserves special attention as an illustration of the abstract being referred to the concrete. On the one hand, Hartshorne is here giving a statement of the "human" situation in the "grades of being." Indeed, these "grades" are the implied context within which human thinking occurs. The "grades of being" scheme is developed in *Reality as Social Process*: . . .[47]

I. Lowest Grade: Superiority to *No* Others,
Least Being.
  i infinitesimal: the *reflexive*, self-unequal, dynamic form.
    The relative or concrete minimum (e.g., a consciousness closer than any assigned distance to unconsciousness; or the scale of beings as approaching, or advancing from, nonentity as lower limit).
  n null: the *non-reflexive* or static form
    The absolute or abstract minimum. Nonentity.

II. Middling Grade: Superiority to *Some* Others,
Ordinary or *Imperfect* Being.

[45] *Ibid.,* p. 54 ff.
[46] *Ibid.,* pp. 47-48.
[47] RSP, p. 116. Also BH, p. 274.

r relative: the *reflexive* form
>   Ordinary concretes (e.g., a man).

a absolute: the *non-reflexive* form.
>   Ordinary abstractions (e.g., honesty).

III. Highest Grade: Superiority to *All* Others,
Transcendent or Perfect Being.
>   R *Relative* (in eminent sense; superrelative): the *reflexive* form
>> The concrete maximum; the self-surpassing surpasser of all. (God as self-contrasting life, process, or personality.)
>
>   A *Absolute* (in eminent sense): the *non-reflexive* form.
>> The abstract maximum; the self-unsurpassing surpasser of all others. (God as mere self-identical essence abstracted from the fullness of His accidents, the contingent contents of His awareness.) [RSP, 116].

This scheme presents a more exact picture of what is intended by the notion of man as one who has his biological being in a context that extends both above and below. Again, the centrality of the distinction between the abstract and the concrete appears. Moreover, in the formal analysis human thinking itself is given a context.

On the other hand, the *biological* principle is an attempt to refer abstractions to man as the point of reference for human understanding. A man understands on the basis of his concrete humanity. "There can be humanity without John Jones. No real relation of humanity to Jones is conceivable but only a relation of Jones to humanity. The concrete really embodies the abstract . . ." [PSG, 131].[48] In saying "thought can never be other than some form of *imaginatively extended adjustment* to an environment," Hartshorne is establishing a background for his extensive use of human analogy. Analogical thinking is important to Hartshorne's treatment of theological topics. In this thinking Hartshorne prefers "analog-

---

[48] It is further pointed out that "it is only a manner of speaking to say that the abstract 'is embodied' in just this particular concrete or that. 'The number *two*' is not a different entity because at a given moment someone embodies it by putting down two dots. But a set of dots must be different according as it does or does not embody the number two. This analogy suggests that the nonrelative (absolute) is the abstract rather than the concrete . . ." [PSG, 131-132].

ical" to "symbolic" [LP, 140]. The point here is that the concrete reference of analogical thinking is clarified by the biological principle.

The *value* principle has already been discussed as aesthetic evaluation, "For value is essentially unity-in-variety . . ." [BH, 212]. Here, thinking as valuation presupposes freedom to choose between true (not illusory) contrasts.[49] Clearly, the contrast inherent in the value principle demonstrates the fundamental character of the distinction between the abstract and the concrete. This distinction is fundamental in Hartshorne's understanding of the nature of thinking.

In sum, the analysis of the function of the relationship between the abstract and the concrete yields the conclusion that in Hartshorne's thought the relationship is A) C. This relationship, which is itself an abstract theory, provides a method of descriptive characterization or identification. Actual occasions remain internally fixed after having occurred but externally available as future possibilities. More than one occasion may, however, be the subject of a given characterization by virtue of the distinction between *Identität* and *Gen-Identität*. The inclusiveness of concrete actualization is a "real" addition to the whole and could not be otherwise without inverting A) C. Because the concrete is intuitively given, thinking must have the concrete as its reference, and stands within the concrete as A) C. The four methodological principles—empirical, rational, biological, and value—illustrate this fundamental relationship.

A) C is nothing less than the key methodological principle of Hartshorne's thought. As a principle for philosophical thinking it is the basis upon which Hartshorne evaluates Husserlian essence, Heideggerian existence, the Peircian continuum, and Whitehead's actual occasions. In Husserl and Heidegger one detects movement

---

[49] This is the basis of Hartshorne's critique of Brand Blanshard's *The Nature of Thought*. Review in *Philosophische Rundschau* (3 Jahrgang, Heft ½, 1955), pp. 119-120. Here Hartshorne says (p. 120): "Is not contrast the principle of all meaning, so that necessity is nothing without accidents?—In reality only the concrete general is given; over against this abstract universals could only signify degrees of unreality. Every distinction between more or less true or real is developed in this way" (trans. R. J.).

toward the concrete, but movement finally checked by the limits of idealistic and existential subjectivity. The criterion by which Hartshorne measures the problem of subjectivity is clarified by Peirce's continuum. The continuum expresses the inclusive potentiality of the concrete without suppressing actual diversity. Every dimension of the Hartshornian concrete—time, intuition, sociality, existence, actuality, objectivity, passivity, continuity, memory, metaphysics, change, freedom, abstraction, identity, immortality, necessity, and thinking—describes some aspect of reality after the fashion of A) C.

In Whitehead, except for "eternal objects," each dimension of the concrete receives systematic metaphysical description. Hartshorne's method is embedded in Whitehead's metaphysics, and one can accurately call Hartshorne a Whiteheadian. It was in Whitehead that Western philosophy achieved concreteness. Though phenomenology and existentialism were steps in this direction, they could not account for more than concrete particulars.

Development of Hartshorne's method in the light of the work of a phenomenologist, an existentialist, a pragmatist, and a process philosopher has shown the similarities and differences in each dialogue. It is helpful, however, to sharpen that method in a formula: A) C. This is a method forged in the temporal relativity of movement toward the concrete: it embraces relativity, but is not lost in relativity. Because A) C embraces the relativity, contingency, temporality, and secularity of our time, it can be applied with understanding to modern problems. In order to clarify the meaning of A) C and to address one of the many problems facing modern man, the application of Hartshorne's method to theology should be explored. It is in theology that Hartshorne has made his most original contribution. Adventure into the concrete has produced a method for approaching Hartshorne's concrete God.

II
Concrete Possibilities

6

The Death of a Classical Abstraction

The time of the death of God became possible because of an impossible God. This God, a classical construction, could not live with history because He smothered its reality with His overbearing absoluteness, eternality, and necessity. If we are to speak of God now, even the most formal ontological statements must be grounded in the concrete.

THE PROCLAMATION of the death of God in the twentieth century has stirred genuine and widespread interest in the question of God. One of the results has been a new sensitivity to the variety of ways the term "God" is used. In the study of Hartshorne's thought, one must first of all have the sensitivity to see that he is *not* using the term in what might be called its ordinary abstract sense. Ordinary abstract usage contains many features which Hartshorne rejects, such as a merely immutable God. The first task is therefore to clear the air of what Hartshorne does *not* mean by the term "God." This clearing occurs in his attack upon classical theism. This attack suggests that Hartshorne is a death-of-God theologian. If the concept "death" in "the death of God" refers to the failure of the classical theological construct, then Hartshorne is indeed talking about the death of God. He believes classical categories render God lifeless by defining away change and freedom. Again, if God's "death" refers to an actual participation by God in the suffering and death of man, there is a second reason for calling Hartshorne a death-of-God theologian. Two of the men in the twentieth century who are taking Christian history, for example, the cross, most seriously are Thomas Altizer and Hartshorne. Both can point to the historical events of the biblical faith because the abstract God of classicism no longer stands between them and the cross.

There is also good reason to distinguish Hartshorne's attack upon classicism from the theology of the death of God, especially as understood by Altizer and William Hamilton. Hartshorne's concrete God can die only in the sense that He participates in particular deaths. Participation in particular deaths and sufferings is possible for the concrete God because He has a contingent relative side as well as an abstract existence. Only God's changing relativity participates in death. His abstract ontological necessity, *that* He exist, His necessary being, is not subject to death. Such a death would be the death of the logical necessity that some possibilities in reality are actualized. Denial of even the possibility of God, the positivistic option, seems less than convincing to Hartshorne. Hartshorne believes contingent existence, the kind required by a God who could die in His totality, "is a defect" [AD, 99]. The concrete God truly has "greatness," which means "better than anything contingent can possibly be" [AD, 99]. Hartshorne has perhaps the most elaborate argument for contingency in God of any modern thinker, but contingency always applies to *how* God exists, not whether He exists. On the contrary, to Altizer and Hamilton, God must have been contingent in every respect in order for His death to be historical.

There is a long tradition, the Augustinian one, in Western theology that upholds the noncontingency of God—a tradition crowned in Anselm's ontological argument. But as Tillich argued in his famous essay, "Two Types of Philosophy of Religion," the difficulty of appreciating the noncontingency of God in Augustinian tradition is compounded by our inheritance of the dissolution of ontology and God in the Thomistic tradition. We are so accustomed to thinking of God as a being among beings (whether under us, over us, behind us as a first cause or ahead of us as a teleological goal) that we can vividly imagine the death of God. But Hartshorne is not a death-of-God theologian precisely because he does not think of God as a being among beings.

A second reason for distinguishing Hartshorne's attack on classical theism from the theology of Altizer and Hamilton is that they believe God's death to be an actual occasion. They insist God's death is not the death of a concept, but a real event. Hartshorne, on the other hand, is speaking of the failure of a concept, a fairly well-defined theological construction. Thus, Hartshorne means that it is man's thinking which has failed. Hartshorne must agree with Schubert M. Ogden when the latter says, ". . . the problem now confronting us is posed, not by the death of God, but by the demise of a 'cast of thought,' of some particular conceptuality through which the witness of Christian faith has traditionally been expressed."[1]

In the time of "the demise of a 'cast of thought,' " Hartshorne understands God as concrete changing reality. Socially conceived, God is supremely relative to creation, interacts with all reality and exceeds all abstractions. Sometimes he calls God's supreme social relativity, "surrelativism,"[2] the notion that divine relativity is infinite. Unlike finite relativity, the kind ordinary beings experience, divine relativity means God really interacts with, is really contingent upon every event in the universe. Surrelativism is compatible with "panentheism," another way in which Hartshorne states his theological alternative to the abstract God of classicism.[3] "Panen-

---

[1] Schubert M. Ogden, *The Reality of God* (New York: Harper & Row, 1966), p. 19.

[2] "Surrelativism" refers to the highest grade of reflexive being, classification no. 3, in the "grades of being." This is "the concrete maximum; the self-surpassing surpasser of all. (God as self-contrasting life, process, or personality)" (*see* Chap. 5).

[3] The term "panentheism" is not original with Hartshorne, as he is aware. It was perhaps first used by Karl Christian Friedrich Krause (1781-1832), a member of the school of Fichte and Schelling. *See* Heinrich Schmidt, *Philosophisches Wörterbuch* (New York: Mary S. Rosenburg, 1945), p. 237. Hartshorne refers to Krause in "The Kinds of Theism: A Reply," *Journal of Religion*, XXXIV, No. 2 (April, 1954), 127. Hartshorne's own full definition of panentheism is as follows: "panentheism: (Gr. pan, all; en, in; theos, god) The view that all things are within the being of God, who yet is not merely the whole of actual things. If God were merely the system of actual things, then should a different system be possible, it would be possible that God should not exist, or should not be himself. Hence either God must be a purely contingent being, and anything might happen to him, including his destruction, or all things, just as they are, are necessary. On either construction God and other things are upon the same metaphysical level, whether of pure contingency or of pure necessity. Panentheism holds, on the contrary, that the self-identity of God is independent of the particular things which exist and the particular totality they form, and that consequently God may exist necessarily, although all other

theism" means that the world is in God, but not strictly coincident with Him because He exceeds the world. Because God is actually relative to what happens in the world, He changes when the world changes. Being-in-God does not mean being in an unchanging abstraction; it means being in the changing concrete whole. *That* God is changing and supremely relative does not change. It is only in this abstract sense that God is merely absolute and immutable. Thus, "the demise of a 'cast of thought' " does not mean that Hartshorne rejects the ontological necessity of God. It means that a particular set of theological propositions is inadequate for the theologian in his most basic task, to speak of God. In Chapter 7 a more constructive description of the concrete God will be offered; but first: Exactly why has classicism failed? This is the other side of the question: Why do we need a concrete God?

Hartshorne searches widely to find adequate symbols to express his conviction that the idea of abstract God has failed. For example, in 1941 he published the following scheme to classify logically alternative ways of thinking of God:

---

beings exist contingently. God exists, to be sure, in a different state for every difference in the existing whole, for he is that whole, but it is a different state of the same being or of the whole as having a flexible selfhood, the individual essence of which is unaffected by the accidents of existence. This makes the inclusive whole analogous to a human personality, which contains many things not essential to its self-identity. A man is the sum of things which fall within his experience, but he is more than that sum, and many an item could have been missing (or have been replaced by another) without making his self-identity impossible. Panentheism claims to reconcile the legitimate motives of ordinary pantheism (God is simply the de facto—or the eternal—whole of things) and the contrary extreme (things other than God are in no way parts of his being). Panentheism admits that there is in God something independent of particulars, but holds that this something is merely the "essence" of God whose entire nature includes also accidents, each of which is the integration of all the accidental being in a given state of the universe. Panentheism sees in God not just another example of whole or totality, unity in multiplicity, but the supreme and most excellent example, as He is the most excellent example of 'goodness,' 'knowledge,' and other conceptions. This supreme example as such deserves to be interpreted with care, and not (as commonly happens) according to casual associations, of such words as 'all,' 'universe,' 'whole,' 'parts.' " From *An Encyclopedia of Religion*, ed. Vergilius Ferm (New York: The Philosophical Library, 1945), p. 557.

Group	Symbol	Case	Symbol	Interpretation
I	(A)	1	A	Absolute perfection in *all* respects.
II	(AX)	2	AR	Absolute perfection in *some* respects, relative perfection in all others.
		3	ARI	Absolute perfection, relative perfection, and "imperfection" (neither absolute nor relative perfection), each in *some* respects.
		4	AI	Absolute perfection in *some* respects, imperfection in all others.
III	(X)	5	R	Absolute perfection in *no* respects, relative in all.
		6	RI	Absolute perfection in *no* respects, relative in some, imperfection in the others.
		7	I	Absolute perfection in *no* respects, imperfection in all. [MVG, 8]

Explanation of Symbols: A stands for absolute perfection, R for relative perfection, I for the joint negative of A and R, X for the negative of A (and thus for the disjunction of R and I), and (A) or (X) for the factors occurring throughout a group. [MVG, 9]

Division of alternative ways to think of God, "an entity somehow *superior* to other entities" [MVG, 6], into seven cases reflects Hartshorne's effort to discover implicit meanings "hidden" in traditional terms. He thinks that without such a scheme traditional descriptions of God like "perfect being," "finite God," and "absolute" remain "hopelessly ambiguous" [MVG, 10]. Having shown sensitivity to ambiguities before reducing ways of thinking of God to three main groups, Hartshorne then argues that only one of the three options must be true. Either (A) correlated with absolutism, Thomism, and most European theology prior to 1880; or (AX) correlated with "much contemporary Protestant theology, doctrines of a 'finite-infinite' or perfect-perfectible God"; or (X) correlated with merely finite God, polytheism in some forms—or atheism must be true [MVG, 11-12]. The last option, (X), could not be the concrete God because He is hardly God. The first possibility, (A), is the abstract concept, which fails because no relativity, X or R, is involved. Hartshorne admits that in doctrines of Incarnation this problem, (A), is "in a fashion" recognized; but he insists, ". . . the point to weigh is whether any concept of God is philosophically or religiously defensible that does not make a logical place for such a union of absolute and relative by rejecting case one as simply an error . . ." [MVG, 16].

Calling "case one" (A) an error means the 1941 scheme builds upon the problem of absolutism or, conversely, a dearth of relativity in God. So far the abstract God is inadequate, then, because He is *merely absolute*, having no logical place for the kind of relativity required by something like an Incarnation in history. Hartshorne developed the problem of abstract absolutism in his 1946 article, "Relative, Absolute, and Superrelative: The Concept of Deity."[4] Development of the meaning of the term "concrete" has already been the occasion for our use of his "grades-of-being scheme" from this article (*see* pp. 76-77). Now, it might be viewed as an especially clear statement of the problem of the abstract God.

In 1946 Hartshorne employs the term "nonreflexive." "*Relativity is the inclusive, concrete conception;* non-relativity or non-reflexiveness . . . is the reduction of this concrete conception to a partly negative and more abstract case" [RSP, 115]. Nonreflexiveness signifies, however, only that another term for abstract absolutism is introduced; the problem is structurally unchanged. Hence, "That the absolute is the *non*-reflexively superior suggests that the merely absolute is the relative with the omission of something, and thus that relative is the more concrete, and absolute the more abstract, category" [RSP, 114]. Being more abstract, the nonreflexive absolute fails to achieve the kind of rich perfection attributable to superrelative divinity. The weakness of the abstract God resides, then, in the fact that abstract absoluteness is not true greatness. If

---

[4] *The Philosophical Review*, LV, No. 3 (May, 1946), 213-228. Also *see* RSP, Chap. 6.

God could supersede Himself, He would escape the problem of absolutism and become superrelative ("God as self-contrasting life, process, or personality"). Abstract absolutism, on the other hand, means God is "fixed" or "static," so that He cannot surpass even Himself; He cannot grow; the absolute God interacts with nothing, is reflexive toward nothing. There is nothing with which He might interact!

Nonreflexible absolutism can be readily illustrated by thinking of the problem of will. If there were a divine fixed will (whatever the term "will" might mean under such conditions), how could it decide anything with respect to relative history without to some extent interacting with history? How, for example, could an absolute God have decided to send a son into history at some point in time? Moreover, how could historical creatures follow such a will, which presumably would be omnipotent? Would not the absolute have to be less than absolute in some degree if creaturely wills were to be real? The problem is: God's will is so absolute that man's will disappears.

In some form nearly all recent commentators on the subject of God and the absolute have attempted to circumvent the problem of the nonreflexive absolute. This is, for example, one facet of Emil Brunner's objection to idealistic absolutism (Hegel). Brunner fears that thinking of the Christian faith as a universal immediately available to all in its absolute form overrides the uniqueness of faith. Revelation, he believes, is not an absolute universal "to be experienced *semper et ubique* by everybody, but a unique, definite, concrete occurrence."[5] Hartshorne shares Brunner's concern that uniqueness not be lost in an absolute universal—an absolute that becomes, as Brunner phrases it, "a certified minimum."[6] Such a "minimum" is inadequate because it is only an abstract absolute. Hartshorne can agree with Brunner that "behind every 'ism' there stands a faith, and one too that makes a 'whole out of a part,' an absolute out of a relative—not merely conceiving, but at the same time ordaining."[7] The differences in theological perspective from which

[5] Emil Brunner, *Philosophy of Religion,* trans. A. J. D. Farrer and Bertram Lee Woolf (London: James Clarke & Co., 1958), p. 50.
[6] *Ibid.*, p. 48.
[7] *Ibid.*, p. 183.

Hartshorne and Brunner point out the problem of absolutism are considerable, but *that* Hartshorne shares this concern with other contemporary thinkers demonstrates that others share Hartshorne's conviction that the abstract nonreflexive absolute is an inadequate theological object.

In 1953 Hartshorne joined with William L. Reese to publish a second major scheme in which the problem of the abstract God is isolated [PSG, 15-25]. Here the key problem is classical eternality, or emphasis upon the eternal with varying degrees of attention to other possible qualities in God, such as temporality. The scheme runs:

E   Eternal—in some (or, if T is omitted, in all) aspects
     of his reality devoid of change, whether as
     birth, death, increase, or decrease

T   Temporal—in some (or, if E is omitted, in all) aspects
     capable of change, at least in the form of
     increase of some kind

C   Conscious, self-aware

K   Knowing the world or universe, omniscient

W   World-inclusive, having all things as constituents
     [PSG, 16]

When E, T, C, K, W are taken together, they are another way of defining panentheism or surrelativism.

The overriding single characteristic of classical theology is eternality, ultimate reality as nontemporal. Every theistic subdivision, Ancient or Quasi-Panentheism (E, T, C, K, W; Ikhnaton; Hindu Scriptures; Lao-tse; Judeo-Christian Scriptures; Plato), Aristotelian Theism (E, C; Aristotle), Classical Theism (E, C, K; Philo; Augustine; Anselm; al-Ghazzali; Maimonides; Aquinas; Descartes; Leibniz; Kant; Channing; von Hügel), Classical Pantheism (E, C, K, W; Asvaghosha; Sankara; Ramanuja; Spinoza; Royce; Jeffers), Emanationism (E; Plotinus), and Temporalistic Theism (E, T, C,

K; Socinus; Lequier) exhibits the E factor, or eternality [PSG, xiii]. Classical doctrines of God include all other aspects at one extreme (E, T, C, K, W) and no other aspects (except E), as in Emanationism, at the other extreme. Hartshorne finds a vivid illustration of this problem in Plotinus. Plotinus is historically significant partly for his influence upon Christian thought through Augustine.[8] His chief value to the 1953 scheme, however, lies in the force with which he represents eternality, or the E factor, to the exclusion of T, C, K, and W. Admittedly, Plotinus has a "language of consciousness," but Hartshorne and Reese are convinced that conscious volition is overcome, and unity is "superior to all multiplicity and duality; ergo, our supreme reverence must be for something held to be wholly super-conscious, supercognitive, and super-volitional" [PSG, 212]. The practical result, they believe, is that Plotinus wishes us to become "as unitary, and changeless and immaterial as possible. This would mean (it seems) exalting mathematical truth over historical truth . . ." [PSG, 219]. Because of his drive to achieve unity and the abstract "One," Plotinus is understood to smother concrete diversity and mutability. Instead of using abstractions to explore the concrete, Plotinus uses the abstract to seek the abstract, "ultimately, the emptiest abstraction of all, bare entity or being or something" [PSG, 220]. In correlating the problem of Plotinus in this way, Hartshorne's discussion in *Philosophers Speak of God* in effect represents God as C) A, and it follows that C) A is the domination of eternality in the classical mode of thought. If this is a correct interpretation of Plotinus, without doubt the declaration that the abstract dominates the concrete means eternality dominates history.

Of course, the problem of abstract eternality is not confined to the scheme developed in *Philosophers Speak of God*. A modern

[8] Speaking of Augustine, Etienne Gilson remarks, "It is natural that historians should disagree on the part played in his religious evolution by the reading of some of Plotinus' works. Here, as in many other cases, doctrinal interest interferes with objectively historical interpretation. Yet, all historians agree that the technical formulation of his doctrine betrays a marked neoplatonic influence. His own narrative in *Confessions*, VII, 9, 13, more than confirms the reality of the fact." (*History of Christian Philosophy in the Middle Ages* [New York: Random House, 1955], p. 70.)

approach to the problem of the domination of living concrete history by abstract "eternal" categories appears in Hartshorne's debate with Paul Tillich. In his essay "Tillich's Doctrine of God,"[9] Hartshorne raises several questions in which the underlying theme is his conviction that Tillich's theology is too abstract. More specifically, the abstract God in Tillich's thought tends to gain ascendancy over the concrete. This is what lies behind Hartshorne's remark (made over a decade after these questions were raised) that Tillich "never clearly envisages the issue between classical and neoclassical views . . ." [LP, 144]. That is, Hartshorne thinks Tillich does not adequately understand the difference between the classical eternality of C) A and the neoclassical temporality of A) C.[10] The question that Hartshorne considers most crucial is why Tillich rejects or fails to adopt "the principle of process, that the togetherness of what-does-not-become and what-becomes itself becomes. . . ."[11] The principle of process is the way the abstract "what" is included in the concrete, which "itself becomes." On this basis the question of "literal" reference is addressed. Hartshorne's early criticism of Tillich's doctrine of God assumes that Tillich identifies God with being-itself. This opinion appears to be based on Tillich's assertion to this effect in Volume One of *Systematic Theology*.[12] Hartshorne modifies his position after reading Volume Two, in which Tillich says the statement that God is being-itself "is both non-symbolic and symbolic."[13] Hartshorne later admits, "I have dealt, perhaps with insufficient subtlety, with Tillich's view . . ." [LP, 9]. But as late as 1966 Hartshorne's assessment of Tillich's theology hinges

[9] *The Theology of Paul Tillich*, I, "The Library of Living Theology," ed. Charles W. Kegley and Robert W. Bretall (New York: The Macmillan Co., 1952), pp. 164-195.

[10] In Volume Three of Tillich, *Systematic Theology* (Chicago: University of Chicago Press, p. 422), Hartshorne finally finds some modification of Tillichian classicism. But he still maintains, "Individuality and concrete particularity seem to me to need better and more literal recognition than they get . . . from Tillich." "Tillich and the Nontheological Meaning of Theological Terms," *Religion in Life*, Vol. 35 (Winter 1966), 675-676.

[11] *The Theology of Paul Tillich*, p. 194.

[12] Here Tillich says, "The being of God is being-itself . . ." (p. 235).

[13] Paul Tillich, *Systematic Theology*, II, pp. 9-10.

upon his conviction that some theological language is nonsymbolic, so that terms like "relative-absolute" literally describe God.[14]

So long as the question of "literal" reference in Tillich's theology remains unsettled, in the sense that it is not clear which way Tillich moves, this aspect of the issue between Hartshorne and Tillich must remain open. Nevertheless, in Hartshorne's A) C, "literal" refers to the reality of the concrete God who is process itself. The process which "itself becomes" in his question to Tillich is, Hartshorne says, to be taken "as something *indicated* not merely named; process-now, not just process taken generically . . . ."[15] Literal inference is indicated in the sense of pointing to that in which the pointer has his presence. Hartshorne implies that in Tillich's case— regardless of how the question of the relationship between God and being-itself is answered (whether symbolically or nonsymbolically) —abstract naming "indicates" only if it points to concrete process from within. If the name "God" refers to mere being, it is, on Hartshorne's terms, the same as an abstraction referring to an abstraction; and the primacy of the abstract is the mark of classicism.

It is the desire that "God" have a dynamic concrete reference that underlies Hartshorne's opposition to Tillich's "classical" concept of God. In saying that God is present in a way that is more inclusive than "eternal" being-itself, Hartshorne places Tillich squarely in the line of fire of his attack upon Plotinus' eternality and classicism in general. To be fair, it must be remembered, however, that Tillich does not oppose the notion that being-itself has a process-character. When put in terms of A) C, the issue is sharpened: the question is whether A or C is, finally, the inclusive term.

The other side of the coin in the Tillich-Hartshorne debate is the question of time. What of past time? It is, says Hartshorne, time ". . . as measured by our deficiencies of retention of achieved qualities of experience . . . ," which is in question in two senses. In one sense, Hartshorne is saying that Tillich should not assume the "destructiveness" of divine time because of the limitation inhering

[14] Hartshorne, "Tillich and the Nontheological Meaning of Theological Terms," p. 674.
[15] *The Theology of Paul Tillich*, p. 194.

in the finitude from which time must be measured; God's time "is the past in all its determinateness and richness of quality . . . ."[16] Hartshorne opposes the abstract restriction of God's history which results from the limitations of finite memory. The concrete God is not timeless, in the classical sense of the domination of eternality, but "timefull" in that history exhibits "all its determinateness and richness of quality."

The argument that Tillich, with his classicism, prevents the emergence of the concrete God of course does not prevent wide areas of agreement between Tillich and Hartshorne, especially since they both see the importance of an explicit ontology of some kind. Like the contemporary German theologian Helmut Gollwitzer, Hartshorne concurs in Tillich's rejection of the notion of God as an existing being among beings. Gollwitzer, moving within a Barthian circle, says, "if 'being' and 'existence' are names for the things we designate by these terms in the world, God does not exist."[17] The difference between Hartshorne and Gollwitzer in rejecting the necessary existence of God-in-the-world, however, becomes apparent only from their presuppositions.

Gollwitzer is a classicist on at least one crucial point: he holds to a theology of the Word in the Calvinist tradition. He chides those who cannot see that some within Calvinism and Calvinistic Puritanism have acted *because of* "the most stringent teaching on dependence and the most stringent doctrine of predestination."[18] Gollwitzer also thinks that those who have rejected God in order to preserve man's freedom to act have an inadequate understanding of God. Unlike Hartshorne, his solution is to look in neo-orthodox fashion to the Word coming from the biblical proclamation, the classical character of which he preserves by a subtle distinction between knowing and expressing. "The Living Lord," he says, "does not enter into the conditions under which particular being is known, but he does enter into the conditions under which it is expressed. . . ."[19] Gollwitzer here gallantly but unsuccessfully wrestles with

[16] *Ibid.*
[17] Helmut Gollwitzer, *The Existence of God as Confessed by Faith*, trans. James W. Leitch (Philadelphia: Westminster Press, 1965), p. 206.
[18] *Ibid.*, p. 101.
[19] *Ibid.*, p. 147.

the old problem posed by classical presuppositions, which deny any contingency to God. He rejects Herbert Braun's existentialist anthropology, which would make theology completely relative to human self-understanding[20] and which we might call the "Bultmann problem." At the same time he thinks that man's "inevitably anthropomorphic way of speaking" can correspond to the reality of God.[21] The question is whether reality is understood as concrete or as abstract.

To answer this question Gollwitzer must say whether or not man's activity qualifies God. The question can be put this way because a negative answer would imply the eternal God of classicism. And this negative answer must be given because Gollwitzer insists that knowledge of God is possible "only in accepting his self-bestowal, in knowledge in the form of being known . . . in submission to God's judgment."[22] Granting this, why is it necessary to make such an issue over anthropomorphic knowledge? Being known is not knowing! What does man know concretely? What is the concrete act of knowing God if "knowing" is merely being known? At the crucial point, knowledge of God, Gollwitzer's understanding of knowledge collapses into classicism, and the concrete God remains unknown.

Another theologian, also strongly influenced by Barth, who writes of God's concreteness is Eberhard Jüngel. To Jüngel the concreteness of God is revealed in the being of God as historical Lord.[23] Building from Barth's doctrine of the Trinity, he believes that the

---

[20] *Ibid.*, pp. 35 ff.
[21] *Ibid.*, p. 151.
[22] *Ibid.*, p. 207.
[23] Eberhard Jüngel, *Gottes Sein ist im Werden, Verantwortliche Rede von Sein Gottes bei Karl Barth* (Tübingen: J. C. B. Mohr [Paul Siebeck], 1965). *See* especially pp. 41-52, 101-119. Jüngel maintains that his Barthian understanding of the "concrete" Word is not to be confused with Hegel's different way of thinking of God as concrete (p. 43, n. 120). The criterion of Jüngel's judgment is his conviction that the content of God's concrete trinitarian revelation is qualitatively different from the general concretion of the Hegelian *Geist*. It can be argued that Hegel's dialectical expression of the *Geist* is actually all interpretation of the Word of the New Testament, but Jüngel's distinction holds unless Hegel is finally given a Barthian interpretation. Structurally, however, Jüngel should say more of how his version of becoming differs from Hegel's.

concreteness of God can be thought of as residing in the becoming of history, which is the way God's being becomes. "Becoming and being are here originally together since the concrete unity of the being of God is 'a unity of one being' which is always also a becoming one."[24] God's becoming does not make revelation superfluous; it is the mode in which the three ways of God's being are manifest.[25] Jüngel's concern to maintain the unity of the Godhead in the diversity of concrete becoming reminds us that he is dealing with the traditional problem of the one and the many, and that he shares the determination of Nicaea to protect unity and retain the Incarnation as an actual occasion. The question is whether or not Jüngel (and Barth) has really seen the problem of classicism.

Jüngel explicitly rejects Hartshorne's (and Schubert M. Ogden's) attempt to think of the being of God as an abstraction from His becoming. Against Hartshorne, Jüngel insists, "*Gottes Sein ist als solches konkret . . . .*"[26] Making God's being concrete raises the question of the difference between being and becoming. Does Jüngel mean $A = C$, or has God no abstract necessity? Surely the contingent concrete is not necessary in any particular manifestation. That some contingencies concretely occur is necessary, but when Jüngel assigns concreteness to the being of God he seems to mean that the "how" of a particular actualization, the trinitarian *historical* revelation, is necessary. From Hartshorne's point of view this confuses God's abstract necessity with His concrete contingency so that history loses its vital principle—freedom. Has not Jüngel continued the classical tradition by making a particular form of eternal being dominate in such a way that *real* concrete becoming is impossible? Atlhough he disagrees with Gollwitzer's interpretation of Barth at many points, Jüngel seems finally to join Gollwitzer in a scandal of particularity that is really a scandal, a scandal resulting from what the scheme in *Philosophers Speak of God* calls eternality.

In 1961 Hartshorne published a third major scheme in his attack upon the abstract God. This scheme is embedded in his

[24] Jüngel, p. 43. (Trans. R. J.)
[25] *Ibid.*, p. 46.
[26] *Ibid.*, p. 112, n. 148.

works on the ontological argument, especially in *The Logic of Perfection* and *Anselm's Discovery.*

That Hartshorne is continuing a lifelong battle against the abstract God may not be readily apparent when one turns to his renewal of the ontological argument. But just as one can mistake Hartshorne for a metaphysician in the classical mold, so one can misconstrue his latest attention to ontological necessity as simply a return to abstract categories. In fact, in the later part of his life Hartshorne turns to the question of ontological necessity *because* he wishes to free the argument for the ontological necessity of God's existence from the abstractness of classicism. Classicism made the concrete God impossible. It is classical necessity, then, not neoclassical necessity (Hartshorne's reformation in concrete categories), which sets the stage for the demise of God. In the context of Hartshorne's renewal of the "proof," we actually have a fresh restatement of the *problem* of the abstract God.

The beginning point of Hartshorne's treatment of the proofs is clarified if, at the outset, one understands his claim that Barth is right in seeing that Anselm "presupposed faith" [LP, 111]. The importance of presupposed faith should not be underestimated in the work of either Hartshorne or Barth; it is not accidental that both are stimulated, in their basic method, by Anselm. Faith, in a broad sense, is presupposed when Hartshorne finds himself in accord with Anselm's attitude toward the unbeliever. "The problem of unbelief is a pure problem of meaning and self-understanding, not of what the facts happen to be. Knowing this is a real aid to belief. It reduces the question to one of sincerity, clarity, and self-understanding, in depth, of our own thought" [LP, 111]. In this sense Hartshorne can well say with Anselm and Barth, "I believe in order to understand."

Because self-understanding is for Hartshorne a standing in the concrete, it is helpful to compare this method to that of Rudolf Bultmann. At first glance, the spirit of Bultmann's theological method lives in different haunts from the spirit of the "proof," which tends to be associated more with classical metaphysics. Yet, when one remembers that A) C means a rejection of such metaphysics, and that both Bultmann and Hartshorne presuppose concrete faith (differing partly in content), it is not inappropriate to mention their similarity on this point. As far as Christian theology is concerned, Hartshorne would oppose neither the spirit nor the language (i.e., "concrete") of the following from Bultmann's *Jesus and the Word*.

> ... when I speak of the teaching and thought of Jesus, I base the discussion on no underlying conception of a universally valid system of thought which through this study can be made enlightening to all. Rather the ideas are understood in the light of the concrete situation of a man living in time; as his interpretation of his own existence in the midst of change, uncertainty, decision; as the expression of a possibility of comprehending this life; as the effort to gain clear insight into the contingencies and necessities of his own existence.[27]

Bultmann implies that "a universally valid system of thought" is abstract, while temporal existence is concrete. One might say that Bultmann means something different by these terms; perhaps so. This is far from evident when one carefully observes how the word "concrete" functions in the passage quoted above. It might be further argued that Hartshorne's "rationalism" is precisely an attempt to establish a "universally valid system of thought in the rationalistic sense." At times, this almost seems true, but when A) C is taken seriously, with all its implications, the charge loses force.

Hopefully, this brief comparison of Hartshorne with Barth and Bultmann clarifies the *Ausgangspunkt* for the proofs of God's existence. Indeed, Hartshorne believes the proofs are relevant in that "Their function is to elicit the content of a realization of God which, as a distinguished British philosopher, H. H. Price, has recently maintained, is in the depths of every man's experience."[28] Thus, "The proofs are *reductio ad absurdum* arguments directed against alleged alternatives or substitutes for theism. If successful,

[27] Rudolf Bultmann, *Jesus and the Word*. Trans. Louise Pettibone Smith and Eunice Huntress Lantero (New York: Charles Scribner's Sons, 1958), p. 11.
[28] Hartshorne, "A Philosopher's Assessment of Christianity," *Religion and Culture: Essays in Honor of Paul Tillich*, ed. Walter Leibrecht (New York: Harper, 1959), p. 173.

they leave the theistic idea as sole residual legatee, after it has turned out that apparent alternatives are not genuine, since experience furnishes no coherent meaning for them."[29] Philosopher Merold Westphal argues that Hartshorne's method of reduction down to a "sole residual legatee" is not valid because no positive inference follows: "that there is no longer a reason to deny X does not by itself entitle us to infer X."[30] This overlooks the way in which Hartshorne uses the notion of inference. Hartshorne remarks, "We do not exclusively infer God, we experience Him spiritually and intellectually" [AD, 170]. I interpret this to mean that logical inference is a method of removing abstract notions which interfere with intellectual apprehension of the concrete. Hartshorne hints he might go even further—"Bonaventura and Malebranche even emphasize the direct awareness of God to such an extent that the argument is no longer an inference at all, but merely the recognition of the divine givenness as self-existent" [AD, 170-171]. Clarification of the concrete givenness in which the logician stands as he speaks not only means inference is contingent upon intuitive verification; it means that there is a given, a concrete reality to intuit. This is the point David Platt misses when he complains that Hartshorne provides no given.[31] Logical structures and inferences are possible in Hartshorne's thinking precisely because the concrete is given as the inclusive reality containing abstract exercises. Both Westphal and Platt underestimate the role of the concrete in Hartshorne's treatment of the ontological argument.

It is this same concrete givenness that must be kept in mind when one reads Hartshorne's formal statement of the ontological argument in his chapter, "Ten Ontological or Modal Proofs for God's Existence" [LP, 28-117]. Hartshorne expresses the meaning of God in terms of perfection, which he defines as "modal coincidence" interpreted "under the analogy of infallible knowledge"[32] Perfec-

---

[29] *Ibid.*

[30] "Temporality and Finitism in Hartshorne's Theism," *The Review of Metaphysics*, XIX, No. 3, Issue No. 75 (March, 1966), 553.

[31] David Platt, "Some Perplexities Concerning God's Existence," *Journal of Bible and Religion*, XXXIV, No. 3 (July, 1966), 251.

[32] Modal propositions have to do with the assertion or denial of the possibility, contingency, or necessity of their own content. Hartshorne's understanding of modality follows "Becker's Postulate" in which

tion, he argues, is intelligible on religious grounds. " 'God is perfect,' in the religious sense, means, He can be worshipped without
incongruity by every individual no matter how exalted" [AD, 40].
The question arises: What is worship? With Tillich, Hartshorne
finds the clearest answer in the Judeo-Christian text. "To worship
X is to 'love' X with all one's heart and all one's mind and all one's
soul and all one's strength. Perfection is the character which X
must have to make sense out of this" [AD, 40].

Hartshorne takes his cue from Anselm's "definite logical discovery" that "Perfection (in the theological sense) belongs indeed
to a different logical type from ordinary predicates; and its existence
cannot be a purely contingent question, but must involve either a
positive necessity or a negative one (i.e., an impossibility). . . ."
[LP, 33] Hartshorne claims that Anselm left the issue vague because
he was assuming the classical notion of perfection taken from Greek
philosophy rather than "the Gospels and the Old Testament." In
other words, Anselm assumed C) A.

Implying that his own source is at least consistent with "the
Gospels and the Old Testament," Hartshorne proposes that the
argument's object, "such that none greater is conceivable," requires
a neoclassical interpretation. In this interpretation Anselm's formula
means: "God cannot conceivably be surpassed or equalled by any
other individual, but He can surpass himself, and thus His actual
state is not the greatest possible state." The neoclassical interpretation is just what is clarified by A) C.

In our discussion in Chapter 7 of Barth's treatment of Anselm's proof of *Proslogium* 2-4 in terms of the Name of God, in the
sense that Anselm was "witnessing to the faith," we will see the

---

"modal status can be affirmed or denied in the mode of necessity only"
[AD, 39]. In making this point he cites R. Carnap, *Meaning and Neces-
sity* (Chicago: University of Chicago Press, 1947), pp. 185-186; A.
Church, "A Formulation of the Logic of Sense and Denotation," in
Structure, Method, and Meaning: Essays in Honor of Henry M. Sheffer,
ed. P. Henle (New York: Liberal Arts Press, 1951), p. 22; Henry S.
Leonard, "Two-Valued Truth Tables for Modal Functions," in *Struc-
ture, Method, and Meaning: Essays in Honor of Henry M. Sheffer*. G. H.
von Wright, *An Essay on Modal Logic* (Amsterdam: North-Holland
Publishing Co., 1951), pp. 66-77. [AD, 39-40]. For a summary of
Becker's postulate, see John Cobb's review of *The Logic of Perfection*,
" 'Perfection Exists': A Critique of Charles Hartshorne," *Religion in
Life* (Spring 1963), pp. 294-304.

proof treated as Christian doctrine. It is consistent with an expression of Christian faith even in its most formal statement by
Hartshorne:

'q' for '$(\exists x)\ Px$' There is a perfect being, or perfection exists
'N' for 'it is necessary (logically true) that'
'$\sim$' for 'it is not true that'
'v' for 'or'
'$p \rightarrow q$' for 'p strictly implies q' or '$N \sim (p\& \sim q)$'

1. $q \rightarrow Nq$ "Anselm's Principle": perfection could not exist contingently
2. $Nq\ v \sim Nq$ Excluded Middle[33]
3. $\sim Nq \rightarrow N \sim Nq$ Form of Becker's Postulate: modal status
   is always necessary
4. $NqvN \sim Nq$ Inference from (2, 3)
5. $N \sim Nq \rightarrow N \sim q$ Inference from (1): the necessary falsity
   of the consequent implies that of the antecedent (Modal
   form of modus tollens)[34]
6. $NqvN \sim q$ Inference from (4, 5)
7. $\sim N \sim q$ Intuitive postulate (or conclusion from other theistic arguments): perfection is not impossible
8. Nq Inference from (6, 7)
9. $Nq \rightarrow q$ Modal axiom
10. q Inference from (8, 9) [LP, 50-51]

The three assumptions of the argument, steps (1), (3), and
(7), are central to the present investigation. To what ground do
these assumptions make their appeal? This ground is explicit in
(7), and confirmed in a statement made in the paragraph following
the logical formulation. "To me, at least, the assumptions are intuitively convincing, provided perfection is properly construed, a
condition Anselm did not fulfill" [LP, 51]. Because of A) C it is
possible to say something about what Hartshorne means by "intuitively convincing."

---

[33] Hartshorne understands the Law of Excluded Middle to say
that an individual is in a given respect either P or not P. *See* "Tillich
and the Nontheological Meaning of Theological Terms," p. 678.
[34] There are "Two ways of reasoning from a conditional proposition or consequence. The *modus ponens* from the *consequence* and the
antecedent infers the consequent; the *modus tollens* from the consequent and the antecedent infers the falsity of the antecedent . . ." (*Dictionary of Philosophy and Psychology*, ed. James Mark Baldwin [Glou-
cester, Mass.: Peter Smith, 1960]), Vol. II, p. 94.

In the body of Hartshorne's thought, intuition has clearly emerged as the immediate experience of the concrete whole. Does not this suggest that the function of the logic of Anselm's argument is to point toward the concrete whole by means of abstract characterizations? What else could the appeal to intuition mean? This suggests that no matter how strict or necessary modal statements are, they are analogical abstractions. Hopefully, this is not taken as a dismissal of the significance of logic, but as an attempt to understand the place of logic in the "scheme of things." Such logic is clarified when, citing the role of intuition and faith in the proof, Hartshorne remarks, "When Wittgenstein says, 'theology is grammar,' he is really agreeing, insofar, with Anselm. The remaining issue is, how correct is the grammar?" [AD, 54]. Note carefully that it is at the point of "seeing" how correct the grammar of theology (logical expression about God) is that "an element of intuition, faith, insight, what you will beyond mere formal reasoning, is inescapable. But so is it in mathematics itself . . ." [AD, 54].

Theologian John Cobb finds Hartshorne's argument (which he says is convincing in many respects) relativized in two ways. On the one hand, he points to the ambiguity of "the meaning of strict implication, decision systems, logical and factual truth, necessity, and Becker's postulate."[35] This is a forceful suggestion. For example, there appears to be a "shift" in the meaning of necessity when one reaches step (7).[36] Yet, there is a reason why Cobb's charge loses some of its impact when viewed from the standpoint of the present analysis. The reason is that logical assertions are explicitly grounded in intuition. Hartshorne says, ". . . analysis of the idea of perfection will, I think, show that it can only be understood as a consciousness of the required intuition."[37] Further, "It is to be remembered that intuitions are on many levels of conscious distinctness. We do not have such an adequate intuition of divinity that we can simply read its nature by mere inscription. We have to

[35] Cobb, " 'Perfection Exists': A Critique of Charles Hartshorne," p. 299.
[36] This was suggested to me by Bradford Dunham, symbolic logician, now with I. B. M. Research Laboratory, Yorktown Heights, N. Y.
[37] "Hartshorne to Ebbinghaus on the Ontological Argument," I, No. 4. This article was kindly supplied by Professor Hartshorne in mimeographed form.

heighten our awareness of the intuitive content by reasoning. This is the function of the theistic arguments."[38]

What does this understanding of the functions of reason in theistic arguments mean in the face of Cobb's charge of ambiguity? Primarily, it means that the ambiguity of logical construction *qua* logical construction is admitted in principle because logic is grounded in the continuity of all concepts which arise out of intuition. To Hartshorne logic is dependent upon intuitive confirmation; therefore, it is to intuition, and not to the exact distinctness of abstract logic, that one must go to discuss ambiguity. Cobb's charge appears to presuppose that there is an abstract order of some kind that is not ambiguous. Moreover, it is assumed that this order or necessary arrangement could illustrate logical construction in a way that would not have some ambiguity. Hartshorne could not accept this presupposition because of the nature of the intuitable concrete. If A) C were reversed, and the kind of knowledge that theistic arguments demonstrate were grounded in the abstract, then Cobb's charge of ambiguity would be devastating. This is another instance in which Hartshorne is misunderstood unless the function of the relationship between the abstract and the concrete is conceived after the fashion of A) C.

On the other hand, Cobb points out that the meaning of existence "shifts with the ontology involved."[39] Indeed, the point of Hartshorne's reinterpretation is to shift the discussion from the context of an ontology of being in the classical sense to an ontology of becoming in the neoclassical, panentheistic sense. Hartshorne would not deny Cobb's point; he intends it. This is not a case of whether the ontology is shifted, but of whether or not linguistical abstractions are sufficiently univocal to "carry meanings over" into other ontologies. Thus, it appears that Cobb's second point resolves itself into the first. In both cases Hartshorne is using abstract logical reasoning "to witness to" the reality of God in which he intuitively believes the world concretely to stand.

Another line of attack is employed by Julian Hartt: "Let us assume that as abstract God is pure ideality. So far . . . God is a

[38] *Ibid.*, p. 5.
[39] Cobb, " 'Perfection Exists': A Critique of Charles Hartshorne," p. 300.

name for this mode of being; and so far there is no good reason for saying this mode 'exists' rather than 'is what is.' "[40] This is illustrated by the notion that justice, an ideal abstraction, "does not entail an existential judgment."[41] Consequently, it has nothing to do with religion.[42] Hartshorne replies that the suggestion "that deity might, like justice, be an unactualized ideal having being only as such (as an abstraction) merely amounts to the declaration that the proof is invalid."[43] He continues: "I define 'existence' in general as *that* the abstraction, whatever one is in question, is 'somehow concretized'; and I distinguish the necessity (in the divine case) of the *that* from the contingency of the *how*."[44] The point is that "Hartt seems to envisage the line between necessary and contingent as coming, not between that and how, but between both, on one side, and the bare unembodied abstraction, divineness or perfection, on the other."[45] This illustrates Hartshorne's recourse when stating the proof.

Still another attack comes from David Platt's suggestion that Whitehead's procedure of combining metaphysical and "suggestive empirical considerations" brings one closer to the concrete God than Hartshorne's recent preoccupation with the ontological argument.[46] He finds a corresponding obscuring of concrete confrontation with God because "at best a proof can only give us an abstraction."[47] From what has been said about the place of the proof and abstract thinking in Hartshorne's philosophy it should be clear that Hartshorne knows the ontological argument is an abstraction. Moreover, he could hardly disagree with Platt's doubt that anything "we come up against" could exist necessarily. Precisely because God's existence is not a thing among things, it qualifies for necessary existence. Platt seems to be asking the proof to produce something like a personal encounter, a religious experience. Such

[40] Julian Hartt, "The Logic of Perfection," *The Review of Metaphysics*, XVI, No. 4 (June, 1963), 756.
[41] *Ibid.*
[42] *Ibid.*
[43] Hartshorne, "Abstract and Concrete in God: A Reply," *The Review of Metaphysics*, XVII, No. 2 (December, 1963), 290.
[44] *Ibid.*
[45] *Ibid.*
[46] Platt, "Some Perplexities Concerning God's Existence," p. 247.
[47] *Ibid.*, p. 251.

confrontation may be associated with the abstract reasoning of the proof, but it is hardly fair to test an ontological proof on these grounds.

In a sense Platt's charge that the proof is superfluous is true. All modal statements are made by beings already standing in the concrete about which they abstractly speak. The best alternative to logical consistent clarification of the concrete by abstract constructions is not, however, merely an existential confrontation which probably has difficulty distinguishing among idols. The function of ontological necessity as a categorical way of ruling out idolatry in Hartshorne's thought bears some similarity to the intention of Rabbi Richard Rubenstein, who writes: "Before God it is difficult for us to elevate the trivial to the central in our lives. The old Hebraic understanding of the meaning of idolatry is important for an understanding of the meaning of God as the focus of ultimate concern. Idolatry is the confusion of a limited aspect of things with the ground of the totality."[48] The alternative could just as well be an irrational silence without theology or philosophy or any language. Platt does not have to return to Whitehead to find a "given" out of which one speaks of God while standing "in" Him. Hartshorne's concrete God is certainly presupposed when the proof is discussed, but this does not make speaking (or proving) superfluous; it makes it possible! Intuition and faith could confirm or deny abstract propositions only if they were real before the fact. Hartshorne is not even talking about factual confirmation of modal statements about God. He remarks, ". . . we have defined deity in purely generic or a priori terms. For what empirical fact would be needed in order to form the idea of knowing itself?" [AD]

In sum it is in the light of A) C that Hartshorne's rediscovery of the ontological proof of God's existence is intelligible as an attack upon classicism. If the abstract were assigned some kind of ontological status in its own right, abstract logical construction would represent a return to the kind of objective metaphysics against which the primacy of the concrete stands. Yet, since Hartshorne's use of logic follows from his basic understanding of the

---

[48] Rubenstein, *After Auschwitz: Radical Theology and Contemporary Judaism* (New York and Indianapolis: Bobbs-Merrill Co., 1966), p. 238.

"place" of the abstract, the "proof" must be understood in this way. Hartshorne's interest in Anselm's ontological proof, and his neo-classical reinterpretation of that proof in terms of concrete process, are methodologically founded in A) C. Necessity would take on its smothering classical form only if A (C rendered contingency empty. Speaking of the necessary existence of God in the neo-classical sense avoids trying to find something necessary in history, the realm of contingency. Classical necessity is a characteristic of the abstract God because it confused God's existence with the *how* of His actual life. Neoclassical necessity is a solution to the problem of the classical God because it removes the question of necessity from the realm of particular beings in the world.

Whether the language employed is "absolutism" (1941), "eternality" (1952), or "necessity" (1961-1965), Hartshorne's driving concern is to show the failure of the abstract God of classicism. This does not mean that these schemes lose their individual significance, because each one does demonstrate a dimension of the problem to which the concrete God is an answer. This problem was summed up recently by a sign someone put on my office door: GOD ISN'T DEAD. HE JUST DOESN'T WANT TO GET INVOLVED. The abstract God cannot "get involved"—He is dominated by classical abstractions which make historical involvement impossible.

7

God as Concrete Reality

The concrete God is the inclusive whole in which history lives. When history changes, God changes with each event. Limited by the uncertainty of the future and the reality of freedom, He is related to every happening. He accepts historical decisions as real and contains them everlastingly in Himself. In this way God loves the world by actually participating in time. Although God is contingent upon how events occur, that *some* events occur is logically necessary and herein lies the abstract necessary uniqueness of the concrete God.

IN THE AGE of the death of God, the theological ethos gives the impression that theology has moved into an unseeing temporality. This is the temporality of existential subjectivity, estrangement, loneliness, relativity, absurdity, despair, and a loss of purposeful existence. In this situation the concrete God easily seems to herald the collapse of all certainty. The quest for certainty of an Augustine or a Descartes appears finally abandoned. Such a notion is false, however, and it will be the task of this chapter to demonstrate that in Hartshorne's work the relativity of our age is fully embraced, even championed, while at the same time a fresh way to understand certainty unfolds.

In the discussion of the abstract God the key problem was eternality. It is not surprising, then, that modern solutions to the problem of classical theism all appeal in some sense to temporality. For example, Hartshorne likes to emphasize the reality of time in the work of Nicolas Berdyaev. Note, however, as in the commentary in *Philosophers Speak of God*, that the other characteristics of God (E, C, K, and W) are also found in Berdyaev's theology. The other characteristics of God are possible because time, not eternity, is primary. The concrete God is primarily temporal, but not exclusively temporal. After the fashion of A) C temporality includes eternality. This relationship between time and eternity is the basic reason Hartshorne can agree when "Berdyaev speaks frankly of a divine history, a divine becoming, divine need, and, above all, divine suffering" [PSG, 285-286]. If temporality did not ontologically include eternality, these "temporal" categories employed by Berdyaev could not be taken seriously. How, for instance, could one make sense out of eternal history? Is not history temporal by virtue of its own "event" character? If historical happenings were already in God's eternity, what could it mean to say they happen in the here and now of history?

The dominance of time means human and divine history accrue together. Accruing history has an ontological advantage over history supposedly unfolding out of an eternal will. In accruing history, events can be real and everlasting without having been "in" abstract eternality. The dominance of abstract eternality means nothing new happens; therefore, the abstract God kills history before being killed by history.

Hartshorne notes that Whitehead and Berdyaev "agree that God has an abstract aspect which is absolute, strictly eternal; but they insist that in His full concrete actuality He is receptive to the world's life, so that all creative action contributes to the divine consciousness."[1] Creative action affecting the divine consciousness would be meaningless if the divine consciousness were already eternally fixed. Only if temporality is real to God does it make any sense to say that human creativity has significance. How could one make a contribution of any kind to that which is complete? Human creativity had to kill the abstract God in order *to be*.

Temporality is the dominant theme in the theology of Berdyaev, but only in the work of Henry Nelson Wieman does time (T) emerge to the complete exclusion of other theological categories. "For H. N. Wieman, God, or 'creativity' or 'the creative event,' whatever else he or it may be, is the producer, or the production or emergence, of unexpected, unpredictable good" [PSG, 395]. How

[1] Hartshorne, "Whitehead and Berdyaev: Is There Tragedy in God?" *Journal of Religion*, XXXVII, No. 2 (April, 1957), 74.

this represents a sharp veering away from Hartshorne's notion of the temporal concrete may be seen by asking what role man plays in creativity. The answer is: "Man is regarded by Wieman as a passive factor in the event from which good emerges so that it is not really man who clarifies, carries forward, and implements the idea; this is the function of God or creativity" [PSG, 396]. Wieman assigns man a passive role instead of one in which his activity is a contribution to accruing reality. Hartshorne's implication that man is man through the contribution he makes, such as the writing of a poem (the results of which he admittedly can only partially foresee), means employing abstractions. Thus, it is the abstract that is omitted by Wieman. In other words, Hartshorne's opposition to Wieman may be expressed as an opposition to the neglect of man's role in abstract expressing. This means that the abstract has been "swallowed up" by the concrete, and eternity by time. Not only is the concrete taken as inclusive, in Wieman, it is taken as all there is.

Wieman tends to consider the problem of abstract identification secondary, making abstract knowledge difficult to imagine. If the debate between Hartshorne and Wieman may be broadened to the question of the relation of metaphysical knowledge to the datum upon which such knowledge is based, the issue can be focused. In effect, this is what John Cobb does when he maintains that Wieman's emerging process—or as Wieman terms it, "creative interchange"—presupposes an ontology, a metaphysical commitment. Wieman replies to Cobb:

> But it is impossible to develop a metaphysical system without prior commitment to creative interchange. Plato's dialogues are the prime example. Every metaphysical system ever brought to attention in the history of philosophy has been created by philosophers engaged in creative interchange with one another. The remarkable fact is that creative interchange throughout the history of philosophy is always transcending every metaphysical system it rears, going on to create another and then another, down to the most recent constructions in the United States by Paul Weiss and Charles Hartshorne.[2]

[2] H. N. Wieman, "Reply to My Critics," *Religion in Life*, XXXII, No. 3 (Summer, 1963), 460.

From this it appears that Wieman holds Hartshorne's appeal for man's abstract expression to be a metaphysical structure which will be surpassed by "creative interchange." Wieman simply denies that "creative interchange" implies a metaphysics.

Put in terms of God, Wieman's view of time requires that the activity of concrete emergence, God's emergence, overpower the "act" of accepting God as a possibility. Hartshorne notes that such a view is not new for a theologian, but it "used to mean that God does not *receive* satisfaction, because he eternally *has* all satisfaction without needing to receive it. For Wieman, it means that God is simply without satisfaction, experience, feeling, either eternal or received" [PSG, 407]. With the collapse of the abstract it becomes a problem to explain why there are not several "gods" rather than one God, and how such a God would be distinguished from man. The criticism reveals how Hartshorne himself distinguishes God from man—through abstract necessity. Over the years Hartshorne has often been pressed to make this distinction, and his recent studies of ontological necessity reflect his concern to make this distinction clear and forceful.

Hartshorne's opposition to mere abstract eternality, on the one hand, and mere concrete temporality, on the other, emerges in his attempt to combine the merits of both in his constructive program—the dipolarity of God.

Utilizing his neoclassical notion of necessity and a modern penchant for temporality, Hartshorne develops the concrete God through a constructive synthesis. The key to this combination, which he often calls "dipolarity," is his insistence that the concrete temporal must always include abstract eternality or, as we have formulated it, A) C. It is now necessary to discuss the two poles of this formula in theological terms.

From A) C we know that every grade of being (minimal, as in a rock; middling, as in man; maximal, as in God) "has" both an abstract and a concrete dimension. [*See* PSG, 499-514.] In the case of God, A symbolizes the supreme abstraction and C the supreme or superrelative concrete. This means that God's abstract character is qualitatively different from minimal or middling abstraction, providing Hartshorne with a way to distinguish God from the world.

The basic difference between man and God can be seen in this, that whereas the character individual to a man cannot be stated in merely abstract terms, such as good or wise or perverse or foolish (all such abstractions being, for all that could be known, applicable to other individuals), God's character, on the contrary, can be described in utterly abstract terms which yet are unique to him as the one divine individual. Only one individual can ever be omniscient, primordial-and-everlasting, all-loving, supreme cause of all effects, supreme effect of all causes. Only one individual can ever be divine. Here is an extremely abstract character which yet is the defining characteristic of a self—or person. This character, though individual to God, is so abstract or nonspecific that it can be correlated with any possible character you please in its correlate, the world. [DR, 80]

The model used to describe God's abstract character is man. Equipped with a model, Hartshorne analogically raises the notion of character to its highest power. This is not to say that Hartshorne's God is simply a projection by man. Rather, noting that human analogy serves as the basis for Hartshorne's theological judgment (cf. Gollwitzer), it is intended only to bring clarity to the method. As the passage quoted above suggests, the "logic" of saying "only one individual" proceeds on the assumption that we know what an individual is. Description of how God is abstractly superior depends upon some knowledge or awareness of human finitude complete with relative abstractions such as "good or wise or perverse." Thinking of God according to human analogy also requires that the abstract and the concrete be related as A) C. For example, Hartshorne says Anselm's only radical error was "that he never relates the necessary, and therefore abstract, to anything which is more than abstract in God."[3] Anselm does not, in Harts-

---

[3] From Hartshorne's introduction to St. Anselm, *Basic Writings: Proslogium, Monologium, Gaunilon's On Behalf of the Fool, Cur Deus Homo*, trans. S. W. Deane (2nd ed., LaSalle, Ill.: Open Court Publishing Co., 1962), p. 15.

horne's judgment, relate God's necessity to concreteness. He cannot do so, Hartshorne holds, "for neoplatonic theology is committed to the worship of the necessary or eternally immutable as opposed to the contingent or noneternal."[4]

---

[4] *Ibid.* Whether or not Hartshorne's critique of Anselm is based upon a correct understanding of Anselm is a matter for debate. The question to which the debate must address itself is the question of how Anselm himself conceived the nature of God. Did his conception really contain, as Hartshorne charges, "prejudices derived chiefly from Greek and Roman sources . . ."? Perhaps the issue is best focused as a question of what the nature of thinking is. Take, for example, the problem of the nature of thinking as it bears upon the problem of the nature of God in the following passage from Anselm's *Proslogium.*

"Assuredly thou art life, thou art wisdom, thou art truth, thou art goodness, thou art blessedness, thou art eternity, and thou art every true good. Many are these attributes: my straitened understanding cannot see so many at one view, that it may be gladdened by all at once. How, then, O Lord, art thou all these things? Are they parts of thee, or is each one of these rather the whole, which thou art? For, whatever is composed of parts is not altogether one, but is in some sort plural, and diverse from itself; and either in fact or in concept is capable of dissolution.

"But these things are alien to thee, than whom nothing better can be conceived of. Hence, there are no parts in thee, Lord, nor art thou more than one. But thou art so truly a unitary being, and so identical with thyself, that in no respect art thou unlike thyself; rather thou art unity itself, indivisible by any conception. Therefore, life and wisdom and the rest are not parts of thee, but all are one; and each of these is the whole, which thou art, and which all the rest are (Chap. xviii)."

To Anselm, "than whom nothing better can be conceived of" appears to mean unity in God whether or not thinking of God involves the distinctions between life, wisdom, truth, etc. What does this mean thinking is? If one imagines that a temporal sequence makes possible different attributes at different times, the problem of unity and difference, as residing in the same being, only shifts to time. The question is the nature of thinking regarding God Himself, not time. The question is whether distinctions do or do not apply to God. If thinking can occur without the contrast involved in distinction, if unity can be concretely thought, if God in His concrete becoming can at once be conceived as both having and not having distinctions, then the problem is dissolved. In the passage above, Anselm appears either to adopt an understanding of thinking that requires no law of contradiction, or to be truly struggling with a contradiction. If thinking requires contrast, which can issue in real contradictions, Hartshorne has understood Anselm's situation with regard to the nature of "than whom nothing better can be conceived of." Moreover, the problem is just what Harts-

In spite of this difficulty, in Anselm Hartshorne sees a key to understanding the abstract side of God's dipolarity. The pure necessity of God's abstract identity, Hartshorne argues, could not in its abstractness "know" the distinctions in concrete particularity.[5] Assuming that knowledge (like love) must in some sense actually be joined to, and hence enter into, the distinctions adhering in its objects [LP, 36], Hartshorne defends the uniqueness of God's self-identity. This necessity itself "is abstract or impoverished to the uttermost, and only therefore does it conflict with nothing, being the mere point of agreement of all possible truths or realities."[6] If Anselm had related this necessity to more than the mere abstract in God he would have avoided what Hartshorne thinks is Anselm's

---

horne says it is: the problem of the relationship between the abstract and the concrete in God.

If, on the other hand, thinking about the nature of God does not involve logical contradictions because thinking does not involve contrast, then Hartshorne has radically misunderstood Anselm. Clearly, Anselm's methodology places faith prior to understanding. In Anselm's words, "Unless I believed, I should not understand" (Proslogium 1). Yet, it is one thing for faith to make understanding possible and quite another to dictate particular distinctions within understanding. When Anselm says, as in the above passage, "these things are alien to thee," he is making a very specific claim about the nature of God. It appears that faith is not only the ground of possibility out of which thinking proceeds, it gives thinking information that contains specific distinctions. If distinctions from faith may override logical contradictions rendering thinking empty, and if Anselm at least implicitly believed this, Hartshorne has not correctly understood Anselm. Hartshorne thinks that contradictions may be involved in the nature of God, which stem from human thinking, and further, that Anselm was aware of this. The rejoinder that Hartshorne is wrong seems to entail either the assertion that Anselm did not "think" in terms of distinctions, a dubious feat, or that human thinking about the nature of God is finally empty because faith renders it so.

Hartshorne is not saying that "than whom nothing better can be conceived of" is not a reference to God as concrete. Anselm's name for God functions in a dipolar way; the abstract designates the concrete. Hartshorne's objection is not that this is not dipolar, but that the abstract pole unnecessarily influences the concrete. Just as Anselm's understanding of faith seems to carry specific distinctions (such as eternality) over into thinking about God, the abstract seems to introduce certain classical notions into the concrete that it designates. Not only is God named, he is given classical specifications.

[5] *Ibid.*

[6] *Ibid.* This point is often repeated in *Anselm's Discovery.*

114 THE CONCRETE GOD

central failure.[7] In other words, the abstract functions improperly when not related to the concrete. Nevertheless, Hartshorne finds value in the fact that Anselm was speaking not of that which is contingent but of that which is necessary. God's uniqueness, then, appears in His abstract *necessity* [cf. AD, 41ff]. Necessity means neutrality toward any contingent concrete actuality. "The divine necessity is *that* such abstract traits or 'perfections' as 'knowing all there is to know' must be realized in some concrete form, with respect to some concrete world of knowable things, but not necessarily in the form and with respect to the world which actually obtain." [AD, 48]

Three caution signs should be erected at this juncture. First, Hartshorne is using the notion of logical necessity, not to be confused with classical concepts that permitted eternal necessity to smother concrete temporality. Classicism is avoided by Hartshorne's concrete starting point because no ordinary particulars are necessary—only *that something* be. Second, the abstract side of dipolarity should not be rejected out of hand simply because it sounds as though Hartshorne were blandly capturing "the mystery of God"— a rather arrogant enterprise. No essence, he says, "captured in a human concept, could possibly be the entire actual God whom we confront in worship, yet such an essence could very well qualify God and no one else" [LP, 4][8] The third caution is a warning not simply to say that Hartshorne's "abstract" theology is a human concept but does not apply to God Himself.

> That "God" stands for the supreme concrete reality does not prevent the word from standing also for the supreme abstract principle. If the supreme abstract principle were not uniquely divine, then God would either come under no concept and be inconceivable (and the word "God" without meaning) or He would be but another instance of the principle, which would thus in a sense be super-divine. This seems blasphemous. [LP, 5]

<hr/>

[7] *Ibid.*

[8] Hartshorne says such an essence would be an "it though God is not. But the *thou* could include the it, and indeed the personal includes the impersonal, not vice versa" (Hartshorne's introduction to St. Anselm, *Basic Writings*, p. 15). Also *see* Hartshorne, "Martin Bubers Metaphysik," in *Martin Buber*, ed. Schilpp and Friedman (Stuttgart: Kohlhammer Verlag, 1963), pp. 42-61.

In his 1941 scheme developed in the language of absolutism
and relativism, Hartshorne maintains that the concrete God must be
both A and R. This is sharpened if correlated with A) C, so that A
is to A as C is to R. Divine relativity is real and ontologically primary in the concrete God, for several reasons.

First, if God were merely nonrelative, He could not relate to
history. For example, nonrelativity is inconceivable from the standpoint of Christian faith based upon an actual historical Incarnation.
Nonrelativity would not only deny any meaningful content to terms
like "willing," "loving," and "feeling"; it would deny the Incarnation
itself. God cannot be involved in relative history without, to that
extent, being relative. Desire to understand ultimate reality or the
concrete God as relative motivated Hartshorne to prefer Heidegger's "more concrete" language over Husserl's phenomenological
essences (see Chapter 2). This same conviction lies behind his neoclassical restatement of the question of God. Hartshorne finds no
unequivocal way to describe the concrete God that avoids actual
relativity in God. He thinks God is relative to historical actions.
Thus, the being that God abstractly has depends in part upon what
happens in the uncertainty of time. What God will be depends in
part upon what man does. Put in terms of human love, God's love of
one's neighbor is *partly dependent upon* whether or not a "free"
human decision to love the neighbor actually occurs. One must
qualify human relativity with words like "partly," however, because
the neighbor would be in the concrete whole of God's "love" ontologically whether or not one added the relative factor of a human
decision. This means, on the one hand, that love occurs in every
case, ontologically. How much love occurs is relative to free historical decisions. Divine relativity, therefore, means that human
decisions have real ultimate significance.

Second, nonrelativity means that the concrete God is limited
by freedom. Hartshorne may properly be called "a philosopher of
freedom" because even God is relative to what happens in free decisions and chance. Human decisions must be thought of as free if
they are real. Either freedom is available or the term "decision" is
emptied of meaning. Hartshorne is convinced that classical nonrelative theism could not solve the problem of freedom because it re-
fused to allow relativity in God. Since God was nonrelative and
omnipotent, freedom was impossible, because not even self-de-

pendence was allowed in God. If all contingency and chance were removed, everything would be ontologically certain and fixed, leaving nothing for man or God to do. Hartshorne finds confirmation of freedom in the "uncertainty principle" of quantum mechanics, and he has recommended the discussion of the quantum principle by nuclear physicist and theologian William Pollard in *Chance and Providence*[9] as evidence of the realization of compatibility between God and the relativity of real freedom.

Finally, nonrelativity is impossible if meaning is "meaningful." What does meaning mean? In Hartshorne's thought there is a clear connection between the meaning of human meaning and divine relativity. In his view, the bridge between them is the notion of contribution to reality. The purpose of existence is to contribute something worthwhile to the concrete God. If God were not relative to or dependent upon what is contributed, it would make no sense to say a contribution is really made. Since meaning depends upon purpose and requires a relative context, the meaning of meaning stems from making a contribution to one's concrete world. What things "mean" always is affected by purpose plus what happens when events actually occur. If reality is nonrelative, what purpose could life have? What contribution could one make to life that is already fixed in nonrelativity? Such a situation could not be dependent upon anything. It is not unfair to conclude on Hartshorne's terms that without relativity not only would history and freedom disappear, the meaning of meaning would be lost.

Because in its abstract pole "God" stands for the relative concrete reality, a question should at this point be put to Hartshorne. Why not use the term "reality" instead of "God"? From Hartshorne's perspective there are several reasons for using the term "God" instead of "reality."[10] (1) God is more personal. Recall Hartshorne's opinion that Heidegger's categories are an improvement over the more impersonal ways of speaking in Husserl's phenomenology. From the beginning of his career, Hartshorne has

---

[9] William Pollard, *Chance and Providence* (New York: Charles Scribner's Sons, 1958). Hartshorne has reservations about the theological side of Pollard's work.

[10] Also see the discussion of the question of the relationship between God and reality in Chapter 10.

sought concrete, ordinary, immediate, emotive, and personal terms in order to emphasize that the everyday world has ultimate significance. In a neoclassical framework "God" has seemed more meaningful than "reality." Spoken in a classical framework, the same terms would have achieved impersonal results. (2) Communication is a problem. The term "God" establishes communication at the same time it hinders understanding. There is some overlapping meaning between Hartshorne's use and ordinary use.[11] The difference between ordinary and dipolar theology is that dipolarity does not carry forward the abstract God of classicism—here Hartshorne would have to agree—the abstract God is dead. (3) Finally, Hartshorne holds that he is speaking of the object of worship. But who could worship "reality"? If one accepts the importance of worship, as Hartshorne apparently does, how could one reject the history of worshiping altogether by saying God should no longer be worshiped, but reality should? Practically speaking, substitution of "reality" for "God" would probably mean the end of worship.

The question of the use of the term "God" is closely related to Hartshorne's notion of God's abstract side or the name which characterizes God alone. This question can be compared with the procedure of Karl Barth in his discussion of the "Name" of God in Anselm's work.[12] Both Hartshorne's discussion of the abstract character of God and Barth's discussion of the Name of God focus upon what is a more or less neglected point in Anselm.[13] They maintain that the aspect of Anselm that has been most discussed in the many

[11] I have heard Hartshorne insist that he means the same thing really intended by the "man in the street" who uses the term "God" to designate a loving father. The term "father" is of course to be understood symbolically along with such terms as "ruler," "shepherd," and "author." Hartshorne says, ". . . these specific images are logically in a different class from purely abstract categories such as necessary-contingent, absolute-relative, infinite-finite, immutable-mutable, potential-actual. I hold these conceptions can have no useful symbolic but only literal meanings" ("Tillich and the Nontheological Meaning of Theological Terms," *Religion in Life* [Winter 1966], p. 676).

[12] See Karl Barth, *Fides Quaerens Intellectum (Faith in Search of Understanding)*, trans. Ian W. Robertson, from the 2nd ed., 1958 (Richmond, Va.: John Knox Press, 1960).

[13] See Hartshorne's introduction to Anselm's *Basic Writings, op. cit.*, pp. 1 ff., and Barth's *Fides Quaerens Intellectum*, pp. 100 ff.

"refutations" of Anselm's "proof" is actually a secondary matter and cite approximately the same textual evidence. The neglected point appears several times, at least by implication, in Anselm's responses to the monk, Gaunilon, but especially in *Proslogium*, 2-4. Here, as both Hartshorne and Barth note, Anselm moves the discussion of God's existence from the realm of contingency occupied by ordinary realities to the nonordinary realm of necessity. In Barth's words Anselm now "proves" the existence of God "by assuming a Name of God the meaning of which implies that the statement 'God exists' is necessary (that means, that the statement 'God does not exist' is impossible)."[14] Hartshorne would agree with Barth that Gaunilon's questions assume the subject of discussion is the realm of contingency and are, therefore, "merely beating the air."[15]

Hartshorne, like Barth, opposes Gaunilon's "retreat into the impenetrability of the divine wisdom" [LP, 109].[16] This tendency of traditional theology, Hartshorne insists, "concerns the concrete contingent qualities of God, not His necessary essence. It is not so much the abstract or necessary which we cannot grasp—mathematics might have taught us that—but the concrete and contingent in its fullness, whether divine or not divine. Our intellects are at home in the abstract, the concrete is an infinitely-receding goal" [LP, 109]. To be infinitely receding in concrete reality is to be other than the abstract name that human conceptualization utilizes in the name "God." For both Hartshorne and Barth, God in His entire concrete wholeness is unknowable to finite man.[17] Yet, both are willing to speak about God in Himself, to take God as a subject of discussion.[18] This indicates that their study of Anselm has been significant for their thought. Moreover, Anselm's method appears to be compatible to both Hartshorne and Barth. Abstract necessity is in both cases the presupposed "name" for the concrete reality,

---

[14] Barth, *Fides Quaerens Intellectum*, p. 73.
[15] *Ibid.*, p. 79.
[16] Also *see* Hartshorne, "Arthur Berndtson on Mystical Experience," *The Personalist*, xxxii, No. 2 (Spring, 1951), pp. 191-193.
[17] Barth says, "God is known only by God" (*Church Dogmatics*, Vol. ii, Part i, sec. 27, 179).
[18] Contrast the method of Rudolf Bultmann in his programatic essay, "New Testament and Mythology," *Kerygma and Myth*, ed. H. W. Bartsch, trans. Reginald H. Fuller (New York: Harper & Row, 1961), pp. 1-44.

and both are "free" to speak of God because they have clearly
distinguished the abstract from the concrete as expressed in A) C.
The dipolarity of God permits not only identification but theological
speaking.

Moreover, dipolarity means that abstractly God must be above
contingencies such as death in order to be himself, but concretely
He is involved in every death. Abstract necessity stands "above"
death, and here again Hartshorne differs from the theology of the
death of God. If the concrete God could die He would not be God.
Hartshorne sees some connection between his argument from this
necessary role of God's existence and the work of both Barth and
Tillich.

> Barth agrees essentially with . . . this author that Anselm's
> main point is that the thinkability of non-existence is excluded
> by perfection, or by the formula, "that than which no greater
> can be thought." . . . The formula itself, according to Barth, is
> a piece of revelation. . . . There seems to be some analogy
> between this and my adoption of Tillich's proposal to define
> "God" through the idea of worship or unrestricted devotion.
> To be capable of non-existence is to be unworthy of worship,
> and so not God, since the term stands for the object of
> worship. [LP, 113][19]

Is it surprising that Hartshorne finds Barth's assertion analogous
to his own, given Hartshorne's own principle of so-called "unrestricted devotion"? Consider the difficulty of any abstraction being
completely unrestricted. Would it not strain the analogy if "unrestricted devotion" were not historical in some sense? Hartshorne
seems to sense the methodological reason for the analogy but fails
to clarify it. Perhaps he is led to this by his own notion of unrestricted metaphysical propositions.[20] In any case, this should be

---

[19] In *Anselm's Discovery* the term "perfection" as a description of
"that being greater than which nothing can be conceived" gives way to
the term "greatness." For example, "to suppose the validity of Prosl. II
is therefore to admit that the existence, lack of which would contradict
greatness, is not simple, but necessary, existence" (p. 99).

[20] *See* Hartshorne, "Metaphysical Statements as Nonrestrictive and
Existential," *The Review of Metaphysics*, XII, No. 1 (September 1958),
35-47.

taken into consideration in a comparison between Hartshorne and Barth. Moreover, the discussion of Barth, though it assists in understanding the place of Hartshorne's assertions about the character of God's abstract necessity, makes the other side of God's polarity, the concrete side, more crucial.

Just as the abstract aspect of God is His unchanging character, the concrete aspect designates His relative, changing inclusive aspect. Theological assertions seem to be historical in character. If "to historicize" means to abstract from the concrete whole, "historical" may be used in the sense of an affirmation, i.e., not negative with respect to a given reference. Taking the term in this way opens a door to the concrete aspect of God and at the same time maintains continuity with the discussion of an abstract aspect. In fact, this approach seems to add substance to "historical" interpretation when applied to the question of change in God's concrete aspect. Hartshorne says:

> ... to attribute change to God, so far from conflicting with permanence or stability in his being, means rather that nothing positive that ever belongs to God can change, but only the negative aspect of *not yet* being this or that. Except in his negative determinations, his not-being, God is utterly immutable. Yet since negative determinations are inherent in positive, God really is mutable. [MVG, 130]

Determinations implied in positive assertions are not in conflict with concrete change.[21] Change does not mean that determinations are rearranged. Rather, change is additional historical determination. Since change refers to God's concrete aspect, the abstract "name"—God—is not torn apart but enriched by change [LP, 274]. If the relationship between the abstract and the concrete were such

[21] In his early review of Whitehead's *Modes of Thought*, Hartshorne agrees with Whitehead that not only does the concrete not interfere with assertions, it makes them possible. "God is immanent in us through 'intuition of the universe as everlasting process.' ... Without this subconscious or dim intuition, we should be unable even to see other things as equally real with ourselves, for then 'there would be no standard of comparison.' " (*The International Journal of Ethics* [October, 1934], p. 495.)

that abstract assertions were not included in the concrete, but determined it, the ever receding "goal" would be reached and change would cease. Since, however, change refers to God's *not yet*, the asymmetry and indeterminacy of concrete time are maintained.

Philosopher Merold Westphal has argued that Hartshorne has not adequately supported the temporal finitism of the concrete God.[22] God as conceivable in modal categories cannot have (ontologically) temporality because modality is neutral toward temporality. Contrary to Hartshorne, Westphal believes, "If one were to speak of the divine consciousness in human terms, and thus temporally, he would say that God knows which possibilities will be actualized." Westphal seems to think we can speak of God in some other terms than human ones. What would these be? It is precisely in human terms that all humans speak of God, including Hartshorne when he says, ". . . not even God can be conceived to know as actual what is merely potential" [LP, 37]. The root of Westphal's objection to Hartshorne's temporal God is nourished by an imported dichotomy between divine and human terms. Even deeper, Westphal misreads Hartshorne's understanding of potentiality. Hartshorne allegedly thinks that possibility in God means contingent knowledge *of a particular*, such as the book *The Logic of Perfection*. It is understandable why modal descriptions of real possibilities cannot produce temporality when the terms (possibilities) are understood to entail particular actualities. Temporality is never entailed by modality—this would mean A (C. Eternity, modality, necessity, and all abstractions are *subsequent to* what happens temporally.

Rejecting ontological coincidence between human and divine knowledge, Westphal can find little support for divine dependence in Divine Relativity. But it is precisely the being of man in God (ontologically, not just logically) that makes divine dependence the same as human dependence. If he would follow Hartshorne's A) C, Westphal would have to admit that the admission of human dependence *is* an admission of divine dependence. Knowing another human being means (strictly implies) dependence upon his existence in the knowing relationship. Since God includes the world

[22] Merold Westphal, "Temporality and Finitism in Hartshorne's Theism," *The Review of Metaphysics*, xix, No. 3 (March, 1966), 550-564.

in which this dependence is actually happening in His becoming, God is to this extent dependent. More dependence than this is not required to establish dependence. Excepting God's knowledge from man's dependent way of knowing does not solve the problem of man's tendency to make God in his own image. It creates the problem of knowing what one might possibly mean when he says God knows without actually being dependent when (temporally in successive reactions to actual novelty) He knows. In Hartshornian terms Westphal has not only derived divine dependence, he has made the meaning of divine knowing (and loving) strange indeed.

On Hartshorne's terms, there is one way finally to describe God's concrete wholeness which affirms and respects the concrete as a receding goal. This is to say that God is love.

> Only "love" is an abstraction which implies the final concrete truth. God "is" love, he is not merely loving, as he is merely righteous or wise (though in the supreme or definitive way). This is because in love the ethico-cognitive and the aesthetic aspects of value are both expressed. The lover is not merely the one who unwaveringly understands and tries to help; the lover is just as emphatically the one who takes unto himself the varying joys and sorrows of others and whose own happiness is capable of alteration thereby. Of course, one could distinguish between the abstract invariable lovingness of the perfect lover, and the concrete varying love-experiences he has of his objects in different stages. But love is the one abstraction which makes it almost entirely obvious that there *must* be such a distinction between the generic unchangeable factor and the total value enjoyed. It is not an accident that love was the abstraction least often appealed to in technical theology, though frequently suggested in the high points of Scripture and other genuinely religious writings. [MVG, 111-112]

Building upon the concrete as love is intentionally ethical as well as aesthetic. Hence, Hartshorne's remark, "Owing largely to Greek influences, the medieval theist overlooked the essentially ethical meaning of the divine constancy as posited by Hebrew writers."[23] Hartshorne generally views the eternal and immutable

---

[23] Hartshorne, "Ethics and the New Theology," *The International Journal of Ethics,* xiv, No. 1 (October, 1934), 94.

character of Greek philosophy as an inversion of A) C. In appealing to love as the ethical character of God as expressed in Hebrew
Scriptures, he thinks that the inclusiveness of the concrete whole is
effectively described as opposed to being prescriptively inclosed.

God as love involves the aesthetic because He expresses the
aesthetic principle of unity-in-contrast through His "valuation of
the world" (Whitehead). Valuation of the world entails an understanding of life as "at least mainly an affair of love . . . love of man
for man, or man for woman, of human beings for the subhuman or
the superhuman" [BH, 258]. The aesthetic life as minimally an
affair of love can be taken in the full ontological sense. Love, as the
abstraction most adequately designating the inclusive concrete of
God, is ontologically grounded after the fashion of A) C. It follows
that both the ethical-cognitive and the aesthetic dimensions expressed in the term "love" are ontologically in God. In Hartshorne's
thought the ethical and artistic functions of life are ontologically
contained in the concrete.

Valuation of the world also "implies the possibility of free
decisions among really open possibilities . . . not exclusively by one
agent, God, but by many agents."[24] How, then, are free agents
"included" by God's concrete reality? Hartshorne answers that
"this corollary of freedom need not prevent the many agents from
being included within the one supreme agent."[25] The reason is that
God is love means that he could not make the decisions which his
included creatures must make to be creatures (or anything) and
still be love. To love a person "is to respect his freedom and to
accept his decisions as objects of appreciative awareness."[26] Love
involves passivity even in God; thus, "by a willing passivity, He
accepts and experiences these decisions as ours."[27] "Passivity *is*
activity so far as it is receptive to, or engaged in taking account of,
the activity of others; and the higher the activity the more compre-
hensive the receptivity."[28] With respect to Christianity, Hartshorne

[24] Hartshorne, "A Philosopher's Assessment of Christianity," *Religion and Culture: Essays in Honor of Paul Tillich*, ed. Walter Leibrecht
(New York: Harper, 1959), p. 168.
[25] *Ibid.*
[26] *Ibid.*
[27] *Ibid.*
[28] *Ibid.*, p. 169.

concludes, ". . . the Christian must think of the divine as the all-inclusive reality. For to recognize anything as real outside God is to express at least some slight interest in it, an interest by hypothesis not directed to God. An all-inclusive interest cannot have a less than all-inclusive object!"[29] Apart from the distinction of A) C, all-inclusive interest might imply that the all-inclusive object is "contained" by the interest. A) C makes it clear that, on the contrary, this is an analogy which points. The result is that human freedom is intelligible as occurring in God's concrete becoming because God is not a finished product.

To be passively in faith is to be intuitively within the concrete whole while trusting that one's free contributions to the dynamics of that whole are valuable and real. One is what he does; therefore, real decisions must be real if the decider is real. Faith is ontologically necessary for the decider.

One cannot choose not to have been in the history of choice. The denial of choice is a choice. Hartshorne's ontological faith is logically necessary in a similar way. One has no choice about standing in the concrete history of God (to describe it in theological language). Denial of faith in God is tantamount to denial of existence in reality since God is reality. Refusing to use theological language may have definite advantages, but to Hartshorne, shifting to another "manner of speaking" does not change reality. The reality that does not change is changing reality. The concrete God changes with every historical event; but *that* He is changing never changes.

The task of thought is therefore twofold: to clarify the reality out of which the thinker or decider speaks and to add to reality one's real decisions. Adding to concrete history is the same as adding to God, who is partly constituted by what man does. This would, of course, be impossible if God were a completely unchanging being. The abstract God rendered decisions by man logically impossible and meaningless. The concrete God is limited by freedom and the contingencies of time, thereby giving human decisions meaning.

Moral responsibility takes on real significance in the life of the concrete God. Being free, man acts either responsibly, taking

[29] *Ibid.*, p. 167.

into account his being with others in faith, or irresponsibly, as if others (and himself) are insignificant. The practical criterion for moral action therefore is one's vision of the concrete whole of God. One's action toward his neighbor becomes one's action toward himself and God, because his neighbor is a part of that which constitutes the self and God. Again, no law (except this one) can be absolutized, because the concrete God could never include a set of commandments as valid for all time in a world continually changing. Having stated the ontological priority of being in the concrete, Hartshorne's theology becomes consistent with a "situational" or "contextual" ethic. He would differ from the position of, say, Joseph Fletcher's situational ethics only in the formation of the "flexible" norm. Fletcher appeals to the New Testament norm, *agape*. Hartshorne might agree with the spirit of *agape*, or love, but the concrete God is a broader vision than Fletcher's Christian context. This raises the question of the relationship of the Christian faith and Hartshorne's concrete God. Before we turn to this question in the next chapter, a summary of conclusions about the concrete God is in order.

1. The concrete God, unlike His abstract classical predecessor, is historical. He changes with the changes of history even when historical events involve suffering. As in Berdyaev's view of God's participation in time, temporality now ontologically precedes eternality. This does not mean, however, that history is "abstractly blind," a danger if temporality destroys all abstracting. Hartshorne cannot, therefore, follow Wieman into the complete contingencies of "creative interchange." Classicism-nonrelativity makes history impossible; complete relativity destroys thought and language.

2. Hartshorne's solution of classicism, on the one hand, and modern relativity, on the other, is the dipolarity of God. God has two poles: an abstract pole, which is the logical necessity that some events be actualized; a concrete pole fully contingent upon what happens in the universe. The two poles are related as A) C.

The abstract side of God's dipolarity provides Hartshorne with a way to distinguish God from the world through His completely nonspecific character. In Anselm he finds one who understood God's logical necessity in spite of Anselm's inability to relate such necessity to the concrete because of classical presuppositions. As the only reality fulfilling the requirement of neutral necessity toward variable relations, God obtains an abstract identity. Theological speaking therefore becomes a possibility when one realizes that abstractions are addressed to God's necessary essence and not to His concrete fullness. Such a God is logically noncontingent, making His death inconceivable.

On the concrete side of dipolarity, God's partial death and participation in the suffering and joy of history is conceivable; in fact, necessary. God cannot be unrelated to the events of the universe and still be God. This means that God is "alive" only if He is changing with the changes of history. His future must be as undetermined as the universe's future and as free as the universe's freedom. When novel events occur they change the reality of God out of which they act by adding to His reality. This means that God and the universe are interdependent and involved in significant interaction. God loves the universe as it loves Him through the process of evaluation. This means that the purpose of life is to contribute to the concrete whole, a contribution made meaningful because it really affects ultimate reality. What God will be is partly up to man, who has an intuitive awareness of his being in the becoming of God. Man's ethical responsibility is thus to love God by loving the constituency of the universe. His decision to act according to his vision of the concrete God is itself real, because man is himself partly constituted by his decisions made in the particular contexts of existence.

8

Jesus Christ: An Actual Occasion

As one of the events in history demonstrating the sympathetic involvement of the concrete God, Jesus Christ shows divine love. This is most evident in the event of the cross because here, as elsewhere, God really shares in the sufferings of man.

NOTING EXISTENTIALISM'S TENDENCY toward subjective understandings of man, Schubert M. Ogden proposes that theology look to Hartshorne's analysis of God as a corrective.[1] Ogden is concerned because theology influenced by existential thinking ceases to address its proper subject, God. Theologians, he thinks, have focused upon human "decisions" and "encounters" in the here and now of selfhood at the expense of adequate attention to the doctrine of God. For this reason, Ogden suggests, Hartshorne's dipolar theism represents a reservoir of possibilities for a thirsty subjectivism. Although the theology of Rudolf Bultmann, for example, adequately describes the situation of man, in Ogden's opinion it requires the complement of something like Hartshorne's concrete God.[2] Ogden

---

[1] Schubert M. Ogden, influenced by both Bultmann and Hartshorne, begins this task in his essay, "Bultmann's Demythologizing and Hartshorne's Dipolar Theism," *Process and Divinity*, ed. William L. Reese and Eugene Freeman (LaSalle, Ill.: Open Court Publishing Co., 1964), pp. 493-513, and continues its development in *The Reality of God* (New York: Harper & Row, 1966).

[2] Hartshorne, as was seen in Chap. 2, is also aware of the problem of subjectivism in existentialism.

thinks, ". . . the chief distinction of Hartshorne's achievement is that he has succeeded in working out with an unprecedented scope and depth precisely the kind of philosophical theology to which Bultmann's concerns clearly point, but which he himself has barely more than postulated in his theory of analogy." Moreover, as in the following, Ogden finds his proposal clarified by the distinction between the abstract and the concrete in the case of both Bultmann's understanding of man (following Heidegger) and Hartshorne's understanding of God.

> Just as Bultmann argues that there can be "a science that speaks of (sic human) existence without objectifying it to worldly being," so Hartshorne argues to exactly the same effect about divine existence. And the reasoning is precisely identical: God can be the object of philosophical explication without in any way being objectified to worldly being because what philosophy seeks to explicate is not God as concretely actual, but rather God's abstract essence—just as, by analogy, the object of existential analysis is not man as concrete existence (*Existenz*), but rather the abstract form or principle of such existence (*Existentialität*).[3]

Ogden correlates the Heideggerian distinction between two kinds of understanding, *existential* and *existentiell,* which Bultmann utilizes with Hartshorne's use of the abstract and the concrete. Thus, "Hartshorne could perfectly express his point by simply applying analogically the Heideggerian distinction between 'existence' and 'existentiality.' The theme of philosophical theology is not the divine 'existence,' but the divine 'existentiality.'"[4] In short, Ogden proposes that the Christian faith look to Hartshorne's analysis of God in terms of A) C as a complement to the Heideggerian-Bultmannian correlating analysis of man in terms of *existential* and *existentiell.* Ogden's primary reservation about the availability of Hartshorne's doctrine of God for Christian theology

---

[3] Ogden, "Bultmann's Demythologizing and Hartshorne's Dipolar Theism," pp. 506-507. Ogden is quoting Bultmann, *Kerygma und Mythos,* II, ed. H. W. Bartsch (Hamburg: Herbert Reich-Evangelischer Verlag, 1952), p. 187, with italics deleted.

[4] *Ibid.,* p. 507. Ogden notes that the Heideggerian-Bultmannian equivalent to *Existenz* in Hartshornian language is "actuality."

is that "Hartshorne has not devoted the same care and attention to the doctrine of man that he has devoted to the doctrine of God. . . ."[5] Since there is a correlation between fundamental dimensions of Heideggerian-Bultmannian and Hartshornian thought, a corrective resource for Hartshorne would be the correlating one. Instead of treating the humanity of Jesus in terms of Heideggerian-Bultmannian categories, the analysis can proceed in terms of A) C. Just as existentials adhere in existence, the abstract adheres in the concrete. "Existence" is primary for Heidegger and Bultmann in a way that correlates with the primacy of the concrete in Hartshorne.

Since A) C offers a correlation with the existential understanding of man, it is a simple matter to build upon Ogden's suggestion. The preceding chapters began the task of speaking of God. The purpose of the present chapter is to start back down the steps and draw out Hartshorne's position on the man Jesus Christ. This is possible because (1) Hartshorne's method, A) C, may be applied to any reality; (2) he does offer some comment upon Jesus Christ; and (3) if one follows his methodological principles, it is legitimate to extend his position hypothetically. Hypothetical extension of Hartshorne's method into a Christology means, then, that a second step is taken beyond Ogden's suggestion. The first step, development of the doctrine of God, has been accomplished by Hartshorne himself.

Unlike Bultmann, Hartshorne is a philosopher. It is not surprising, therefore, to hear him say, "I have no Christology to offer. . . ."[6] We are at least mildly surprised when he goes on to remark, ". . . nor do I wish to criticize any."[7] Just as antitheater plays are still theater and no-fashion is still fashion, Hartshorne's no-Christology theology remains a type of Christology. Admittedly, his explicit comments upon Jesus are neither plentiful nor constructive in a systematic fashion. Even those that do appear tend to concentrate

[5] *Ibid.*, p. 512.
[6] Hartshorne, "A Philosopher's Assessment of Christianity," p. 179.
[7] *Ibid.*

upon one facet of a doctrine of Jesus Christ to the exclusion of many of the issues crowding the history of theology. Nevertheless, when the obvious entwinement between the history of the doctrine of God and the history of the doctrine of Jesus Christ is taken into account, the claim that no Christology is criticized is surprising. To be sure, no Christology is criticized if a critique must be a formal and explicit presentation. Nevertheless, the critique is there, and is a topic for Christian theology.

Implicitly, Hartshorne has much to say concerning Jesus Christ. In order to hear what this is, one has merely to agree that Jesus Christ is, in some sense, involved with the concrete world, the world that Hartshorne takes as the presupposition for abstract speaking. Granting this, the Christian theologian now has a stake in the philosophical critique of the classical tradition in which earlier theological expressions are couched. This is not to say that the reality of God stands or falls with the outcome of such a critique, but rather that the Christian theologian has a concern with the way in which the language of the world does or does not adequately express the reality he wishes to describe. The massive polemic that Hartshorne marshals against the classical understanding of God also represents a critique of the classical understanding of Jesus Christ.[8] It does not matter if such a critique is largely implicit.

Hartshorne's consistency is indicated by the one facet of the understanding of Jesus Christ to which he gives most of his explicit attention, namely, Jesus as God's suffering love.

. . . there is one aspect of the view that God was incarnate in Jesus which I do wish to mention. Jesus was a man who suffered, mentally and physically, in intense degree, and not alone upon the cross. Thus his acceptance of suffering symbolizes the supreme value of humility. The first of men dies the death of a slave. But should we not go further? Jesus was termed the Christ, the self-manifestation of God. Yet, according to many theological and philosophical doctrines, being di-

[8] In addition to "A Philosopher's Assessment of Christianity," also *see* Hartshorne, "Philosophy and Orthodoxy," *Ethics*, LIV, No. 4 (July 1944), 295, and Hartshorne, *Reality as Social Process* (Glencoe: The Free Press and Boston: The Beacon Press, 1953), p. 535.

vine means precisely, and above all, being wholly immune to suffering, in any and every sense. In that case, the Stoic or Buddhistic sage would be more nearly divine than was Jesus.[9]

Hartshorne is not saying Jesus is "more nearly divine" because suffering is good. Such an interpretation neglects the polemical tone of this passage. God's suffering in the man Jesus is good only in the larger context of God's love. Classicism in Christology meant that God's suffering love was logically impossible. It is against this logic that Hartshorne is working, as is clear in the remainder of the passage.

> On the contrary, as we have already seen, reasons can be given for positing supreme passivity, as well as supreme activity, in God. We have also maintained that all things, of any importance whatever, must be recognized as literally embraced in the divine reality. But surely suffering has some importance. Hence there must be suffering in God. If it be not so, then to wish to remove suffering must be to feel an interest that is not an interest in God. We should, I think, take literally the saying, "Inasmuch as ye have done it to the least of these, ye have done it unto me" where "me" refers to God Himself, and not to any man as man, not even Jesus. Not, indeed, that deity is to be conceived as thirsty, say, in the sense of having a human body, deficient in moisture, as His very body, but that the feelings of suffering involved are somehow within the divine experience, as analogously the sympathetic spectator of a thirsty man imaginatively shares in his sufferings. In the divine case, however, there is not mere imagination, but sheer, intuitive participation.[10]

Intuitive participation is concrete sympathetic involvement. Thus, the facet of the doctrine of Jesus Christ upon which Hartshorne centers is Jesus as concretely representative of God's contingency and passivity. God literally suffers. "Inasmuch as ye have done it to the least of these ye have done it unto me." God "intuits and thus shares in our tragedies."

An example of the way in which this understanding of Jesus stands as a part of Hartshorne's over-all critique of classicism appears in his posing of the question of the suffering of Jesus as a

[9] "A Philosopher's Assessment of Christianity," p. 179.
[10] *Ibid.*

problem for Thomism. "The Thomistic God has no sorrow, only joy —and this joy owes nothing to ours. Of course, if God is taken, via the incarnation, as identical with the human Jesus, then he does sorrow, but by definition he is then not the Thomistic God."[11] The problem Hartshorne sees in the Thomistic God is, finally, that God's passivity is not recognized, and this is indicated by the deletion of actual divine suffering in God.

To Hartshorne the symbol best expressing the way in which God participates in the sorrow and joy, wealth and burden of the world is the cross, "a sublime and matchless symbol of this . . ." [MVG, 165]. "The cross may be taken as a symbol in that Jesus, in accepting such a fate, made it as clear as any man could that his own escape from suffering was not the major consideration."[12] To Hartshorne this remains true regardless of being "partly nullified by theological efforts to restrict suffering and sympathy to God as incarnate."[13] Altizer's assertion that God died in the Incarnation has the same basic intention—witnessing to the total involvement of God in the world. From Hartshorne's perspective Altizer simply takes God's suffering on to death, a move that neglects transcendental necessity.

Taken together, the references for which the cross is a symbol may be expressed in one word: love. Hartshorne argues that "it makes it sensible to say that we love the inclusive reality and that it loves us" [LP, 101]. To anyone who objects that love is an empirical idea too restrictive to be an adequate designation for "inclusive reality," Hartshorne replies:

> I can only deny this flatly. Human love is a particular form, but the manner in which it figures as base of our analogy is logically non-restrictive, even though in psychological probability (in the way our imagination works) some restrictiveness may be more or less inevitable. Whatever is special or odd about human love is precisely what the analogy makes ir-

[11] Hartshorne, Discussion: "Reflections on the Strength and Weakness of Thomism," *Ethics* (October, 1943), 54.
[12] Hartshorne, "The Kinds of Theism: A Reply," *Journal of Religion*, XXXIV, No. 2 (April, 1954), 131.
[13] *Ibid.*

relevant. Finitely flexible love (inevitably with arbitrary limits of flexibility) is one thing, infinitely flexible love is another. It may be unimaginable, but we are here conceiving, not imagining. To say that love must be limited in flexibility is merely one of the many ways in which the positivistic alternative to theism may be put. [LP, 101][14]

In any case, Hartshorne, who once defined love in general as "sympathetic rapport" [PPS, 13], finds a matchless symbol in the specific event of Jesus on the cross. The cross as the symbol of God's love is based upon the actual occurrence of that love in Jesus who "as literally divine loves men, really loves them . . ." [MVG, 165]. Hence, "Instead of simply *adding Jesus to an unreconstructed idea of a non-living-God*, should we not take him as proof that God really *is* love—just that, without equivocation?" [MVG, 165]. Thus, the cross, of God's love, transcends symbols—it is an occurrence which, as actual, is consistent with the reality in which it stands and, as symbolic, is an indication that that reality is best understood as being like the love shown in the cross. Jesus is *literally* divine in that He is God loving—not merely like God, but as a part of God. Jesus is *symbolically* divine in that His actual love analogically points to the whole of the reality of God as love.

Occurrence involves real novelty; Jesus, as the occurrence of God's love, could not be prescriptively contained in a God of absolute self-sufficiency. Jesus' work, like the work of all creatures, contributes to the reality of God. Yet, Jesus' cross is also the supreme symbol of God's love for the creatures—His actual love. This understanding of the work of Christ underlies Hartshorne's question about the doctrine of the Trinity. How can God, understood as self-sufficient in trinitarian formulations, love His creatures without receiving their love? The love of God is incompatible with divine self-sufficiency. The Christian solution is obviously to abandon the self-sufficiency of God as a religious article and affirm the love of God as a Christian possibility. Even the secularist can accept this

[14] This is one example of Hartshorne's general practice of speaking of man and God together (here in unrestrictive love). This practice lies behind Ogden's insistence that "in his own way, Hartshorne endorses the motive of Karl Barth in urging the *analogia fides* against the *analogia entis* of traditional philosophical theology" ("Bultmann's Demythologizing and Hartshorne's Dipolar Theism," p. 509).

argument. All he has to do is consider ordinary love as a contribution to reality. When he loves he inevitably loves reality because all objects of love are "in" reality (even imaginary objects are "really" held). Theologically, God is related to the creatures' interest through the kind of love that actually occurs in Jesus. Jesus as literally divine expresses God's interest through actually loving His creatures. Man literally (panentheistically) expresses the love of the creatures for God through actually contributing to God, i.e., proving "that God really is love—just that, without equivocation. . . ." Jesus actually loves, hence contributes to God by loving the creatures who are panentheistically in God.

What has been said to this point follows clearly from Hartshorne's central interest in the Incarnation as a concrete occurrence. God has sympathetic intuition with the creatures, as expressed in Christ suffering and consummately in love. Two other doctrines which Hartshorne explicitly treats may follow less obviously from his central understanding. These are *personal immortality* and *prayer*, two topics he discusses in "A Philosopher's Assessment of Christianity."

Hartshorne's major criticism of what he takes to be the "bookkeeping sense" of personal immortality, i.e., God as rewarding and punishing in "exact proportion to the past deeds of the agent himself," is that such a conception "seems incompatible with the nature of existence."[15] Exact proportions are foreign to actual social existence because of the reality of chance.[16] "Acts bring consequences in the course of social interaction, to which every agent, and not simply God alone, contributes decisions. The world is not a police court, nor anything much like it."[17] To illustrate this problem and his suggested solution, Hartshorne again uses a human analogy, in this case a parent. Like a human parent God must permit his children to reward and punish within freedom; otherwise life would be a meaningless determinism. In this scheme God's justice is not something all-powerful, because of the limits of real freedom. But

[15] Hartshorne, "A Philosopher's Assessment of Christianity," p. 176.
[16] *Ibid.*
[17] *Ibid.*

His love "is all-sufficient, and it *is* His justice"; therefore, Harts-horne sees "no reason to suppose that endless prolongation of individual existences is necessary or desirable simply in order to make the laws effective."[18] Neither, we may suppose, would a doctrine of the "endless prolongation of individual existence" be a part of Hartshorne's implicit Christology. Since Jesus Christ *is* God's love and God's love *is* His justice, Hartshorne's Christology requires no additional notion of personal immortality.

Although no addition is required, *within* the being of God in Jesus Christ a doctrine of personal immortality remains. Immortality resides in the concrete event of Jesus Christ and in those concrete events of history toward which the name Jesus Christ abstractly points. Hartshorne thinks this doctrine of personal immortality is consistent with the nature of existence in the sense of Whitehead's doctrine of the objectively real immortality of the past.[19] This means that "God does not lose elements from His experience, does not forget what He has once enjoyed, but with ideal perfection of vividness retains it forevermore."[20] Hartshorne adds, ". . . there is a divine evaluation of such treasure, a consciousness of what it contributes or fails to contribute (in comparison with what may have been possible for us)."[21] From this it follows that "there is indeed a 'divine judgment' upon our lives. . . ."[22] Out of this concrete situation a purpose for existence evolves in the notion of contribution.

> Those who are willing to contribute poorly will "have their reward"; they will not have enjoyed the sense of contributing adequately which they might have enjoyed. Why ask for a motive for loving God, and for making service to Him the ultimate end? Either the motive for loving God is His lovableness, or it is something else. If it is His lovableness, then that is sufficient, and all that is required is to make men

---

[18] *Ibid.*, p. 177.
[19] *Ibid.*
[20] *Ibid.*
[21] *Ibid.* Elsewhere Hartshorne remarks, "Whitehead's God *values our values as integral to his own.* He suffers in our sufferings, as well as enjoys in our enjoyments" (Communication: Rejoinder: "Ely on Whitehead," *Journal of Liberal Religion,* v, No. 2 [September, 1943], p. 98).
[22] *Ibid.*

as aware of the divine good as possible. If the motive must be something else, then God is deficiently lovable, which is blasphemous.[23]

Further than this Hartshorne refuses to go. He does not offer an opinion on whether or not there is individual survival after death in more than an "objectively real" sense.[24] He says, "I am saying only that I see no religious or philosophical necessity for the idea, which has often promoted selfishness rather than neighborly love."[25] Hartshorne also recognizes the danger of the opposite extreme—foolish altruism, "extravagant absorption in the destiny of others . . ." [MVG, 147].

How does personal immortality relate to Jesus? Because Jesus is literally a concrete occurrence, it would be consistent to say that He is personally immortal just as other occurrences are immortal in God. Jesus obtains everlasting presence through His own actuality. And because past occurrences can be nothing other than concrete history, men live in the reality of Jesus Christ simply because it occurred. It is possible to see Jesus as an indication that God is love because past actualities remain present possibilities through their immortality in God. Hartshorne could agree with Barth when he says, "Things exist on the basis of the possibility of God, but on the basis of this possibility alone."[26] Past occurrences also "live" in the memory of man, but only in a finitely deficient way [LP, 293]. Nevertheless, man intuitively participates in the concrete whole of reality, and thereby every occurrence in that whole (the concrete God) may be said to be a possibility for man. The point is that these possibilities are everlastingly (not eternally) a possibility for man. If they were eternal they could not happen as novel events in history. Everlasting events are occasions which at some time have not yet happened, but which remain forever once they do happen.

Having concretely occurred, the event of Jesus Christ stands in God in the same way in which all other events are immortally in

23 *Ibid.*
24 *Ibid.*
25 *Ibid.*, p. 178.
26 Karl Barth, *Church Dogmatics*, III, Part 2, p. 154.

Him. This means that Jesus Christ is one of the concrete occurrences of history, each of which has its own unique quality. How, then, is Jesus unique? What is to separate the event of Jesus from, say, the event of Aristotle? On Hartshorne's terms both have their being in God. Perhaps one should say that they have their becoming in God. Both have the uniqueness of their own concrete event. The event of Aristotle is unlike any other event, owing to its own novelty. It is this novelty that makes Aristotle uniquely Aristotle. The event of Jesus Christ is unlike any other event, owing to its own novelty; hence, this novelty makes Jesus uniquely Jesus. So far the uniqueness of Jesus is established according to the same' principle as the uniqueness of Aristotle. Here uniqueness means different in the *same way* that all concrete occurrences are different. On Hartshorne's terms qualitative difference appears to be limited to the ordinary distinctions of concrete existence, except in the nonordinary case of God. Uniqueness could only take on the special uniqueness of God to escape finite uniqueness. If "Jesus Christ" is only an abstract designation for God's necessity, He is unique in a qualitative way, but He is no longer historical. On the other hand, if Jesus Christ is a concrete occurrence in the history of concrete occurrences (which are individually contingent) Jesus' uniqueness occurs in the same way that Aristotle's uniqueness occurs. When Hartshorne speaks of the symbol of the cross, he generally refers to Jesus as an illustration of that which makes God supreme, hence, supremely unique. When describing the occurrence of Jesus as a concrete event in its own right, he speaks of Jesus as being unique in the same way that Aristotle is unique.[27]

On Hartshorne's terms even resurrection would be the same in the cases of Jesus and Aristotle. By virtue of the principle of objective immortality, both Jesus and Aristotle would be "resurrected" into eternal life if resurrection means being everlastingly in God.

[27] Given this understanding of uniqueness Hartshorne could accept Van A. Harvey's conclusion about Christianity's historical destiny: "It is most faithful to that destiny and the image of him who initiated it when it simply accepts and rejoices in that destiny and ceases to claim for this historical reality an exclusiveness that, when claimed, surrenders the very truth to which it witnesses" (*The Historian and the Believer: The Morality of Historical Knowledge and Christian Belief* [New York: The Macmillan Co., 1966], pp. 288-289).

This would not only occur after death, but would occur during life in that every concrete event is everlastingly in God. To establish a doctrine of resurrection in which Jesus is *"the* resurrection" of all reality would mean deletion of concrete historical particularity in favor of abstract symbolic designation. In other words, so long as Jesus remains concrete, His resurrection goes the way of all concreteness.

This Christology may be illustrated by returning to the other item Hartshorne explicitly mentions—prayer. Discussion of prayer in turn involves the nature of theological speaking, and this must be grounded in Hartshorne's understanding of the linguistic character of human consciousness. Man's linguistic character itself must be founded in faith; hence, prayer arises from the concrete ground of faith.

Hartshorne remarks, "If anything is Christian, it seems that prayer must be."[28] This is held to be consistent with God as "conscious of us, and of our thoughts and feelings. To be sure, we do not need to put these thoughts or feelings into words for God to know about them."[29] This sets the stage for a statement of Hartshorne's views on the relationship between language and theology, a matter of contemporary concern.[30] Speaking of thoughts and feelings panentheistically in God, he says:

> But we do need to put them into words if they are to take on distinct and conscious character, rather than remaining inchoate and subconscious. *For human consciousness is essentially linguistic.* If, then, our relation to God, our response to Him, which religion holds is to be the inclusive response, is not to remain lacking in conscious clarity it must take on verbal form. But such form must consist either in talking, if only to ourselves, about God or else of talking to Him; it must be either

[28] Hartshorne, "A Philosopher's Assessment of Christianity," p. 178.

[29] *Ibid.*

[30] *See* for example, *New Frontiers in Theology: The New Hermeneutic,* II, ed. James M. Robinson and John B. Cobb (New York: Harper & Row, 1964).

in the third or in the second person. Yet, since third-person statements are natural only in the absence of the party concerned, and since God is never absent but always in effect a witness and auditor, it is the second person that is appropriate. Hence prayer is rationally justified.[31]

To deny verbal form to prayer is "to remain lacking in conscious clarity" in relation with God. The essence of human consciousness is itself linguistic; therefore, to become consciously aware of God, man must speak about or to Him. This assertion involves the notion of the "hermeneutical circle" in which it is necessary already to know reality in some sense in order to recognize it when it does appear.[32] Hartshorne would agree, and can say that God is already known intuitively as that in which the speaker stands, and the act of speaking is the act of bringing knowledge of God into "distinct and conscious character." To refuse to speak would be to refuse to be conscious man, because "human consciousness is essentially linguistic." To refuse to speak to God, on Hartshorne's terms, would be to refuse to address the reality in which one stands.

It is this understanding of the relationship between the conscious and the unconscious in theological matters that stands behind Hartshorne's claim that, because the motive for loving God is God's lovableness, "all that is required is to make men as aware of divine good as possible." This clarifies the definition of faith given earlier, namely, "the acquirement, on the more conscious level, of that integral adjustment to the whole of things which inherited impulse furnishes to all creatures below the conscious level." This, Hartshorne continues, agrees with his contention "that God is experienced, not just proved indirectly. . . ."[33] Standing in the

[31] Hartshorne, "A Philosopher's Assessment of Christianity," p. 178 (italics added).
[32] An example of the "hermeneutical circle" would be Carl Michalson's description of Bultmann's theological method: "The act of preaching presupposes that a word that has been heard will make possible the hearing of the word" ("Theology as Ontology and History," *New Frontiers in Theology: The Later Heidegger and Theology*, ed. James M. Robinson and John B. Cobb (New York: Harper & Row, 1963), I, p. 143.
[33] Hartshorne, "A Philosopher's Assessment of Christianity," p. 179.

concrete God means *everyone* has faith! This is true in the same way in which thought is grounded in experience and the abstract is grounded in the concrete. Thus, "one man may surpass another, not so much in the clarity of his thought concerning God as in the vividness and steadiness of his perceptual experience of the divine. 'Blessed are the pure in heart, for they shall see God' is not necessarily contrary to reason, and may even receive some support from it."[34] Elsewhere, Hartshorne argues that the reverse might also hold. The pure in heart "*may* have light to throw upon truths otherwise likely or perhaps certain to be missed or seen less clearly" [MVG, 67]. Herein, Hartshorne posits the limits of abstract reason because reason may lead man astray. In formulating his conscious objectives a man "is capable of departing widely from his proper place in the scheme of things, making himself, as it were, less than a man."[35] Out of the same freedom and history, a man is also able to hold the vision of God's actual love in Jesus Christ and other events in his consciousness.

Conscious reasoning can point man toward his "ground" as well as away from it. The very possibility of misguided reason thus gives Hartshornian faith a positive role in two senses of "positive." On the one hand, the more conscious "adjustment to the whole of things" seems to entail the positing of linguistic conventions because man's consciousness is essentially linguistic. The assumption here is that a word is a characterization or a designation involving an abstraction from the whole of concrete possibility. To be consistent Hartshorne would have to say that faith entails the positing of conscious limits that sufficiently designate the whole. The test of faith would consequently be the intuitive realization of God. On the other hand, faith is positive in the sense of being an affirmation that points to God as love. If this seems extreme, it is intentionally so. Expressing faith in this way, Hartshorne attempts to go beyond impractical vagueness in search of a living faith that is "more definite than the mere general faith that somehow it is all right for us to live and try to do our best" [RSP, 67]. Faith is grounded in the definite experience of God. Thus, ". . . if one admits that experience is ultimate but denies that loving experience is anything but a spe-

---

[34] *Ibid.* The biblical quotation is Matthew 5:8.
[35] *Ibid.*

cial case, the answer is that mere experience apart from any social-sympathetic character is just as unidentifiable as mere being apart from experience" [MVG, 346-347]. If the fundamental experience is God as love, then faith as "an integral adjustment" would have to integrate according to this experience. Hence, to posit faith is to affirm God. It is therefore possible for "Jesus Christ" to symbolize being in God because of the logical necessity of prior concrete faith.

Although Hartshorne does offer an explicit definition of faith, his primary concern, especially in "A Philosopher's Assessment of Christianity," is to point out those doctrines in which he finds some degree of rational justification. He concludes, "I discern some degree of rational justification for a religion of complete, all-inclusive devotion to One in whose Life all actualities are embraced, to whom prayer may properly be addressed, and whose loving acceptance even of our sufferings is supremely symbolized in the human life depicted in the Gospels."[36] On the surface, this appears to put traditional doctrines such as prayer to the test of reason. The odd thing about such a conclusion is that reason and faith ultimately have the same ground, i.e., intuition of the wholeness of God. As the discussion of prayer demonstrates, when both reason and faith posit a Christian doctrine as the framework out of which they are speaking, it becomes difficult on Hartshorne's terms to distinguish between reason and statements of faith. This lies behind Hartshorne's question, "Is it not reasonable to suppose that a closer relationship between science and religion, or reason and faith, is what is required?" [LP, 6-7]. Both appear to be the act of bringing the intuited whole into conscious awareness.[37]

Hartshorne does think that "The traditional problem of faith and reason is indeed profoundly transformed by the new metaphysics which posits in God a relative, contingent, temporal aspect and holds that this aspect is the concrete actuality of deity" [RSP,

[36] *Ibid.*, p. 180.
[37] Hartshorne's method is reminiscent of Friedrich Schleiermacher in the centrality of feeling and immediate God-consciousness. Cf. Schleiermacher, *The Christian Faith*, ed. H. R. Mackintosh and J. S. Stewart (Edinburgh: T. and T. Clark, 1960). *See* especially p. 206.

171]. Once again, when faced with a fundamental problem, Hartshorne turns to the relationship between the abstract and the concrete. When put in these terms "reason deals with the universal and
abstract; the wholly particular and concrete can only be intuited.
Thus, insofar as faith, or life-trust, has something particular as its
object it transcends rational evidence" [RSP, 171]. The concrete
individual is consequently understood as lying beyond the bounds
of reason, yet, as being the ground of faith. This may be expressed
in terms of an individual man:

> Now each man has to have a sense of his own particular
> value in the universe and for God, and this no science and no
> metaphysics can give him, but only his own awareness of him-
> self, and of the world or God as containing him. Rational
> theology may be able to show that there is a God who cherishes
> all his creatures; but no rational discipline can show there is a
> God who cherishes "me," meaning by me, the precise indi-
> vidual quality, incommunicable in abstract terms, that makes
> me different from anyone else that ever lived or ever could
> have lived. [RSP, 171; cf. RSP, 173]

It follows that reason can know the essence of God "such as all-
knowing, or loving" but cannot fully know concrete particular in-
carnations of God [RSP, 173]. From A) C it follows that faith as
the mode of knowing the concrete is greater than and includes reason as the mode of knowing the abstract. When this distinction is
not clearly made, the relationship between faith and reason quickly
becomes blurred.

Jesus may be known in two modes. He may be known through
the intuition of faith. No abstract term can match the depth of
intuitive understanding. This does not mean that abstractions cannot describe at all—description is their very function [RSP, 173]. On
Hartshorne's terms abstract theological description would not end
when encountered by the concrete dimension of Jesus; it would
begin. Because abstractions are only abstractions that are always
contained in the concrete, the concrete represents an ever new possibility for speaking. Still, abstract speaking follows upon and is
contingent upon the intuited concrete world of social process,
which, as in the philosophy of Peirce, may be conceived as a continuum. The reality toward which the name "Jesus" points is known

intuitively through ontological overlapping (*see* Chap. 3). Jesus is intuitively known in the same way that faith is inevitably present. The function of theological abstractions is, therefore, to know essentially what is already known intuitively. When theological statements "call the name of God" they know the essential or immutable aspect of God. The basis of this abstract knowing is intuitive faith just as the basis for the abstract is the concrete after the fashions of A) C.

Such an understanding of faith moves beyond immediate intuition toward the realm of linguistic abstractions. What, then, is the relationship between the general fact of immediately intuited faith necessary to thinking and living, and "conscious" faith involving linguistic abstractions? In Hartshorne's words the latter is distinguishable from the former in that it involves "the choice of *which* faith, which verbal and intellectual and perhaps institutional, ritualistic, and artistic form of expression and intensification we shall seek to give the faith we inevitably have" [RSP, 173]. In other words, Hartshorne uses faith in two senses, but the concrete *that* of faith includes the second sense, the more abstract conscious expression (which faith). Without distinguishing between the abstract and the concrete in this way, faith as the intuited experience of a particular occurrence would readily be confused with a given description of that occurrence. Concretely, everyone stands in faith by virtue of his participation in reality; abstractly, one may speak of a particular faith—Protestant, Catholic, Jewish, Buddhist, Muslim, Hindu, Nationalistic, Racist, Communist, etc. Such a distinction also serves to preserve the distinction between the necessary and the contingent which has already been shown to be central to Hartshorne's doctrine of God. Concrete faith is necessary, but abstract faiths are historical contingencies. On Hartshorne's terms this means God remains while religions, nations, races, and ideologies fade.

Utilizing "an" abstraction based upon "a" concrete occurrence, Christian theology employs a characterization entailing both strict and genetic identity when it characterizes its subject as "the" event or occurrence of Jesus. Strict identity would be said to inhere in each of the concrete occurrences that, taken together, make up the reality to which the abstract "Jesus of Nazareth" or "Jesus Christ" refers. Jesus Christ is the generic term that designates a certain series of concrete events. As an abstraction from those events it characterizes in the way any name characterizes. Thus, on Hartshorne's terms, it would be misleading to speak of "the concrete occurrence of Jesus" if this meant that only one event is thereby designated. The only way to speak of Jesus as "an" event would be to intend the name "Jesus" to refer to one occasion, such as the cross, to the exclusion of other occurrences that might be included, such as His trial and death.

There is a sense in which a single occurrence such as the event of Jesus' death on the cross may be said to be culminative of all the occurrences for which the name "Jesus" stands. This line of interpretation permits Hartshorne to take this occurrence as the concrete basis for the cross as a supreme symbol. However, according to the doctrine of strict identity, each event occurs or becomes actual in a way that involves its own novelty. This means that if the cross is taken as the culminative event, it is an embodiment of the "many plus one." That is, following Whitehead's "novel intuition," the cross would have to be understood as also being unique in itself and occurring out of freedom, hence, excluding total predictability (see Chap. 4). Herein, the asymmetry of time is maintained because the event of Jesus' death would be internally related to the events of His life, and the events of His life would be externally related to the event of His death.

The problem of how many events the name of Jesus covers is, nevertheless, ontologically secondary. Abstract names can only point toward concrete reality. Abstract residence in ontological wholeness is the basis which continually "informs" the conscious novel realization. When the name Jesus is used as an indication that God is love, love from God ontologically informs the name. Whether or not the user is consciously aware of everything that the name historically designates, every occasion that actually occurred in Jesus' lifetime remains secondary. In the original quests of the historical Jesus, there was a tendency to overlook the limitations of conscious knowledge about historical realities that have ontological priority.[38] Ontologically, the one to whom the name is spoken already intuitively knows that God is love. This knowledge makes possible the recognition of Jesus as the act of God's love. One can know Jesus as the love of God only if he already understands love to *some* extent.

Again, this knowledge does not mean that the occasion of "Jesus" is "finished." To say this would be to forget that names are "abstractions from" concrete occurrence, an occurrence in which God became something He had never been before; novelty literally occurred.

> Concerning the question of literalness in theological concepts, I wish (with apologies to him) to urge Barth's procedure (when taken to task for treating God in terms of personality). He said, I believe, something like this: We know what personality is because we know God; our understanding of human "personality" is derivative from revelation. Similarly, I suggest, we know what human temporality is because we have (to use Tillich's word) an "ecstatic" sense of divine temporality. The past, *the* past, is not, even for us, simply our past, the mere content, even the possible content, of our memory and reconstruction from monuments and documents. *The* past past "as it really was" transcends all human access in every precise aspect. It is the actualized life of God, to which at every moment new additions are made.[39]

"Jesus" or "the cross" becomes what it is, not only in itself, but also in terms of its function in concrete relationships. This becoming achieves new reality in each additional relationship, and this addition literally increases that to which abstract designations refer. Hence, "Jesus" or "the cross" could not be exhausted because the strict reality to which each refers is continually increased, just as "the many become one and are increased by one." When the Christian faith, which Christian symbols express, changes, it changes by

[38] See Albert Schweitzer, *The Quest of the Historical Jesus*, trans. W. Montgomery (New York: The Macmillan Co., 1961).

[39] Hartshorne, "Tillich's Doctrine of God," p. 179. Hartshorne is referring to Tillich's special use of the term "ecstasy" in Tillich, *Systematic Theology* (Chicago: The University of Chicago Press, 1951), I, pp. 111 ff.

addition. If these symbols are conceived in such a way as to preclude additional enrichment, abstract immutability or eternality destroys the historical relativity of Jesus.

In sum, the following points emerge as an outline for a Hartshornian Christology.

1. Ogden's suggestion that Hartshorne's dipolar theism can complement the subjectivist analysis of man by Bultmann is an invitation to build a Hartshornian Christology as well as theology. This is facilitated by the correlation between the Heideggerian-Bultmannian distinction between *existential* and *existentiell* and A) C. A) C, or Hartshorne's basic method, therefore provides an approach to Jesus Christ that is structurally similar to the work of existential thinkers, but an approach that avoids the pitfall of subjectivism. The concrete God's dipolarity avoids thinking of the Christian faith exclusively in either subjective or objective categories.

2. Hartshorne's characteristic treatment of the figure of Jesus in terms of sympathetic suffering, i.e., God literally suffering with man, becomes clearer in the light of A) C. Literal suffering as concrete occurrence may signify God's entering into man's suffering because of the shared experience possible in concrete intuition. If the suffering of Jesus were only abstractly like the suffering of man, the relationship between God and man in Jesus would also be abstract. If, however, the abstract characterization of God as the one who loves man by suffering with him is seen as being contained in a concrete event, it is no longer abstract. If the event of Jesus' suffering were simply a way of speaking about God, not a concrete occurrence, no ground for understanding the Christian message would be available in man's immediate experience. A) C provides Hartshorne with a way to speak of God's actual love being literally with man through suffering with man.

3. Following (2), it is clear how the cross as the supreme symbol of God's love is "grounded" in the concrete occurrence of God's suffering with man. The symbol of the cross can function as a symbol because what it symbolizes is concretely known, not merely knowable. As a receding goal the concrete would never be wholly knowable, but would be available for finite conscious knowing because it is an abstract symbol for the "truth" in which man already

stands. In other words, the symbol of the cross obtains force and ultimate meaning because it is grounded in the necessity of God. As a symbol, it remains contingent, just as any other aspect of the world is contingent. Contingency is not its downfall, but that which permits its truly divine function. If the cross in itself were necessary, on Hartshorne's terms, the relationship between the abstract and the concrete would be reversed, and it would not be a symbol because it could point to no necessary ground. However, when understood as being abstract in itself, the cross properly functions as a symbol and it is just this that A) C clarifies.

4. A) C also clarifies the abstract "place of literal." "Literal" means actual concrete occurrence. God Himself is affected by a literal occurrence. He actually becomes that which He has never been before. In the concrete event of Jesus Christ, God literally becomes that which He has never been before. As love, this event or occurrence is that which happened; i.e., a real addition to reality was made, and the happening demonstrates God as love. In this happening divine love is literally changed by the addition of Jesus Christ. Thus, "literal" signifies concrete change by addition in God. All reality stands in God; when God is literally changed, all reality is literally changed. Moreover, since the present is everlastingly in God, all reality stands in that part of God's changed reality to which the name "Jesus Christ" points.

5. Obtaining everlastingness through concrete occurrence, each person becomes immortal in the way that Jesus Christ is immortal. "Personal" designates the concrete occurrence of a person in the same way Jesus Christ designates the concrete. Personal immortality literally occurs when the concrete happens. Personal immortality in itself is an abstract designation for a concrete reality. It is, on Hartshorne's terms, not that which is merely to be obtained; it is that which is obtained when history happens. Without A) C personal immortality may be taken as a future abstract goal. When A) C is fully taken into account it becomes the present and past concrete reality. The orientation shifts from life that wishes to be in God, to life witnessing that it is already in God. Justice, then, refers not to an otherworldly heaven, but to the situation of present life.

6. On Hartshorne's terms man obtains consciousness of his

being-in-God when he prays. Christian prayer is prayer that expresses being-in-God with reference to Jesus Christ. Because conscious prayer utilizes linguistic abstractions which are grounded in a concrete continuum in which creatures ontologically overlap, prayer may actually change the reality to which it is addressed. Prayers bring to consciousness praise or concern that has an accessible object. When the Christian prays he "acts out of" the reality of Jesus Christ in which he stands. Yet, he intuitively knows that by virtue of the concrete situation in which he stands, his prayer adds to that to which it is addressed. Thus, even though prayer utilizes abstract characterizations, validity resides not in abstract accuracy but in concrete reference.

7. Since the mode to which Christian concepts refer is the concrete, it is correct to center Christian affirmations in the "experience" of Jesus Christ. Christian abstractions become intelligible to the world by virtue of the reference to the same experience that one has prior to abstract knowledge. On Hartshorne's terms the ground for Christian theology is personal experience. Through personal experience, the Christian realizes the necessity of God. This does not exclude realization of God at any point in the chain of being; it simply declares such experience to be personal in the case of man. Here, theology is the conscious pointing to concrete possibility, namely, the possibility of Jesus Christ. The task of Christian theology is not to bring to the hearer the experience of Jesus Christ, but to point out that the hearer already "has it." That is, the concrete experience of Jesus Christ as an actual occurrence in God is the inevitability to which Christian theology points. Hence, Christian faith is experienced before it is named by Christian theology. Christian faith must be ontologically prior to abstract naming in the same way that the concrete is ontologically prior to all abstract naming.

9

The Church:
A Concrete Response

The Church is that body of men who take Jesus Christ as their reference. Their unity may be taken as symbolic of the unity all men have
in the concrete God. Since all men are in God, no reason remains for
absolutizing institutional boundaries. Neither is there cause to act toward any human on earth as an outsider. Just as Jesus cannot show the
love of God without actually entering into the sufferings of the world,
the Church can express its mission only through love in and for the
world.

THE CHURCH has been the most static of human institutions. How
could it have been otherwise with a theology built upon an
unchanging God? Signs of thaw point toward a springtime of
possibility, but until the conceptual abstractions underneath the
surface are recast, really recast, only fringe changes can occur. It
is for assistance in this most basic theological task that churchmen
may look to Hartshorne's process theology. Although Hartshorne
offers even fewer explicit statements on the Church than on Jesus
Christ, his views can be developed along three lines: Christological
foundation, ecumenical suggestion, and ethical implications.

In Jesus Christ as an actual occurrence of God's concrete being with
man and in the cross as the supreme symbol of God's sympathetic
love of the world is a foundation for a Hartshornian doctrine of the
Church. This is not simply to say, Jesus is the founder of the Church.

As Dietrich Bonhoeffer says, "Jesus Christ was no more a founder of the Christian religious community than he was the founder of a religion. The credit for both these things belongs to the primitive church, that is, to the apostles."[1] Bonhoeffer's point is dependent upon a clear distinction between revelation and religion in order to declare the occurrence of Jesus Christ "the" new reality, not only "a" new reality.[2] On this basis Bonhoeffer thinks the relation between Jesus Christ and the Church is twofold: "1. The Church is consummated in Him and Time is annulled. 2. Within Time the Church is to be built up on Him as the foundation. He is the Church's historical principle."[3] (1) remains a problem; (2) parallels the possibility within Hartshorne's thought to think of the Church as a concrete response to the actual occasion of Jesus Christ. Bonhoeffer's twofold distinction is a point of entry to the discussion of Hartshorne's understanding, because in overcoming the ambiguity of the notion of Jesus as founder, he employs a distinction between the abstract absolute and the concrete relative. In (1), the "Church is consummated in Him" means "Time is annulled." Here, "annulled" time means temporality loses its force. "In Him" is a characterization that identifies God. "In Jesus Christ" could be substituted for "in Him," because Jesus Christ is the reality in which the Church is consummated, and all that is "in" the Church is thereby "in" God. The result is a "Church-in-theism" rather than a panentheism.

But what happens to time when "the Church is consummated in Him"? Consummation annuls time. This was the dimension of classical theology that on Hartshorne's terms made classicism abstract. The characteristic of classical theology was abstract eternality because time was "annulled" in the sense of "destroys the force of." Annulment means the abstract contains the concrete. Hartshorne would not object to the presence of the E factor, or eternality. His objection would be that here the abstract side of the Church is conceived in such a way as to destroy the force of time.

---

[1] Dietrich Bonhoeffer, *The Communion of the Saints: A Dogmatic Inquiry into the Sociology of the Church*, trans. R. Gregor Smith (New York: Harper & Row, 1964), p. 111.
[2] *Ibid.*, p. 112.
[3] *Ibid.*

On Hartshorne's terms it would be more accurate to describe the Church as time-full than as time-annulling. Time-fullness would mean that "the consummation of the Church in Him" refers to a concrete occurrence in time without annulling time. Everlastingness flows from time, not the reverse. If the reverse were true it would be difficult to call the occasion of Jesus Christ an occasion, since a nontemporal occurrence is meaningless. Hartshorne might agree with Bonhoeffer that there is an eternal factor, a "name of God," but he could not agree that this implies the annulment of time.

Bonhoeffer's second way of understanding the relation between Jesus Christ and the Church (which is really incompatible with the first) represents the concrete side. Now "the Church is to be built upon Him as the foundation," but within time, and "He is the Church's historical principle." Hartshorne would hardly disagree with this so long as being in time is not understood as having a strictly determined present or future. This is the concrete side of God's polarity because the concrete is historically prior. It is prior not only chronologically but theologically. The act of God in the occurrence of Jesus Christ is temporally time-full. In other words, here the abstract name, the Church, has its concrete reference, the historical occurrence, Jesus Christ in the world. The Christian may be said to stand in this concrete event when he responds to Jesus Christ. The Church would, therefore, best be conceived as a fellowship of those responding to Jesus.

There is one point about the notion of "being in Jesus Christ" as a concrete actual occurrence which should be clarified. Hartshorne would require that either "being in" refers to standing within that to which the cross refers, or "being in Jesus Christ" means being in His Church. These conditions arise because of, not in spite of, the concreteness of Jesus. Within the concrete temporal sphere the asymmetry of time must be maintained. If the Christian is "in Jesus Christ," and this means being in a concrete event, how is it possible to maintain both externality and internality? Being in Jesus Christ means the cross is the symbol of response to this concrete event. The churchman is one who expressly recognizes Jesus Christ as the supreme symbol of his participation in God (cf. Tillich). Since Christ is thereby recognized as "an abstract symbol for the concrete reality," no time problem arises. Being embodied in the concrete, the Christ is an indication that God is love and sympathetically is with the Church. Care should be taken to specify the symbolic character of the Christ to insure that it is not logically destructive of the time toward which He points. Symbolically, then, the Christian is "in Christ," in the way that the concrete is "within" that to which an abstraction may refer. Internality and externality become a problem only by moving to the concrete historical event of Jesus.

The concrete Church is related to Jesus Christ as the present is related to a given past occasion. Looking forward from Jesus to the present, Jesus is external to present realization. From Jesus' point of view the present would be future and thereby externally unknowable so long as it remains future. Of course, discussing Jesus' point of view is only a manner of speaking, because we are bound by the present. On Hartshorne's terms, to be in Jesus Christ must mean to be in Him as a possibility for present realization. This does not exclude living in all other events of history with varying degrees of consciousness of those events. For example, Americans stand just as "really" in the event of Abraham Lincoln as they do in the event of Jesus. The difference comes in the significance attached to each event. On Hartshorne's terms all men, including Lincoln and Jesus and even the villains of history, are "sons" of God and "in" the Father.

As a concrete possibility, Jesus is actually that in which the Christian stands. The Church is consequently composed of those who internalize Jesus as a possibility for present living. Such internalization becomes the basis for the Church as a community among communities so long as historical possibilities other than Jesus are also realizable. If Jesus internally contained the Church, A) C and the asymmetry of time would be violated; internality and externality would be hopelessly confused. So far as the Christian is primarily concerned as Christian, Jesus Christ would be *his* possibility.

Fundamentally, the identity of the Christian Church rests upon the strict occurrences that manifest belief in Jesus Christ. As a series of occurrences having a common reference, but each also containing individual differences, "Church" meets the requirements of "genetic." Hence "Christian Church" is the genetic name for that series of occurrences taking Jesus Christ as their point of reference. Under this definition it would not matter what specific form a given Church event took. It could be occurrence of a hymn of praise, occurrence of a sermon, occurrence of a social concern, etc. The only logical requirement would be reference to Jesus Christ.

Little more than suggested directions are offered here, but before leaving the discussion of the relationship between the Church and Jesus Christ, what of the question of authority? To the extent that authority implies absolute causal or determinative relationship (if such would truly be "relationship"), ecclesiastical authority would be dubious indeed. For example, what would apostolic succession[4] mean in a view of history that introduces real freedom at every point? It is one thing to say that history is the reference for ecclesiastical authority in general. It is quite different to say that a given succession of occurrences necessarily sanctions Church authority. Without this distinction the assertion that God "acts" in history is quickly confused with the assertion that a given succession of occurrences necessarily "contains" those "acts" to the exclusion of others. The latter assertion would invert A) C and thereby destroy the meaning of the free act to which the Church witnesses.[5]

It is also an additional claim to say that authority derivable from a given historical occurrence is final. Hartshorne might accept

---

[4] W. Norman Pittenger's definition of apostolic succession will suffice here: "The continuity of the Christian ministry is expressed by traditional Catholic groups in their doctrine of apostolic succession, which in Roman theology tends to be understood as the historical sequence of the three orders of sub-deacon, deacon and priest (in the two grades of priest and ordaining priest or bishop); in Anglican theology a bishop, priest and deacon; and similarly in the Eastern Orthodox Church. Particular stress is laid upon the function of the bishop, especially in the Anglican and Orthodox communions. Among Protestant groups, Presbyterians have a theory of apostolic succession which locates it in the Presbyterate functioning as a whole, or in an episcopal capacity. The entire conception of apostolic succession is defended, by all groups maintaining it, as a means of securing the purity and continuous character of a body especially for the purpose, namely the ministry from above rather than evolved from congregations. This continuity is traced back to Christ and his apostles" (*An Encyclopedia of Religion*, ed. Vergilius Ferm [New York: The Philosophical Library, 1950], p. 34).

[5] Cf. Schubert Ogden, "What Sense Does It Make to Say God Acts in History?" *The Journal of Religion*, XLIII, 1 (January, 1963), 1-19.

the notion of finality in the sense of strict unchangeable identity; having happened, nothing changes. That which has occurred has happened once and for all and is irrevocable. As an irrevocable occurrence, the event to which the Church refers is unique. Yet, on Hartshorne's terms, every event is unique; otherwise it would have no qualification for being *this* event over against *that* event. Abstract identity would destroy particular concrete occurrence if each occurrence were not a "receding goal" of particularity over against all characterizations. The question of authority rests on whether or not an occurrence is unique in a way that exceeds this kind of uniqueness.

If finality is taken to mean unique finality exceeding the uniqueness of particular concrete events in general, Hartshorne would be hard pressed to say what this could mean. The finitude of historical events would be violated if one historical event were taken as unique in a qualitatively different sense. Strategic essential differences remain, but on a finite plane, because Hartshorne has no trouble saying God Himself is final in a way that ordinary events are not. As was observed in the discussion of God, finality results from God's unique necessity. All lesser realities are contingent, since on Hartshorne's terms no contingent concrete historical occurrence, no Church, derives its reality apart from its "being in God." No single historical occurrence contains the whole of God in itself either quantitatively or qualitatively. The reference of Church authority is God, but inasmuch as any "manifestation" or "revelation" of God is contingent, no human institution could claim final authority. Such a claim would itself be idolatrous. The inaccessibility of God's concrete occurrence in the past, plus the implication that He is becoming, renders finite claims of finality (apart from the sense explained above) impossible. If such a claim of finality were made, "the fallacy of misplaced concreteness" would appear. The proper relationship between the abstract and the concrete would be inverted so that an abstraction from the concrete whole of social reality would itself be declared the whole.

If one argues that A) C as necessarily being A) C is consesequently itself an idolatrous proposition, something should be said to indicate just what the relationship between metaphysical and ecclesiastical authority is. As a metaphysical description, A) C

remains necessary in the way in which all abstractions are necessary. A) C is to the real what John Jones is to the actual man whom
we thus describe. It is necessary that John Jones remain John Jones
if we are to name this series of occasions. Likewise A) C "necessarily" points or functions if metaphysical propositions are necessary
descriptions of reality as a whole. If one argues that metaphysical
propositions themselves are impossible, this is itself a necessary
general claim. Since metaphysical propositions are necessary general claims or descriptions, the denial is self-contradictory. The
denial of metaphysics is metaphysics. Metaphysics derives its authority from such logical persuasion. If logic itself subsequently
becomes uniquely necessary, as opposed to functioning as description, then God's uniqueness is usurped. "Infallible human knowledge" is another form of idolatry. As we have seen, Hartshorne's
use of A) C is not finally grounded in self-evident necessary
uniqueness—surpassing all finitude—but in faith. Hence, underneath its logic, A) C is a statement of faith, just as underneath its
claims, the authority of the Church is a statement of its faith
expressed in its response to actual historical occasions.

In sum, to Hartshorne, Church "authority" would be proclaiming more than claiming. It would be witness to the witness of Jesus.
In naming the name by which it refers to God, the Church is
analogically pointing more than apostolically proving. Abstractly
proclaiming Jesus to be the Christ, the Church points to the concrete
experience of Jesus.

The aspect of the Church which commands Hartshorne's most
explicit interest is the question of ecumenicity.

> Today, there is much earnest endeavor to mitigate the
> disunity of the Christian Churches. The attempt to find a
> common doctrine about God is not, it is recognized, the sole or
> perhaps the chief objective of this "ecumenical movement."
> Still, few would wholly repudiate such an objective. I believe
> that present-day metaphysics can offer some assistance toward
> its (never to be wholly complete?) achievement. [RSP, 145]

The preceding chapters have shown what Hartshorne has in
mind when he suggests "that present-day metaphysics can offer

some assistance" in the matter of the "Ecumenical movement." If we utilize A) C, some of these offerings can be delineated.

First, the notion that reality is social process contains a basic clue for ecumenical thinking. Who would argue that the many divisions within the Church have nothing to do with metaphysics, which has absolutized various forms of abstract being? Certainly, the completeness, the nonhistorical character, implied in the assertions of various denominational structures results from metaphysics of being as opposed to becoming. If denominations "become," how could they be absolutized sufficiently to become "grounds for separation"? Would not becoming imply an openness that would preclude the kind of certainty required for most divisive dogmas?

In the reality of social process the past is determined, is fixed, but the future is open. Just as God cannot know the future which is not yet actualized, human institutions, including credal and denominational determinations, cannot fully anticipate future requirements. The future of human institutions is contingent upon free decisions as reality becomes something new in every moment. Absolutization of institutions, such as ecclesiastical organizations, is idolatry because only God is necessary. This is true even if human institutions claim divine support. Hartshorne puts it this way:

> Clearly, an ecclesiastical organization claiming revelation may or may not represent the pure in heart, and if it claims infallible revelation, some of us would be inclined to see in this very claim itself the expression of pride rather than of purity. Human reception of divine messages is not, it seems, itself divine, and only as received is the message available.

The ecumenical point is that, since doctrines and institutions become, it is possible (1) for them to be open to one another as they are open to the future, and (2) not *being* complete in themselves, they may *be-come* together.

Second, the notion that reality as social process exhibits a continuum represents a ground for ecumenicity even though the Church is only part of reality. On Hartshorne's terms each group and subdivision would be considered more intelligible when understood as lying on a continuum of possibilities. By the same token, understanding between Reformation and Catholic forms would be in principle more possible. This is the ground that ecumenical discussions might imply, and the ground that would give them promise. Of course there is always the danger that continuity will be forgotten after ecumenical consolidation, and the problem would then become separation between Church and world. Too much unity in the institutional Church could well contribute to the neglect of ontological continuity between Church and world.

A third resource closely connected with both the notion of becoming and the continuum is Hartshorne's explicit concern with the question of ontological unity. This is focused in his essay, "Total Unity in Russian Metaphysics" [LP, Chap. 11]. Here ontological unity is expressed in ecclesiastical terms:

> Another still more characteristic notion of Russian philosophy is that of ontological unity, solidarity, "consubstantiality." This applies on several levels. There is the unity of the human race, perhaps in the Church as the Body of Christ. Even those Russian thinkers who follow Leibniz most closely—Kozlow, Askoldov, Lopatin, Lossky—all abandon the radical pluralism of that philosopher, all admit "windows" in the monads; and while this has been a common trait of most neo-Leibnizians, some of the Russians carry it exceptionally far. The consubstantiality of persons in the Trinity is taken by Florenski to imply consubstantiality in general. [LP, 266][6]

Hartshorne presumably accepts some notion of general consubstantiality. In the following paragraph he argues, ". . . togetherness must be something, a real property of the creation, or of God, or a third something on its own. . . . In some sense 'pan-unity' or 'total

[6] Hartshorne does not here indicate to what extent he adopts the notion of "the unity of the human race, perhaps in the Church as the Body of Christ." Clearly, he advocates the "unity" of the human race, but it is not clear whether "perhaps" means a possibility for him or for Russian philosophy. That "the Church as the Body of Christ" can symbolically stand for the unity of humanity seems to be confirmed elsewhere [LP, pp. 243 ff.]. On the other hand, he could merely be indicating the view of one of the Russians about whom he is speaking. For example, L. P. Karsavin says, "The Church is the Body of Christ, the perfection of the world saved by the Son of God. . . ." (N.O. Lossky, *History of Russian Philosophy* [New York: International Universities Press, 1951], p. 309).

unity' is an inevitable doctrine" [LP, 267]. Hartshorne thinks the concrete reality of God must be considered the inclusive reality, or else something (perhaps the Church) is greater than God. In the light of our discussion of the function of abstract identity as characterization of the concrete, compare Hartshorne's statement to the understanding which Lossky attributes to Florenski:

> Victory over the law of identity, a creative transition from one's self-containedness into the real of "the other" and a real discovery of oneself in that other is a fundamental truth expressed in the dogma of consubstantiality (*homoousia*). The conception of consubstantiality must guide us both in considering the relation between the Three Persons of the Holy Trinity and the relations between earthly creatures insofar as they are individual and seek to realize the Christian ideal of mutual love.[7]

Is it any wonder that Hartshorne is intrigued by such thinking? The doctrine of consubstantiality approximates what Hartshorne would take the ontological unity of the Church to be. Since Hartshorne's ontology of reality as social process bears much resemblance to the doctrine of consubstantiality within the Church, reference reads in both directions. Unity within the Church correlates with unity in general, and vice versa. In order to avoid confusion, Hartshorne parenthetically adds "the point is not that only one entity is 'real,' but that one entity must really include all the others. A relation being only as real as its terms, a really all-inclusive entity must have real entities to include." [LP, 276][8]

The specific point with regard to ecumenicity is that agreement is not to be found so much in lowest common denominators among creeds or authoritative structures as in underlying ontological real-

[7] Lossky, p. 181.

[8] Hartshorne is not the first to argue for the interdependence of the one real unity and individual members. This reflects the traditional philosophical problem of the one and the many dating back to the Pre-Socratics. For a later statement compare, for example, Cusa's remark, "Negue potest esse multitudo, quae non participet unitate." Nicolai De Cusa, *De venatione sapientiae*, ed. Paulus Wilpert (Hamburg: Verlag von Felix Meiner, 1964), p. 90. I am indebted to H. L. Bond for this reference.

ity. This attracts Hartshorne to the Russian understanding of the Church. "The Russian view of the Church," he says, "is not that of an 'authority' wielded by officials or even councils, but a community of members forming a spiritual organism in which they reach a level of life involving integral experiences of the nature of reality" [LP, 264]. In this sense, Hartshorne concludes, "Faith calls us to a life of freedom, rather than 'obedience' " [LP, 264]. It follows that the ontological principle to which various Churches should look for ecumenical guidance is not obedience to past authority, but faith in freedom.

The aesthetic principle of unity-in-diversity represents a fourth metaphysical resource for ecumenical discussion. An immediate advantage appears in greater coherence represented by ecumenical unity. On Hartshorne's terms it is a principle of coherence that "the interpretation of the parts of the aesthetic whole" means that "the perception of each includes the perception of all" [PPS, 160]. Look at a single color in a picture, and "the surrounding colors remain included, at least in the 'fringe' of this act of attention, so that the separate colors are never seen purely in themselves but always as differing from, contrasted with, or akin to, neighboring colors" [PPS, 160]. Unity-in-contrast may be interpreted in the ecumenical discussion as meaning that the beauty of religious experience in any one denominational situation is increased by the presence of surrounding denominations. Hence, other Church forms are necessary to aesthetic enjoyment. Rather than viewing those outside as either unnecessary or irrelevant the churchman would of necessity have to admit both necessity and relevance. To Hartshorne, "contrast," the ground for thinking, requires unity, and when this unity appears (without erasing contrast) aesthetic enjoyment occurs.

But a problem arises, because the reference of the Church is God. Abstract denominational fragmentation could have a serious effect on one's "conscious" awareness of divinity. To Hartshorne the ultimate concrete unity is God. The greatest aesthetic experience would have God Himself as the unifying factor. If denominationalism had the effect of "closing out" some part of the whole concrete reality, its aesthetic possibilities would be accordingly restricted. Striving after unity would not have mere unity as its purpose. Pure unity would no more be desired than the artist surveying a land-scape simply would wish to unify all its parts. The artist and the ecumenical thinker seek a new creation, creation guided by the awareness of God as *the* possibility (not that man can create God wholly—he can only add to Him). Taking God as his vision, each human creator has greater possibility before him as his inspiration. If theological visions quarantine men within lesser realities, aesthetic possibilities are diminished. Ecumenical change, maintaining contrast, occurs by the addition of novel forms. Once changes occur, new aesthetic experience of God becomes a possibility for future experiences. The vision of the aesthetic possibility of God could mean that total deletion of the Church is desirable and perhaps leads to a new form of theocracy. If denominationalism chaotically fragments the unity of divine possibility, church members might, by leaving the church, transcend church life and thus heighten their religious experience. It depends on how effectively the Church contributes to a vision of the love of God.

Unity-in-contrast might also be taken as an argument *against* ecumenicity. Ecumenicity could destroy the contrast required for aesthetic religious experience. In the light of the problems inherent in abstract monopolarities, such a warning should be carefully heard. Moreover, unity-in-contrast is itself an abstract description and is "not any definite unity in contrast or any absolute sum of such unities (which would have neither unity nor contrast since it would be nothing), but the purely general requirement, let there be as much unity in contrast as possible" [MVG, 228-229]. Understanding the abstract character of unity-in-contrast does not, however, remove the logical requirement that concrete differences always be real. No principle could function properly in Hartshorne's thought if it, like Plato's forms, rendered concrete particulars unreal.

Concrete contrasts remain real whether or not they are properly conceived for aesthetic experience. Practically speaking, the pluralism of the Church is not the problem. The problem is how to see God as diversity's necessary ground. When the vision of the concrete God does appear, when abstract limitations are transcended, ecumenicity may present the concrete possibility of the aesthetic experience of "being in God" as different churches are in God. If diversity of Church forms were not the case, and essential unity prevailed, the problem to be approached would be different.

Instead of concerning oneself with unity, attention would be focused upon concrete diversity. In the latter case the concrete could be the ground of nonecumenicity. Hartshorne, tending to assume too much diversity as the problem, seeks unity. All social unity is grounded in the continuum of concrete possibilities (the concrete God), including the possibility of Church unity.

Little has been said to indicate the ethical implication of Hartshorne's thought. Such a procedure has been merely arbitrary, but it is appropriate that the subject is finally addressed under the general rubric of the doctrine of the Church. Building upon A) C there is strong basis for a Hartshornian ethic.

In his essay "Tragic and Sublime Aspects of Christian Love" [RSP, Chap. 8], Hartshorne again turns to the cross as a symbol of divine suffering. Now he holds that "It also indicates the root cause of suffering. The world is tragic because the creatures are partly free, within limits making their own choices." It is illusory to conduct oneself as if this radical freedom were not present, and as if it did not often issue in tragedy. The assassination of President John F. Kennedy might be taken as an example of such tragedy. Nevertheless, freedom is not the full explanation, and it is to the crucifixion of Jesus that Hartshorne has recourse.

> The Cross symbolizes something further. Those who crucified Jesus were not acting wholly in the dark. The world is tragic, not only because conflict is inevitable between free and ignorant beings, but because there is an inner conflict in men between their will to serve a common good and their desire to promote a private or tribal goal. Some conflicts are chosen where a less destructive, more fruitful form of interaction is known. The crucifying of Jesus, we feel, must have embodied somewhere, in someone, a deliberate choosing of the greater evil and the lesser good. This is sin, the supreme tragedy. [RSP, 149]

The freedom to sin helps to explain the cross. (This is not blandly to explain "the mystery of the Cross." As concrete occurrence it would in principle remain partially inexplicable. This is only to indicate in the way abstract discussion indicates.) Hartshorne is critical of liberal religion for failing to take sin and evil seriously.[9] He suggests that a closer reading of Reinhold Niebuhr would have helped to prevent such a failure.[10]

In developing his doctrine of sin, Hartshorne employs A) C.

> We also see, from the Gospel story, that the root of sin is not just man's animality, his so-called lower nature of physical desires. No such desire put Jesus on the Cross. No, it was the higher nature corrupted and twisted; it was in the name of God that the Son of Man was turned over to the Roman crucifiers. He was a blasphemer. And those who so judged were, they thought, seeing the matter through God's eyes, as it were, defending the divine honor. In short, they were, in self-assumed function, the deity. This self-assumption of divine functions is perhaps the most basic sin. We can all of us see the possibility of it in ourselves. We should like to seem infallible, omnipotent, absolutely righteous, at least in some sphere. [RSP, 149]

Assumption of absolute righteousness (or absolute anything) is, in effect, the smothering of the concrete. This is accomplished through the inversion of A) C. It follows that, as in the passage here cited, one way to understand Hartshorne's concept of sin is to view it as the idolatrous inversion of A) C. Indeed, if God is the receding goal of concrete wholeness, the root of sin is the attempt to be God through the deification of an abstraction. Taking Jesus Himself as a deified abstraction could be sinful idolatry as well.

Although it roots in freedom and sin, the cross can, nevertheless, remain a symbol of divine love. Saying "remains," of course, does not indicate how God is present, but that *He is*. Hartshorne maintains that in every case biblical sayings that affirm divine

[9] Cf. Hartshorne's review of John Elof Boodin's *Religion of Tomorrow* (New York: The Philosophical Library, 1943), *Ethics*, LIV, No. 1 (October, 1943), 233-234.

[10] *Ibid.* Also *see* Hartshorne's review of A. Campbell Garnett's *A Realistic Philosophy of Religion* (Chicago: Willett, Clark and Co., 1942). After praising much of this latter book, Hartshorne remarks, "Perhaps the liberal optimism, the stress upon human potentialities for good, is not fully balanced by awareness of the tragic depths and unquenchableness of the springs of human evil—Niebuhr receives only a footnote" (p. 62).

immutability are, as the contexts indicate, referring to God's ethical aspect, "not his total being" [RSP, 151]. Abstractly, God is named love; concretely, God is experienced as love. When love happens the ethical activity of the Church or of man in general appears. Christian love comes, as the following passage indicates, not in God's abstract identity (which may have power as a guiding vision), or from a supernatural occurrence, but in concrete interactivity with the work of Jesus in the world.

> Jesus was a being whose experiences succeeded each other in time. To all appearances he was no more "immutable" or "timeless" than the rest of us. Moreover, our forefathers declared that the Church was the "mystical body" of the life of Christ in history, and that his body is temporal. Each of us, by contributing to the life of the Church, contributes to the life of Jesus and so to the life of the deity. [RSP, 150]

On Hartshorne's terms, the Church would understand its ethical directions to be founded upon real contribution to God. Reality as social process, combined with the ethical dimension of concrete emergence as sympathetic vicarious love, plus free decisions, gives the basis of a Hartshornian ethic.

Recall that thought can only expand, generalize, extrapolate, and abstract; it follows that "thought can arrive at no world other than a world of feelings, with their relations, aspects, varieties, and so forth," which Hartshorne observes "is in one respect, the social view of reality." Generally, this is "thinking about" the intuited social whole; specifically, it means employing abstract concepts to designate social love as the ethical function of the Church within the larger whole. Inasmuch as the Church stands with the concrete whole, it exemplifies sociality. Not only does the Church exemplify; Hartshorne thinks that religious ideas, specifically Protestant ones, depend on the Church. He says, ". . . the social importance of religious ideas seems to be dependent upon their embodiment in religious institutions" [RSP, 145].

In expressly taking a Protestant position on social questions, Hartshorne attempts to avoid what he considers the lack of freedom in Roman Catholicism. The foundation of this opinion is clear in his essay "Politics and the Metaphysics of Freedom."[11] Here three ideas that interfere with the social concept of freedom are given: (1) limiting freedom to man; (2) interpreting present decisions as being fully determined by one's present external situation plus one's own past; (3) supposing that God "limits our actions in a non-social way." The Church, like the political sphere, must overcome these three interferences if it is to express the sociality that Hartshorne understands to be the basis of ethical operations.

In the "chain of being," man was shown as an example of the middle grade between the subhuman and the superhuman. Hartshorne believes freedom properly characterizes lower forms, and that his principles in general are exemplifiable in them. We may suppose that his ornithological writings are more than a hobby.[12] The study of birds is consistent with his concern for the universality of freedom. It is, however, the other direction along the "chain" that most interests us here. The Church as a human institution points to being in God when it points to Jesus Christ. The ethical implication is that the social concern of the Church is grounded in God. Man's being is no more intelligible apart from God than any reality is without at least a faint awareness of its context. God is the presupposition of the ethics implied by the notion of the Church as "a community of members forming a spiritual organism in which they

---

[11] In *Enquête sur la Liberté*, Fédération internationale des sociétés de philosophie. Publié avec le concours de l'u. n. e. s. c. o. (Paris: Hermann & Cie, Editeurs, 1953), pp. 79-85.

[12] Hartshorne's publications on ornithology are as follows: "First Encounter with Hawaiian Songbirds . . ." *Elepaio* (Hawaii), XII, No. 12 (June, 1952), 76-78. "A Foreigner's Impression of the Lyrebird's Singing," *The Victorian Naturalist* (Australia), LXIX, No. 5 (September, 1952), 73-74; "Musical Values in Australian Bird Songs," *The Emu* (Australia), LIII, Part 2 (June, 1953), 109-128; "The Monotony Threshold in Singing Birds," *The Auk* (U.S.A.), LXXIII, April, 1956, 176-192; "The Phenomenon of Bird Song," *The Emory University Quarterly*, XII, No. 3 (October, 1956), 139-147; "Some Biological Principles Applicable to Song-Behavior," *The Wilson Bulletin* (U.S.A.); LXX, No. 1 (March, 1958), 41-56; "The Relation of Bird Song to Music," *Ibis* (Great Britain), C, No. 3 (1958), pp. 421-445; "Freedom, Individuality, and Beauty in Nature," *Snowy Egret* (Rome, Ga.), XXIV, No. 2 (Autumn, 1960); Review of *A Treasury of New Zealand Bird Songs: An Album of Three Records, The Wilson Bulletin*, LXXII, No. 4 (December 14, 1960), 421-422; "Sketch of a Theory of Imitative Singing," *The Oriole* (U.S.A.), XXVI, No. 2 (June, 1961), 23-27.

reach a level of life involving integral experience of the nature of reality" [LP, 264].

Since man's free actions presuppose being in God as the concrete whole, *literally*, just as Jesus Christ literally loves, social acts affect God. Thus, "every moment of our lives contributes a unique quality to the divine experience, and the finer the quality the richer the life of God, so far as derived from us" [RSP, 151]. In God, human acts add to history. "The past, we can now feel, is not empty, but is the inconceivable beauty and sublime record of all experience in the divine memory. And *we* have made a little of that imperishable beauty, and perhaps also have tinged it imperishably with tragedy" [RSP, 151]. To do unto others is to do unto God. This social view of being in God has definite meanings in practical situations, as Hartshorne illustrates:

> In a certain great city veterans and Negroes are in especially desperate need of housing. The cry goes up from property owners, "yes, housing for veterans, perhaps housing for Negroes, but not in our neighborhood." Some of these persons are doubtless Church people, and probably more of them believe there is a God. But how many have thought to themselves, that it is not just veterans or Negroes that are seeking houses. It is, as many Hindus would put it, God Himself that is seeking a home. A Christian should say this as well as a Hindu. "Inasmuch as ye do it unto the least of these . . . ." Once more, Christians have symbols which they even yet do not know the meaning of. That other fellow (of whatever social class) whose sonship to God we may abstractly admit, is not just a product of divine power, or just an object of divine well-wishing, but a very fragment of the life of God which is made all-inclusive through sympathy. [RSP, 151]

If it is argued that this passage does illustrate A) C, but in fact illustrates that God is A and neighbor is C, then the force of the neighbor's being in God is missed. Take Hartshorne's phrase "a very fragment of the life of God" seriously, since human beings are "self-creative fragments, and not mere external products, of the higher creativity."[13] In the same way that a whole may be said to be constituted by its parts (irrespective of the question of complete

[13] "Man's Fragmentariness," *Wesleyan Studies in Religion*, 1963-1964, LVI, No. 6, p. 28.

ontological coincidence), God is this C, this neighbor. Hence, it is incorrect to interpret this passage as an illustration of God's abstractness. On the contrary, not just symbolically, but concretely and ontologically, God is fragmentarily the neighbor. To this extent unfair treatment of veterans and Negroes, or anyone else, is on Hartshorne's terms ethically wrong on theological grounds.

Another key term in Hartshornian ethics, as in his Christology, is "sympathy." To understand his use of this term today, one must realize that he intends much more than an emotionalistic benevolence. In fact, he remarks that the reminder of divine benevolence or human kinship "gives but little help toward persuading us to deal kindly with one another" [RSP, 147]. Hartshorne finds a more persuasive reason for ethical action in the cross. The following expresses this and provides a proper context for a correct understanding of his use of "sympathy."

> I suggest that much more than divine benevolence or human kinship was symbolized in the doctrine that the man on the Cross was deity. The devotion of Jesus to his fellows was not mere benevolence, a wishing them well, or an eagerness to do things for them. It was a feeling of sympathetic identity with them in their troubles and sufferings, as well as in their joys, so that *their* cause and *their* tragedy became his; and he paid the price of a bitter death, rather than weaken the intimacy of his relation to the human lot, with all its suffering and failure. [RSP, 147]

The ethical act of sympathy concretely expresses ontological participation in (hence, identification with) the intuited whole. The Church would accordingly be understood as "being with" the concrete event of Jesus' love when Christians love.

On the one hand, the Church *is* sympathetic love, which has Jesus as its reference. Taking Jesus as its reference provides the common term for its "corporality." Just as the cells of a human body sympathetically feel one another, the fellowship of Christ has its corporate being through the interchange of love. Inasmuch as God is love and Jesus is "proof" of that love, to take Jesus as one's reference would be to mean that God as love is one's reference. To refuse to love would be to try to stand outside the vision of God to which the cross points. Faith as concrete intuition of God is inevitable; therefore, standing outside the corporate body of the Church would not mean separation from God, but being in God in a different mode. Abstractly, one has the choice of which faith best expresses his concrete faith, and on this secondary level "standing outside the Church" is possible. One could stand outside the corporate body of the Christian faith as an abstract reference to God, but one could not stand outside the concrete source of that reference. The concrete event of Jesus Christ, that which "Jesus Christ" names, would be ontologically a part of the concrete whole. On the abstract level one could stand outside the "name" but not outside what is named (cf. Barth). Ontologically or sympathetically, both Jesus Christ and the Church are in God, but so is all reality. Conversely, therefore, all reality is concretely "with" Jesus and the Church. The ethical act of love is an expression of the theological truth of being. Ethically, love expresses what Hartshorne intends when he says, "Each of us, by contributing to the life of the Church, contributes to the life of Jesus and so to the life of deity."

On the other hand, ontologically grounded sympathetic sociality points to love of the world. If the Church did not love the world, it would not be witnessing to the love for which the cross stands. The world is in God. Therefore, not loving the world means to that extent not loving God. Since Hartshorne understands Jesus Christ as the love of God, and reference to Jesus Christ constitutes the being of the Church, to cease to love would be to cease to be in the Church. The function of the preaching of the Church should be to call to consciousness the being of the world in God, and to indicate love as the ethical expression of that faith. Hence, the ethical direction of the Church is the love of God through love of the world in Him, a concrete response to concrete reality.

Keeping in mind that a Hartshornian doctrine of the Church must, like his Christology, be finally founded upon life in the concrete God, it is possible to enumerate what has been suggested concerning the doctrine of the Church.

1. Correlating with Bonhoeffer's discussion of the foundation of the Church, Hartshorne's treatment of the Christological foundation of the Church maintains a distinction between the eternal and the temporal. However, Hartshorne cannot accept the belief that

the eternal, or abstract, means the annulment of the temporal, or concrete. The eternal (everlasting) aspect of the Church can be conceived only as an abstraction which characterizes its being at any moment of becoming without annulling the way in which time occurs through additional change. This places the question of authority in temporality in a contingent, not a final, light. Being temporally, or concretely, grounded, the absolutization of contingent institutions is most problematical. The only final authority to which the Church has reference is God. No Church organization in itself is finally authoritative. Hence, the function of the Church is to employ analogically Christian symbols in order to designate God. From this function, the Church attains its identity.

2. Since identity results from what becomes, no individual denominational tradition must become in its past or present abstract form. By placing the concrete before the abstract, Hartshorne provides a framework for ecumenical discussion based on the openness of the concrete and the future. Resisting strictly determined abstract "relations," ecclesiastical traditions have no prescribed form which must result. In effect, this means no metaphysical reason should prevent ecumenicity. The Church may become unified because there is no abstract being that necessitates traditional divisions. This does not mean that traditions are irrelevant or that the concrete "many" are crushed, but that they represent possibilities for present and future realization instead of that which must absolutely be actualized. This, of course, summarizes what Hartshorne's thought intends when he finds himself primarily in a Protestant perspective. At the same time, he would insist that Protestant divisions are not "necessary" ones.

The ground to which Hartshorne may appeal is the notion of the continuum. Although concrete becoming represents the actual change that ecclesiastical traditions may undergo, the continuum indicates that the divisions of the Church interrupt pure possibility. The continuity of real possibility implies that "gaps" between institutional differences offer degrees of abstract difference, not absolute separations. Moreover, in the existing forms, a continuum may be posited which indicates that actual as well as possible differences are a matter of degree.

Another way of expressing the unity of actual churches is the ontological unity expressed by the Russian church's understanding of consubstantiality. Here, abstract absolutization of ecclesiastical authority is undercut by vivid, if mystical, expressions of concrete freedom. The freedom to which Hartshorne appeals is concrete freedom. The ontological unity underlying the Church is freedom from the prescriptions of abstract being, not absolute indeterminacy. When Hartshorne appeals to freedom over obedience, he means the freedom of actual possibilities granted by the occurrences of time. Like Berdyaev, he fights obedience to abstract being. On Hartshorne's terms the Church is free for ecumenical activity because it stands in concrete freedom.

Finally, the value of A) C in ecumenical discussions lies in the principle of value itself. Aesthetic possibilities based on ecumenical unity-in-variety emerge when abstract obstructions to unity are transcended. The conclusion is that the ecumenical movements hold out aesthetic possibilities for Christian experience so long as concrete contrast is not extinguished by abstract form.

3. For Hartshorne, Christian ethics derives from the love of God supremely symbolized by the cross. Yet, the cross is an actual occurrence of God's suffering love. Because Jesus of Nazareth is panentheistically in God, God literally suffers with man. The concrete relativity of God means God actually suffers with man. Hartshorne's A) C consequently clarifies the notion of God's suffering love. Being concretely real, the "way" God's love occurs is through Christian ethical action. Christian ethics is, then, concrete suffering love, which refers to Jesus Christ. The naming of the ethical act occurs in the same way abstractions name concrete events, which means identity is derived, not prescribed. Having no prescribed laws defeats legalism.

Based upon freedom, Christian actions indicate that God participates in, but does not control the details of, the sin, evil, and tragedy of the world. At the same time, social life emerges through concrete creaturely participation in the lives of other creatures. Acts done to other creatures are literally done to God. The Church has as its ethical mission the love of God through the love of the world in God. The final insight issuing from Hartshorne's A) C is this: When the Church loves the world, it actually loves God by loving the world.

10

Assessment and Questions

Hartshorne has assisted in the task of turning philosophy back to its metaphysical task and theology back to the doctrine of God. Because of his growing importance in both philosophy and theology, his work should be questioned with a new sense of urgency as the space age dawns.

IT IS BOTH PREMATURE and presumptuous to attempt an assessment of Hartshorne's work when the impact of his thought is only now achieving the prominence it deserves. Nevertheless, most of his prodigious output is already recorded and it seems prudent to begin the task. What is said here, therefore, remains a prolegomenon to future assessment in both philosophy and theology.

Primary emphasis in the present book has been upon Hartshorne's theological accomplishment, but what of his place in modern philosophy? His dialogues with a phenomenologist, an existentialist, a pragmatist, and a process philosopher were selected for examination in Part I partly because they reveal his position vis à vis this much twentieth-century thinking. Of course none of these figures or schools received adequate treatment here, but Hartshorne's unified position toward them is revealing. It shows: (1) a disenchantment with the discreteness of the phenomenological doctrine of essence; (2) objection to the lack of objective criteria in existentialism; (3) agreement with the spirit of Peirce's pragmatism and with the notion of reality as a continuum; (4) extensive agreement with Whitehead's descriptive metaphysics of process.

From these dialogues and the corpus of his work in general,

three definite contributions to the philosophy of the twentieth century emerge. First, Hartshorne has helped philosophers to *return to metaphysics*. Hartshorne himself has never abandoned the metaphysical enterprise, but the influence of his thought has been delayed by a skepticism which only now shows signs of thaw. Hartshorne's persistence during the period through which philosophy has just passed illustrates a strong independence of spirit. Moreover, he had the nerve "to sound quaint" by reintroducing serious study of the ontological argument for God's existence at a time when "philosophers" of every stripe were scoffing at proofs. His resolution has gone far to bring closer to realization Huston Smith's hope that metaphysics "will before long be widespread in the philosophical community." In addition to Hartshorne's constructive contribution, descriptive metaphysics is returning for the very practical reason that a basic examination of fundamental values is resulting from technological secularization. David Hume, Søren Kierkegaard, Bertrand Russell, and Ludwig Wittgenstein tacitly presupposed a cultural metaphysics (while denying metaphysics). Both the success and the failure of their philosophies brought about the need for fundamental metaphysical work.

The secular world resulting from the critique of past value structures is creating a cultural void. As Marshall McLuhan, Herbert Marcuse, and others have sensed, an unplanned techni-metaphysic is filling the void. But without metaphysical guidelines there is little more to do than surrender to history. There is scant philosophical desire to check the "happening" of history by return to some static ideology; nor simply to see what happens (city traffic planners head the latter list). There is, however, a growing search for workable universal concepts. Better abstractions, not no abstractions, have become necessary in order that the concrete may be more clearly seen. The abstractors themselves must be men who, like Hartshorne, have sufficient understanding of concrete faith not to be afraid of the abstract.

Second, Hartshorne is important in the twentieth century not just because of a return to metaphysics, but as a result of the *kind of metaphysics* involved. Following A) C, Hartshornian (like Whiteheadian and Strawsonian) metaphysics is *descriptive*. Consequently, dynamic reality can be abstractly pictured or understood without neglecting the problem of reading into reality prescribed modes which, like the Hegelian *Geist*, can dominate history. Descriptive metaphysics has no reason ultimately to deny change, relativity, contingency, and particularity. Unlike classical metaphysics, C) A, descriptive metaphysics can be open to real freedom and an unrealized future.

The value of abstraction, which can accept modern relativity while still attempting to make some sense of it, is clear. It is no accident that Hartshorne's dynamic philosophy of change is meaningful in a society caught in an ever quickening pace. The river must be dealt with as a river, and no amount of wishing for a past quiet brook will quell the torrent. Hartshorne is able to offer metaphysical guidance because he has abstracted from flowing process; his terms came out of the world of change, and their descriptions are categories "returning to their source." In a world of change we need a philosophy of concrete change. Hartshorne, following Whitehead, offers just such a philosophy.

Hartshorne's third major contribution comes at the point where he builds upon and surpasses Whitehead, namely, in the doctrine of God. Hartshorne has led in the *return of philosophical interest to the question of God*. Above, it was mentioned that Hartshorne renewed discussion of the ontological argument when it was unpopular. His renewal had little to do with the question of popularity. As has been shown, Hartshorne's work on the ontological argument in his later years fits quite nicely into the general direction of his work. It is by no means inconsistent with the concrete faith of his early years; in fact, it develops logically from his lifelong interest in the question of God. Hartshorne's treatment of the doctrine of God is not the result of lack of critical acumen on his part—his critics know that—but stems from his conviction that this question is fundamental to the critical metaphysical enterprise.

Hartshorne has avoided identification with twentieth-century God-structures. Somehow, to the twentieth century, God-talk conjures up either classical theism or modern pantheism, either a Hegelian absolute or an irrational piety. Obviously, Hartshorne's philosophy of religion accepts none of these, but God-talk remains possible on different grounds. These are the grounds here described as A) C. God language is possible because it is truly abstract, truly philosophical, and does not attempt to function "beyond language" in the realm of ordinary existence. Speaking of the divine again becomes a possibility because philosophy abandons positivistic language games and again becomes philosophy. No wonder the empirical spirit could speak only of the empirical; it dogmatically established empirical ground rules which made real philosophical questions (like God) categorically impossible. This paralleled the existential mistake of trying to speak of God in terms of ordinary existence, as Schubert M. Ogden, for example, has seen. Philosophy has paid the staggering price of irrelevance because of this mistake. It can be grateful that Hartshorne and finally a growing number have begun to realize the importance of the question of God and related questions of ultimacy.

Hartshorne's renewal of the neglected question of God for philosophy at the same time answers a crucial need in theology. Theology is currently searching for something beyond either Barth's Christological, Bultmann's anthropological, or Tillich's ontological category. Precipitated by "the death of God" (Altizer, Hamilton), on the one hand, and "secularization" (Cox, and the contemporary German theologian Friedrich Gogarten) on the other, attention to the question of God reflects nothing short of a cultural crisis. The American Olympus is being shaken to its theological roots. Advocates of "the American way of life" are defensive because their most basic institution, Godness, is under siege. Reaction to this attack not only reveals a cultural base in theology, but shows that a particular understanding of God is at issue. To make a long story short, American reaction to radical theology and secularization clearly demonstrated *the cultural God is the classical being among beings, a God who can die.*

Theology's failure to attend to the doctrine of God, plus the cultural crisis, creates a situation to which Hartshorne's work is immediately relevant. This has already been acknowledged in theological circles, and a growing number of theologians reflect an interest in the concrete God. Hartshorne's value does not end with professionals, however; it speaks directly to large-scale cultural problems. On Hartshorne's terms the death of God can be under-stood as a result of C) A, the classical theological mistake. God's demise is therefore to be applauded if we are talking about the failure of the static being which smothered the freedom of man. The death of God as the failure of classicism increases the relevance of the concrete God.

Secularization can also be embraced on Hartshornian terms because the world is panentheistically in God. One might argue that panentheism really entails the rejection of secularity since it understands existence theologically. Such an argument is untenable, however, because it misrepresents both secularity and Hartshorne. One of the basic reasons for secularity is theological disenchantment —a divorce between classical theism and modern needs. Secularity has not yet ruled on neoclassical thought patterns; if it had it would be a "positivistic secularism," not a true secularity. It is one thing to say the old God is dead; it is quite another to say no God is possible. Hartshorne's position is not compatible with positivistic secularism (no God is possible), but neither is secularity, which is basically a search for new meaning. Hartshorne's position is not incompatible with the quest for meaning in technopolis, because his categories are not dependent upon a particular form of being. Hartshorne's concrete God is only nominally the same as the God away from which secularity is moving. Secularity primarily rejects the abstract God, which Hartshorne also rejects. The openness of the future of the concrete God and the openness of modern culture are quite compatible. To dismiss Hartshorne because he describes the secular world in religious language is dogmatic secularism. Indeed, the question is not the "names"; the question is what is named.

Marshall McLuhan has suggested that beneath contemporary aspirations "for wholeness, empathy and depth of awareness" made possible by electric technology lies "a faith that concerns the ulti-mate harmony of all being."[1] His "secular" point is reminiscent of Hartshornian concrete faith, but in the congruence of Hartshorne's perspective with McLuhan's faith one can detect a second major contribution to theological thought by Hartshorne. The issue that

[1] Marshall McLuhan, *Understanding Media* (New York: McGraw-Hill Book Co., 1964), pp. 4-5.

brings this to the surface is the question of the corporality of life entailed in the concrete God. Technological harmony is possible because of theological-ontological harmony.

Corporate harmony, seeing life in one body, is symbolically pictured in Hartshorne's discussion of the theological notion of consubstantiality. Such theological language is possible because reality actually has togetherness in a continuum of possibility. What reason can there be for not combining McLuhan's "technological" faith with Hartshorne's concrete faith as a way of seeing underlying corporality? Instead of this community and that community, one might say with the Hindu, "not this, not that"; all is in one community. This was not possible given classical presuppositions. Theological monists, themselves saturated with scientific method, must surely be impressed by McLuhan's electric corporality. They must be equally impressed by Hartshorne's and Whitehead's achievement of concrete unity without the problems of classical determinism. The concrete God is compatible with much more than ecumenical unity (usually too narrowly conceived anyway); concreteness can well be expressed by the categories of modern technology.

One final contribution represented by Hartshorne's work comes in theological ethics. Based upon unity in the concrete God, Hartshornian ethics is a ground for new morality that is really new. True novelty is possible only where the future is open and free decisions are real; in other words, in a process view of history. Ethics was nonsense given classical prescriptions, but it obtains ultimate significance in neoclassicism. Even God must wait on man's free decisions. This is a frightening thought in an age when human passions are high, human freedoms great, and human destructive capacity staggering.

But just as our ethical capacity for destructiveness is immense, so is the possibility of creative new solutions to world problems like war, food, population, and law. *We can act* for the good because freedom is real. Moreover, mankind's past mistakes really can be taken into account, because on Hartshornian terms history is stored in man's common heritage, the memory of God. Ethics is not merely relative, then; it is possible because of freedom *and* history. What

has happened in the past is a *certainty* upon which present delibera-
tions can be made in spite of the limits of finite perception. Inciden-
tally, technology is gradually narrowing inability to accurately
record, and thereby is giving us an increasingly improved "memory"
of history. On Hartshornian terms one can only conclude that the
better the world is known, the better God is known. The better God
is known (cognitively), the better ethical decisions one is in a
position to make. Cognitive knowledge of the universe is co-exten-
sive with cognitive knowledge of God. Consequently, knowledge is
necessary for right action. Unethical activity resulting from inadequate information can be curtailed by improving the information
base. The underlying value of Hartshorne's concrete God for
information theory impinges on ethics at the point where theologians "divide knowledge." Theological division of knowledge refers
to concepts such as "Christian way of life." From a Hartshornian
perspective ethics grounded in a particular structure (recall
Schweitzer's point that early Christian ethics was interim ethics,
for that time) is too narrow in vision. From Hartshorne's point of
view there can ultimately no more be a Christian ethics or a
Buddhist ethics than a Christian chemistry or a Buddhist chemistry.
The value of Hartshorne's thought to theological ethics is finally
that the whole of history becomes normative instead of some particular history.

One may well speculate whether or not Hartshorne's relativized Jesus represents a threat to the Christian faith. I think the
answer is a ringing Yes!—and a quiet No.

To the extent that Christianity continues to understand Jesus
from the standpoint of abstract categories, such as supernatural
Savior, increased modern knowledge will certainly weaken the emotional hold of Jesus upon His followers. Modern knowledge strips
the believer of simple alternatives and ancient superstitions. Con-
structively, it opens him toward the concrete whole of multiple
choices. For example, knowledge that belief in the virgin birth of
a savior appears in other cultural patterns and in cultures more
ancient than Christianity will surely mellow passion for the virgin
birth as a necessary article of faith. Most of those professing
the Christian faith simply lack such knowledge of concrete history

and culture. Being contained in an abstract limitation always means limited knowledge, but ignorance of competitive or parallel claims may well be partially overcome.

Hartshorne's theology is not a threat to Christianity, because his reinterpretation actually renews the possibility of the Christian faith as a living option. Jesus Christ as an actual occasion makes sense without appeal to special revelation, mystery, paradox, or supernaturalism. Just because Hartshorne's Christology is historical without being exclusive as the *only* reality, possibilities open that have often been closed. Hartshorne redirects Christian goals toward concrete love in the world, but who can demonstrate that this does not capture the real meaning of Christian faith?

If Hartshorne's method, with its attending philosophical reorientation, were adopted by Christian thinkers, what transformations might one expect in the nature of Christian faith?

In the first place, Christian theology would become more *confessional* than it has been. Instead of saying with Augustine that if there is some other "access to the Father" Jesus Christ lived and died to no avail, one would say all that happens occurs in God. Instead of saying "no man cometh unto the Father except by me," one would say there are many ways to participate in the love of God. This general confessional position would exclude no one. Each particular faith, such as the Christian faith, would witness out of its own tradition. Christian preaching would say: "In Jesus Christ the love of God is actual." It would not say that "*only* in Jesus Christ" is the love of God actual. Presumably each faith would witness in its own mode, no faith making the additional claim that its faith is the only true faith.

One immediate practical advantage would come to the Christian devotee from a confessional witness. It would no longer be necessary to suppress the haunting fear, held by many, that the Christian faith is not "true." It would no longer be necessary to consider Jesus as a supernatural God-man. Rather, the Christian could simply witness to the love of God as he perceives it in the man Jesus. Moreover, he would be freed from the fear that his life has no meaning unless his truth claims are true. He could relax his concern that his neighbor should "think as he thinks." If his neighbor should not freely choose to believe as he believes, he would not need to "convert" him. One could certainly share his faith with his neighbor; living itself is sharing or nothing.

A second Hartshornian transformation of Christian theology would entail a corollary of the first, *radical tolerance*. If the individual no longer thinks he has a corner on the market of truth, he is more open to the beliefs of others. Certainly religious intolerance has been a major source of the conflicts between men. Being afraid one "truth" is lost if it is not universally held, men have devised every scheme imaginable to force, cajole, harass and generally persuade others to believe as they believe. On Hartshorne's terms the Christian theologian would be free to share "his truth," but with a radical tolerance of others. There would, I imagine, be only one exception; namely, it is not possible to be tolerant of intolerance itself. So far as possible, tolerance is required, but the passivity of general tolerance would require active opposition to intolerance. Tolerance and slavery, for example, are incompatible; tolerance and issues not involving the "coercion of intolerance" are compatible.

There would be no longer any burning reason to send forth missionaries *to preach the truth*. One might well go to share and help one's neighbor, but not with an eye to saving him from eternal damnation because he is culturally "cut off" from "*the* way, *the* truth and *the* life." On Hartshorne's terms the Christian has reason to accept cultural and religious diversity. He has reason to have a radically tolerant attitude toward non-Christian religions and the cultural pluralism of the world.

Third, because the Hartshornian Christian witnesses out of his own tradition he can take *history* with new seriousness. Hartshornian thought sees history, the actual events which constitute man and God, as the "literal" situation out of which faith must speak. The historical occasion of Jesus Christ is real for the Christian, and it is a part of the history out of which he speaks. No classical categories like "eternality" hide the historical Jesus behind a cloud of abstractions or pious affirmations. He is there in his starkness, in his humanity, in his historicity. The shades of the supernatural are drawn back, and the Christian is free to interpret the inspiration for his particular mode of faith in the categories of human existence. The advantage of this approach, which centers in human understanding, is that man now sees himself in the history of the universe and is not restricted by a particular historical perspective. Speaking out of Christian history does not mean being limited to a particular tradition; particular traditions are only beginning points. Too often Christian history has been taken to mean "only this history." The theology of Rudolf Bultmann tends to be an example of a historical theology which is not historical enough with respect to universal history. Hartshorne's historicity is a corrective to more than Bultmann's existential analysis of man. It is also a corrective to exclusivistic understandings of history. On Hartshorne's terms the historicity of Mahayana Buddhism *also* has theological validity.

Finally, Hartshorne's thought suggests that Christian theology come to terms with the *universe.* Christian concepts have quite understandably been molded in terms of human history. Now, human history is expanding its own vision beyond the bounds of the earth. It is surely a matter of concern to the Christian to reinterpret faith so that it is meaningful in the space age. If Christian theology follows the implications of Hartshorne's thought our horizons will certainly expand into the cosmos. The mythologies of the earth, of human history, may be challenged to describe life in a radically new way. Christians must find ways of expressing faith which speak to the space age. In transforming Christian thinking, Hartshorne's open history of tolerance may be a rich resource.

A) C unlocks the door to Hartshorne's thought, but there is a final way to illuminate the room inside. This is the way of critical questions designed to point out problems requiring future attention. Some of these questions are not clearly within the area explored, but all of them are related to the task of probing into dark corners, perhaps for theological antiques covered by the dust of neglect. Some questions have already appeared, such as whether or not the term "reality" is interchangeable with "God"—and should reality replace the use of the term "God." The criticisms of Cobb, Platt, Westphal, Smith, and Hartt have also been mentioned; but even in a sympathetic study it is good to end with still more questions for future work.

Taking Hartshorne seriously, would not some rather difficult consequences follow from A) C? For example, are there no eternal (not "everlasting") principles? If we mix two parts hydrogen with one part oxygen, we expect to get water. Is not H_2O the eternal principle of water? Of course this question assumes roughly equivalent conditions, but does not the principle always hold?

Hartshorne might respond that the principle came into being when H_2O concretely occurred. What happens in each case merely exhibits the same abstract principle. The principle, he might insist, is derivative. Would this answer satisfy the scientist who conducts the experiment? How would we check the claim that no principle is being followed by the concrete occurrence of water? Hartshorne appeals to intuition; the counterclaim can also appeal to intuition. How can intuition be checked? That the question does arise in this way has implications for the use of A) C in theology, but even theological usefulness may depend upon intuitive agreement. Two contemporary theologians who have been influenced by Hartshorne have designated the question of constant rational principles as an issue dividing them.[2] Schubert Ogden finds that Hartshorne's work sufficiently exemplifies universal principles, and affirms that they are to be embraced. Ogden interprets Hartshorne as affirming the "rational constancy" of the universe and finds this useful in theology. John Cobb also finds such a constancy of fundamental principles and turns (perhaps surprisingly) to Whitehead.[3] He thinks Whitehead's thought more readily lends itself to epochal principles which do not have to be eternally the same, and is consequently more attracted to Whitehead as a theological resource. Parenthetically, we might ask whether or not Ogden and Cobb have correctly interpreted Hartshorne at this point. If they have, the present question may lose its force. Hartshorne has remarked,

[2] This discussion is based upon conversations with Schubert M. Ogden and John Cobb.
[3] Cobb dedicates his book, *A Christian Natural Theology, Based on the Thought of Alfred North Whitehead* (Philadelphia: Westminster Press, 1965), to Hartshorne "To whom I owe both my understanding and my love of Whitehead's philosophy." Speaking of Whitehead's notion of cosmic epochs in which "different modes of order will prevail" (*Process and Reality*, First Harper Torchbook Edition, 1960, pp. 139, 148, 171), Cobb adds, ". . . it is extremely difficult to see how one unchanging order can provide a specific and novel aim to every new occasion" (*A Christian Natural Theology*, p. 155).

... there is no one final system of metaphysics, but an inexhaustible variety of ways of "carving up" the ultimate continuum. Neglect of this fact that the ultimate truths lack the discreteness of discursive thought is a cardinal weakness of Husserl's doctrine of the Wesenschau . . . .[4]

Inasmuch as the argument that Hartshorne's position is A) C is also metaphysical, the question is two edged. In the same way that Hartshorne's statement calls into question "constant rational principles," it calls A) C into question. Again, Hartshorne might say that the formula is derivative from reality, but is not derivativeness of metaphysical principles itself metaphysical? The metaphysical alternative would be that constant principles are not derivative. Can we not ask if the metaphysical principle (that metaphysical descriptions of reality are derivative) is itself subject to change? This question, arising from discussion of A) C, parallels the question of whether or not *the principle* that reality *becomes* itself becomes. The question of metaphysical consistency can be illustrated in contemporary ethics. Joseph Fletcher argues that there are no universal criteria for ethical decisions, with the possible exception of Christian love.[5] I say "possible exception" because the situationists' understanding of Christian love prevents any kind of law from standing above love. The meaning of Christian love varies from situation to situation. The question paralleling the question of metaphysical consistency is whether or not the norm of Christian love is really a norm. This is not to say there must be a norm, and Christian love is not universal enough. Rather, it is simply to ask how the same reality could be present in different situations. The underlying question for Christian ethics is the basic philosophical question of real universals. Hartshorne's concrete-centered theology results in situationist ethics because of the universal principle of change. What would happen to both Fletcher's and Hartshorne's concrete ethics if the principle A) C were itself to change? Following Whitehead, Cobb guards against this possibility as a disruption of concrete novelty, but what if actual occasions change in a new

---

[4] Hartshorne, "Metaphysics for Positivists," *Philosophy of Science,* II, No. 3 (July, 1935), 291.

[5] Joseph Fletcher, *Situation Ethics: The New Morality* (Philadelphia: Westminster Press, 1966).

epoch so that new epochs are no longer possible? There always seems to be one principle that is necessary in order for everything else to make sense, including this principle, but what if this principle ceases to be true?

What is the difference between Hartshorne's concrete intuition and mysticism? This question becomes especially important considering Hartshorne's admitted affinity to Nicolas Berdyaev. One is struck by the similarity between Berdyaev's open appeal to Jacob Boehme's notion of the *Ungrund*[6] and Hartshorne's doctrine of the concrete as the source of possibility. Not only this, but "meonic freedom," Berdyaev's ontology of freedom, seems a fair characterization of both concepts. The differences appear primarily when Berdyaev's poetic expression of Boehme's mysticism is considered. Hartshorne is more interested in the inspirational value of logical construction than in poetic expression. Yet, these are differences in mode of expression. The intuitive or mystical aspects reside more in the realm of the ontological possibility of expression than in the form of expression. When Berdyaev looks into the deep well of nonbeing out of which "being boils," he is looking away from the static limitations of being. But it is just such limitations that give some order to chaos, some law to nature, some abstract understanding to concrete possibility. In the thought of both Berdyaev and Hartshorne, a mystical immediacy hovers over basic method. This results not from attitudes toward metaphysics (Hartshorne's positive, Berdyaev's negative), but from the basis of each method in intuition. The question becomes: How is intuitionism distinguished from mysticism? Both are modes of knowing immediate concrete experience. Hartshorne protects his position with the notion of the definiteness of the concrete; yet, too much discrete definiteness would undercut the continuum, and the problem of ideal essences would reappear. How can Hartshorne's notion of reality as social process avoid backing into mysticism as he defends against ideal essence and abstract pre-eminence of every kind? The obvious answer is an appeal to his rationalism or his positive attitude toward metaphysics, both of which illustrate the role of the abstract. A qualification of this answer occurs, however, because abstractions

[6] Cf., for example, Nicolas Berdyaev, *The Destiny of Man* (New York: Harper & Row, 1960), *passim.*

have no ontological basis in themselves. The question of mysticism is aimed at the depths of the concrete.

The question of mysticism stems from the concrete. Shifting attention to the role of abstraction, Hartshorne may also be challenged on almost the opposite grounds, gnosticism. The direction this question takes is indicated by Hartshorne's interest in logic and the ontological proof of God's existence. His eye often seems to be on "knowledge of faith" as opposed to "faith." This is one interpretation of Jacob Taubes's criticism in his review of *Philosophers Speak of God*.[7] Taubes says: "Mr. Hartshorne's dipolar theology is a dialectic of cognition that tends to an absolute gnosticism."[8] What does gnosticism mean here? Harry A. Wolfson describes gnostics as those "who depreciated simple faith" over against philosophic reason or knowledge.[9] If this is what Taubes intends by Hartshorne's "gnosticism," it means that Hartshorne's notion of intuitive and direct inevitable faith is rejected outright. Rejecting the concrete, the ground of faith clearly would mean Hartshorne is gnostic in the sense that only abstract knowledge remains.

There is, however, another way to interpret the charge of gnosticism. The point might be that dipolarity is "gnostic" because it moves toward gnostic dualism. Hans Jonas maintains: "The cardinal feature of gnostic thought is the radical dualism that governs the relation of God and world, correspondingly of man and world."[10] Recalling Hartshorne's description of man's consciousness in terms of linguistic abstractions drawn from the concrete resources of the world, Jonas gives us a framework in which Taubes's charge may be understood.

Two articles are especially important in answering Taubes. In "God and Man Not Rivals,"[11] Hartshorne opposes a dualism be-

---

[7] *The Journal of Religion*, xxxiv, No. 2 (April, 1954), 120-126.
[8] *Ibid.*, p. 121.
[9] Harry A. Wolfson, *The Philosophy of the Church Fathers: Faith, Trinity, Incarnation* (Cambridge, Mass.: Harvard University Press, 1956), I, 125.
[10] Hans Jonas, *The Gnostic Religion* (Boston: Beacon Press, 1963), p. 42.
[11] *The Journal of Liberal Religion*, vi, No. 2 (Autumn, 1944), 9-13.

tween God and the world. In "The Monistic Theory of Expression,"[12] he responds to the charge of dualism between man and the world by reaffirming the doctrine of the continuum. The best answer Hartshorne has for the dualists, however, is A) C. If the latter answer is sufficient, the charge of gnosticism in the first sense (intellectual knowing) would re-enter. Which way the question of gnosticism is interpreted determines upon which horn of the dilemma Hartshorne is to be questioned. This situation is closely paralleled in William Hamilton's uneasiness about the gnostic problem in Altizer. "At times," Hamilton notes, "Altizer walks very close to the gnostic nay-sayer whose danger he ordinarily perceives."[13] Altizer's dialectic of the sacred and the profane (following Mircea Eliade) seems to Hamilton to contain gnostic overtones in a way similar to Taubes's concern that Hartshorne's A) C "tends to an absolute gnosticism." Taubes's charge actually has more foundation than Hamilton's because Hartshorne has more sympathy for reason and metaphysics than Altizer. But again, Taubes must circumvent the inclusiveness of the Hartshornian concrete because abstractions have no value in themselves. If the abstract and the concrete can be pried apart, the charge of gnosticism does become serious in Hartshorne.

A deeper question is whether "concrete" as a description of the true nature of God interferes with full realization of theological possibility. The concrete God is unlike at least the classical theological object. Is the divine reality best described as concrete? The term "concrete" even has the connotation of unchanging definiteness in much usage. Does the term actually help us out of our conceptual darkness? Could it not be that the concrete God is another metaphysical limitation upon the holy? The answer, like silence itself, is a strange kind of sound. How can any theological description avoid describing since indescribability is a description? The test of theological descriptions such as the concrete God is not whether abstract limitation is avoided but whether the description is adequate. What is the test of adequacy? How can one decide if

---

[12] *The Journal of Philosophy*, i, No. 14 (July 2, 1953), 425-434.
[13] William Hamilton and Thomas J. J. Altizer, *Radical Theology and the Death of God* (New York and Indianapolis: The Bobbs-Merrill Co., 1966), p. 29.

Hartshorne's concrete God is adequate as a description of the real or the holy? Is personal experience (broadly conceived) the measure of adequacy? The question is whether or not the concrete God is consecrated by our experience of reality known through intuition or faith. ("Intuition" in philosophy and "faith" in theology are often functionally the same.) At the same time terms such as "the concrete God" inform us they depend upon experience for their truth. This is not to say with Kierkegaard that truth is subjective personal experience. Experience contains the realm of objectivity. Who we are is contingent upon where we are. What we have experienced depends upon what has happened beyond our control in objective history as well as what we have subjectively caused. The test of the adequacy of the concrete God is history itself.

In a recent paper Hans Jonas set the stage for the question concerning the theological usefulness of philosophical concepts of any kind.[14] Jonas raised the question of what is entailed in such usage in the case of theology and Heidegger. What does theology "buy" when it uses philosophical concepts such as Heidegger's? This same question may easily be asked of the theological applicability of Hartshorne's A) C.

In order to be "an" assertion as opposed to "any" assertion must not at least conceptual limitations be involved? Hartshorne responds that abstract limitations may be inevitable, but this does not mean that concrete reality is subject to the same problem. If we question whether or not "concrete" carries specific connotations, Hartshorne would admit that it does, and insist that the word "concrete" is connotatively limited because in itself it is an abstraction. The question is: Does this beg Jonas' question or answer it?

One of the basic problems of the history of philosophy emerges in the light of A) C: the problem of the one and the many. How can unity be maintained given real diversity, or how can diversity be maintained given real unity? Hartshorne assumes the problem to be insufficient unity and addresses himself to it accordingly.

If Hartshorne's assumption that the problem is primarily unity

14 Hans Jonas, "Heidegger and Theology," op. cit.

is rejected, for a moment, the question is sharpened. Given the Hartshornian method (aesthetically conceived) of seeking unity-in-diversity and diversity-in-unity, his solution is clear. If the assumption of too much diversity is rejected, he would be waiting, in a practical way, to see if the problem becomes the opposite one of too much unity. If a balance of unity-in-contrast (or diversity) appears, the problem would be metaphysically solved as far as Hartshorne is concerned. Yet, does this practical approach really settle the problem of the one and the many? We might persist by asking: *Can there be* unity-in-contrast? This puts the traditional question to Hartshorne in his own terms.

A parallel approach appears when Hartshorne adopts Whitehead's "novel intuition." In the discussion of Whitehead, Hartshorne applauds Whitehead's novel insight that "the many become one and are increased by one." In effect, this means that Hartshorne refuses to treat the question of the one and the many apart from the question of change. I question whether John Lachs takes sufficient account of this point in his assessment of unity in Hartshorne's God.[15] Nevertheless, we may view Hartshorne's adoption of Whitehead's "solution" in itself. This solution solves the problem by going beyond its classical structure. Instead of trying to settle the issue internally in terms of the being of given diversity-in-unity, this solution approaches the issue by working from being to becoming. The one which "is" is the one which the many "become." Does this solution solve the question of the one and the many? Since the concrete is reality in Hartshorne's thought, should not the question of the one and the many be asked in terms of the concrete alone? It is easy to think of abstract unity; what of concrete unity? Hartshorne maintains that a Peircian continuum "holds" the chain of being together. The continuum of possibility is filled with actual events, each having some quality that distinguishes it from all others. Do these qualities constitute discrete reality with unique durations? If so, exactly how does discreteness square with continuity? Hartshorne approaches the problem by calling upon the distinction between possibility and actuality. The continuum is based upon real possibilities; discrete events are ac-

[15] On this point, *see* "Two Concepts of God," *Harvard Theological Review*, LIX, No. 3 (July, 1966), 239.

tualizations. Because of the reality of concrete time, the question of the one and the many now depends upon whether or not one accepts temporal becoming as actualization of possibility. If concrete time is accepted the Whiteheadian-Hartshornian solution sticks. The question of the one and the many is, finally, the question whether or not time is real.

The problems of the one and the many and change are inextricably related. They can be isolated, however, by asking how an entity can "be" and be changing at the same time. To put it in Zeno's well-known terms, how is it that an arrow moves or changes place when it can be argued that it simply is where it is at a given time? If the arrow always is where it "is," does it "become"? Generally speaking, the Greek's solution was that being is real and becoming is illusory.

If anything, Hartshorne's response to the question of change must be taken as the opposite of the Greek's solution. Recall Hartshorne's comment: "Being is intelligible as the abstract fixed aspect is becoming, and eternity as the identical element in all temporal diversity." This seems to mean that becoming itself is real; but if becoming is a process of adding to being (Hartshorne's understanding of change), has the question of change been faced? This is similar to the question that arose in discussing the one and the many. Does change as addition answer or beg the question of change? If change by addition is rejected, what are the alternatives to Zeno's paradox, except perhaps a neoplatonic denial of change altogether? If such alternatives could be found, change by addition would be unnecessary. Be that as it may, does change by addition answer the problem?

Hartshorne studied with Husserl and Heidegger in Germany before returning to Harvard and coming then under the influence of Whitehead and Peirce. This return is symbolic of Hartshorne's movement away from phenomenological (Husserl's) and existential (Heidegger's) ways of asking basic philosophical questions. But what happened to the question that has dominated much of Heidegger's work, the question of being? Both Heidegger and Hartshorne have persistently treated this question in a dynamic fashion. Heidegger uses the dynamic notion of temporality; Hartshorne employs a dynamic of becoming. Nevertheless, even from the standpoint of one of Heidegger's later essays, a question arises concerning Hartshorne's treatment of the question of being. Specifically, in *The Question of Being*, Heidegger says: . . . *the question as to the essence of Being dies off, if it does not surrender the language of metaphysics, because metaphysical conception forbids thinking the question as to the essence of Being.*"[16]

Hartshorne not only is not opposed to "metaphysical conception," but readily employs his own kind of metaphysics such as A) C in theological doctrines. It can be argued that Heidegger's attack upon metaphysics as that which covers up the question of being does not apply to the kind of metaphysics that Hartshorne does. The "dynamic" similarities between the two philosophies have been indicated, since both stress the priority of the concrete. If it can be maintained that Hartshorne's metaphysics causes the question of being to die off in a way that Heidegger's thought does not, then from a Heideggerian perspective Hartshorne's metaphysics *qua* metaphysics is questionable. Has Hartshorne's metaphysics made it impossible to ask the question of being? Perhaps this is another way of asking if the concrete restricts reality (*see* p. 186). Heidegger's way of putting the question smacks of classical presuppositions. Is Heidegger after the emptiest of all concepts, pure abstract being? Pure being could never be *in* the concrete in its necessary form because all concreteness is contingent. Heidegger attempts to avoid the classical question as an abstraction from particular "being-there." From the standpoint of concrete "being-there," no obvious quarrel with A) C appears. But in the analysis of Hartshorne's review of Heidegger's *Being and Time*, it was clear that Hartshorne's understanding of concreteness differs from Heidegger's. Primarily the difference lies in the objectively real continuum in which discrete beings appear. From a Heideggerian standpoint the question thus becomes whether or not the continuum covers beings existentially conceived.

Finally, what of God? Internally, Hartshorne's theology makes sense when developed according to A) C, but what of the larger

[16] Martin Heidegger, *The Question of Being*, trans. with an introduction by William Kluback and Jean T. Wilde (New York: Twayne Publishers, 1958), p. 73.

question, whether or not theology is possible at all? Thomas Huxley once said, "It is the customary fate of new truths to begin as heresies and to end as superstitions." Will all theology eventually be considered superstition? Without doubt Hartshorne's theology amounts to a modern heresy; will it end as an ancient superstition? A few years ago Will Herberg remarked that there was going to be a Whiteheadian renaissance, and then Whitehead (and presumably Hartshorne) would take his place in the philosopher's heaven. Perhaps so; a new reason for the demise of a theologically grounded philosophical system has appeared on the horizon. Till now the problem has been the adequacy of concepts to express holy reality. Now comes the question: Is there holiness? Depth psychology has moved many miles beyond Rudolf Otto's *Idea of the Holy*.[17] Critical thinking now walks boldly into the once hallowed ground of holy mystery. Hartshorne himself has done much to coax holy mystery out of its venerable cave. Harvey Cox is right in saying that theology is now being by-passed, but it can be added that critical thinking will increasingly question the theological interpretation of secularization. Radical theology already seems to have done this.

Since the concrete God is reality itself for Hartshorne, why not call it concrete reality and forget religious dressing? The obvious rejoinder is that theological history carries much intended by the concept of concreteness: for example, love. But why not secularize love, or perhaps accept the thesis that love is already secular? The only significant reason for keeping a theological dressing may be that communication with theologically saturated culture requires it as a practical measure. Hartshorne's God can be understood and defended in secular terms, but is culture sufficiently secular to make such a move practical?

In the spirit of pragmatism, the question is whether God-talk is practical. The dynamics of Hartshorne's system, however, are not really at stake in this question, for it is a question of communicable terms. On this level why not throw out the term "God" altogether? Certainly "God" is more religiously satisfactory than "reality," but why seek religious satisfaction at all? Does it matter that the term

[17] Otto, Rudolf, *Idea of the Holy*, trans. John W. Harvey (New York: Oxford University Press, 1958).

"God" connotes more personal feelings? Is it not possible that our problem is precisely with the religious notion of personal? Being personal, being subjective (admittedly Hartshorne does not mean only this) contributes to world disorder and inability to live by law. Moreover, does being personal suggest that the doctrine of man, even neoclassical man, is worthy of our enduring embrace? Are we clinging to the object of religious language because it is required by our anthropology? It is perhaps ironical to put this question to Hartshorne, a process philosopher, when so many weaker classical notions are still abroad. Nevertheless, even Hartshorne's process philosophy often seems to imply that man as he is known today is what we wish to preserve.

By keeping the term "God" and its implicit religious connotation, is communication strengthened or weakened? Not the least of the considerations that should be made here is the great heterogeneity of world cultures. Hartshorne has long been in dialogue with Buddhism, for example, but to what extent is his religious conceptual framework a Western Christian framework? This is the broad question: Can any particular religion furnish adequate terms for the whole of the planet—or does the fact that all terms communicate special meanings from their cultural context render this impossible?

In raising these questions I have intentionally attempted to play the devil's advocate, not because Hartshorne's system is riddled with difficulties, but because his thought is too important not to be questioned. These questions are merely raised for discussion. I have confidence that Hartshorne will acquit himself well as he has in the past. The questions are therefore two-edged; they are my attempt to nudge philosophers and theologians to engage Hartshorne's thought. They are not aimed at Hartshorne alone but at those of us who have tended to rest in the shade of Hume's skepticism while important metaphysical questions gathered moss. Theologically, especially on the question of God, extensive probing by imaginative and sensitive minds is now required. "Self-evident truths" are still curtailing creative output. By again calling up basic, not symptomatic, philosophical and theological issues Hartshorne has rendered twentieth-century thought a needed service. We are in his debt.

Bibliographies

BIBLIOGRAPHIES

1—The Published Writings of Charles Hartshorne
from 1929 to 1967*

*When articles and essays have been incorporated into books,
the book in which they appear is noted.—R.E.J.*

A. Philosophy

1. Books

THE PHILOSOPHY AND PSYCHOLOGY OF SENSATION. Chicago: The University of Chicago Press, 1934.

BEYOND HUMANISM: ESSAYS IN THE NEW PHILOSOPHY OF NATURE. Chicago: Willett, Clark & Company, 1937.

MAN'S VISION OF GOD AND THE LOGIC OF THEISM. Chicago: Willett, Clark & Company, 1941. (After 1948 published by Harper & Brothers Publishers, New York. After 1964 reprinted by Archon Books, Hamden, Connecticut.)

THE DIVINE RELATIVITY: A SOCIAL CONCEPTION OF GOD. The Terry Lectures, 1947. New Haven: Yale University Press, 1948.

WHITEHEAD AND THE MODERN WORLD: SCIENCE, METAPHYSICS, AND CIVILIZATION, THREE ESSAYS ON THE THOUGHT OF ALFRED NORTH WHITEHEAD. By Victor Lowe, Charles Hartshorne, and A. H.

* I wish to thank Mrs. Charles Hartshorne for furnishing this bibliography, especially with the heretofore unpublished list of reviews.

Johnson. "Whitehead's Metaphysics" by Charles Hartshorne, pp. 25-41. Boston: The Beacon Press, 1950.

REALITY AS SOCIAL PROCESS: STUDIES IN METAPHYSICS AND RELIGION. Glencoe: The Free Press and Boston: The Beacon Press, 1953.

PHILOSOPHERS SPEAK OF GOD. (With William L. Reese) Chicago: The University of Chicago Press, 1953.

THE LOGIC OF PERFECTION AND OTHER ESSAYS IN NEOCLASSICAL META-PHYSICS. LaSalle: Open Court Publishing Co., 1962.

ANSELM'S DISCOVERY. LaSalle: Open Court, 1965.

THE SOCIAL CONCEPTION OF THE UNIVERSE, edited with notes in Japanese by Keiji Matsunobu. Tokyo: Aoyama, 1967. Pp. 78.

A NATURAL THEOLOGY FOR OUR TIME. LaSalle, Ill.: Open Court, 1967. Pp. 145.

COLLECTED PAPERS OF CHARLES SANDERS PEIRCE. Edited by Charles Hartshorne and Paul Weiss. Cambridge: Harvard University Press.

Vol. I PRINCIPLES OF PHILOSOPHY, 1931.
Vol. II ELEMENTS OF LOGIC, 1932.
Vol. III EXACT LOGIC, 1933.
Vol. IV THE SIMPLEST MATHEMATICS, 1933.
Vol. V PRAGMATISM AND PRAGMATICISM, 1934.
Vol. VI SCIENTIFIC METAPHYSICS, 1935.

2. Articles from Journals, Symposia, and Books

Review Article: SEIN UND ZEIT by Martin Heidegger and MATHEMA-TISCHE EXISTENZ by Oskar Becker, from JAHRBUCH FÜR PHI-LOSOPHIE UND PHÄNOMENOLOGISCHE FORSCHUNG, Achter Band, THE PHILOSOPHICAL REVIEW, XXXVIII, No. 3 (May, 1929), 284-293.

"Continuity, the Form of Forms, in Charles Peirce," THE MONIST, XXXIX, No. 4 (October, 1929), 521-534.

"Ethics and the Assumption of Purely Private Pleasures," THE IN-TERNATIONAL JOURNAL OF ETHICS, XL, No. 4 (July, 1930), 496-515.

"Sense Quality and Feeling Tone," PROCEEDINGS OF THE SEVENTH INTERNATIONAL CONGRESS OF PHILOSOPHY, OXFORD, UNIVERSITY PRESS, 1931, 168-172.

"Contingency and the New Era in Metaphysics (I)," THE JOURNAL OF PHILOSOPHY, XXIX, No. 16 (August 4, 1932), 421-431.

"Contingency and the New Era in Metaphysics (II)," THE JOURNAL OF PHILOSOPHY, XXIX, No. 17 (August 18, 1932), 457-469.

"Four Principles of Method—with Applications," THE MONIST, XLIII, No. 1 (January) 1933, 40-72.

"The Intelligibility of Sensations," THE MONIST, XLIV, No. 2 (July, 1934), 161-185.

"Redefining God," THE NEW HUMANIST, VII, No. 4 (July-August, 1934), 8-15.

"The New Metaphysics and Current Problems (I): Medievalism, Humanism, and Beyond," THE NEW FRONTIER, I, No. 1 (September, 1934), 24-31. (II): THE NEW FRONTIER, I, No. 5 (November-December, 1934), 8-14.

"Ethics and the New Theology," THE INTERNATIONAL JOURNAL OF ETHICS, XLV, No. 1 (October, 1934), 90-101.

"The Parallel Development of Method in Physics and Psychology," PHILOSOPHY OF SCIENCE, I, No. 4 (October, 1934), 446-459.

"Pattern and Movement in Art and Science," COMMENT: THE UNIVERSITY OF CHICAGO LITERARY AND CRITICAL QUARTERLY, III, No. 2 (Winter Quarter 1935), 1-2, 11. (see chapter 2, REALITY AS SOCIAL PROCESS)

"Metaphysics for Positivists," PHILOSOPHY OF SCIENCE, II, No. 3 (July, 1935), 287-303.

"On Some Criticisms of Whitehead's Philosophy," THE PHILOSOPHICAL REVIEW, XLIV, No. 4 [whole No. 262] (July, 1935), 323-344.

"The Compound Individual," in PHILOSOPHICAL ESSAYS FOR ALFRED NORTH WHITEHEAD, New York: Longmans, Green and Co., 1936, pp. 193-220.

"The New Pantheism—I," THE CHRISTIAN REGISTER, CXV, No. 8 (February 20, 1936), 119-120. (II), THE CHRISTIAN REGISTER, CXV, No. 9 (February 27, 1936), 141-143.

"The Philosophical Limitations of Humanism," in "A Symposium on Humanism," THE UNIVERSITY REVIEW, III, No. 4 (Summer, 1937), 240-242. (see chapter 11, REALITY AS SOCIAL PROCESS)

"The Reality of the Past, the Unreality of the Future," HIBBERT JOURNAL, XXXVII, No. 2 (January, 1939), 246-257.

"The Method of Imaginative Variations," in "Notes Concerning Husserl," THE JOURNAL OF PHILOSOPHY, XXXVI, No. 9 (April 27, 1939), 233-234.

Discussion: "The Interpretation of Whitehead (Reply to John W. Blyth)," THE PHILOSOPHICAL REVIEW, XLVIII, No. 4 (July, 1939), 415-423.

"A Critique of Peirce's Idea of God," in "Abstracts of Papers to be read at the Joint Meeting of the Eastern and Western Divisions of the American Philosophical Association, Columbia University, December 27, 28, and 29, 1939," THE JOURNAL OF PHILOSOPHY, XXXVI, No. 25 (December 7, 1939), 683-684.

"Husserl and the Social Structure of Immediacy," in PHILOSOPHICAL ESSAYS IN MEMORY OF EDMUND HUSSERL, Cambridge: Harvard University Press, 1940, pp. 219-230.

"Santayana's Doctrine of Essence," in THE PHILOSOPHY OF GEORGE SANTAYANA, The Library of Living Philosophers, II, Evanston and Chicago: Northwestern University, 1940, 135-182.

"The Three Ideas of God," THE JOURNAL OF LIBERAL RELIGION, I, No. 3 (Winter, 1940), 9-16.

"Whitehead's Idea of God," in THE PHILOSOPHY OF ALFRED NORTH WHITEHEAD, The Library of Living Philosophers, III, Evanston and Chicago: Northwestern University, 1941, 513-559.

"Charles Sanders Peirce's Metaphysics of Evolution," THE NEW ENGLAND QUARTERLY, XIV, No. 1, March, 1941, pp. 49-63.

"Anthropomorphic Tendencies in Positivism," PHILOSOPHY OF SCIENCE, VIII, No. 2 (April, 1941), 184-203.

"A Critique of Peirce's Idea of God," THE PHILOSOPHICAL REVIEW, I, No. 5 (September, 1941), 516-523.

"A Philosophy of Democratic Defense," in SCIENCE, PHILOSOPHY AND RELIGION: SECOND SYMPOSIUM, New York: Conference on Science, Philosophy and Religion in Their Relation to the Democratic Way of Life, Inc., 1942, pp. 130-172.

"Elements of Truth in the Group-Mind Concept," SOCIAL RESEARCH, IX, No. 2 (May, 1942), 248-265. (see chapter 3, REALITY AS SOCIAL PROCESS)

"Organic and Inorganic Wholes," PHILOSOPHY AND PHENOMENOLOGICAL RESEARCH, III, No. 2 (December, 1942), 127-136. (see chapter 7, THE LOGIC OF PERFECTION AND OTHER ESSAYS IN NEOCLASSICAL METAPHYSICS)

Discussion: "Is Whitehead's God the God of Religion?," ETHICS, LIII, No. 3 (April, 1943), 219-227. (see chapter 14, REALITY AS SOCIAL PROCESS)

Communication: Rejoinder: "Ely on Whitehead," THE JOURNAL OF LIBERAL RELIGION, V, No. 2 (September, 1943), 97-100.

Discussion: "Reflections on the Strength and Weakness of Thomism," ETHICS, LIV, No. 1 (October, 1943), 53-57.

"A Mathematical Analysis of Theism," THE REVIEW OF RELIGION, VIII, No. 1 (November, 1943), 20-38.

Radio Discussion: "How Christians Should Think about the Peace," by Edwin Aubrey, Charles Hartshorne, and Bernard Loomer. The University of Chicago Round Table, No. 316 (April 9, 1944), 1-20.

"The Formal Validity and Real Significance of the Ontological Argument," THE PHILOSOPHICAL REVIEW, LIII, No. 3 (May, 1944), 225-245.

Discussion: "On Hartshorne's Formulation of the Ontological Argument: A Rejoinder," THE PHILOSOPHICAL REVIEW, LIV, No. 1 (January, 1945), 63-65.

Discussion: "Professor Hartshorne's Syllogism: Rejoinder," THE PHILOSOPHICAL REVIEW, LIV, No. 5 (September, 1945), 506-508.

"Philosophy and Orthodoxy," ETHICS, LIV, No. 4 (July, 1944), 295-298.

"God and Man Not Rivals," THE JOURNAL OF LIBERAL RELIGION, VI, No. 2 (Autumn, 1944), 9-13.

Entries: AN ENCYCLOPEDIA OF RELIGION, ed. by Vergilius Ferm. The Philosophical Library, New York, 1945. Acosmism; analogy; anthropomorphism; anthropopathism; Aristotle and Aristotelianism; Berkeley, George; Carneades; cause; Copernican astronomy; eternal; eternity; ether; etiology, aetiology; foreknowledge, Divine; Gerson, Levi ben; God, as personal; Hume; infinite; Kant, Immanuel; omnipotence; omnipresence; omniscience; panentheism; panlogism; pantheism; Peirce, Charles Sanders; perfect, perfection; Ptolemaic astronomy; Renouvier, Charles; Spencer, Herbert; Spinoza, Benedict; time; transcendence; Whitehead, Alfred North.

Review Article: "Efficient Causality in Aristotle and St. Thomas," by Francis X. Meehan; THE JOURNAL OF RELIGION, XXV, No. 1 (January, 1945), 25-32.

"A New Philosophic Conception of the Universe," THE HIBBERT JOURNAL, XLIV, No. 1 (October, 1945), 14-21. (see chapter 1, REALITY AS SOCIAL PROCESS)

Review Article: "The Philosophy of Bertrand Russell," ed. by Paul Arthur Schilpp, THE JOURNAL OF RELIGION, XXV, No. 4 (October, 1945), 280-284. (see chapter 13, REALITY AS SOCIAL PROCESS)

Communication: "Reply to Father Meehan," THE JOURNAL OF RELIGION, XXVI, No. 1 (January, 1946), 54-57.

"Relative, Absolute, and Superrelative: A Formal Analysis," THE

PHILOSOPHICAL REVIEW, LV, No. 3 (May, 1946), 213-228. (*see* chapters 7-8, REALITY AS SOCIAL PROCESS.)

"Tragic and Sublime Aspects of Christian Love," THE JOURNAL OF LIBERAL RELIGION, VIII, No. 1 (Summer, 1946), 36-44. (*see* chapter 7-8, REALITY AS SOCIAL PROCESS)

"Theological Values in Current Metaphysics," THE JOURNAL OF RELIGION, XXVI, No. 3 (July, 1946), 157-167.

"Leibniz's Greatest Discovery," JOURNAL OF THE HISTORY OF IDEAS, VII, No. 4 (October, 1946), 411-421.

"Ideal Knowledge Defines Reality: What Was True in Idealism," THE JOURNAL OF PHILOSOPHY, XLIII, No. 21 (October 10, 1946), 573-582.

"God as Absolute, Yet Related to All," THE REVIEW OF METAPHYSICS, I, No. 1 (September, 1947), 24-51. (*see* chapter 2, THE DIVINE RELATIVITY: A SOCIAL CONCEPTION OF GOD)

"Two Levels of Faith and Reason," THE JOURNAL OF BIBLE AND RELIGION, XVI, No. 1 (January, 1948), 30-38. (*see* chapter 10, REALITY AS SOCIAL PROCESS)

"The Rationalistic Criterion in Metaphysics," PHILOSOPHY AND PHENOMENOLOGICAL RESEARCH, VIII, No. 3 (March, 1948), 436-447.

"Existential Propositions and the Law of Categories," PROCEEDINGS OF THE TENTH INTERNATIONAL CONGRESS OF PHILOSOPHY, Amsterdam, August 11-18, 1948. Ed. by E. W. Beth, E. J. Pos, and J. H. A. Hollak, Fascicule 1. North-Holland Publishing Co., Amsterdam, pp. 342-344.

"Ein Theologisches Paradoxon nach Arnauld," PHILOSOPHISCHES JAHRBUCH, 59/2 (1949), 250-251.

"Noch einmal die Zufälligkeit der Welt und Notwendigkeit Gottes." Erwiderung an Dr. Ferdinand Bergenthal, PHILOSOPHISCHES JAHRBUCH, 59/2 (1949), 469-471.

"Das metaphysische System Whiteheads," ZEITSCHRIFT FÜR PHILOSOPHISCHE FORSCHUNG, III/4 (1949), 566-575.

"The Synthesis of Idealism and Realism," THEORIA, XV (March 12, 1949), 90-107. (*see* chapter 4, REALITY AS SOCIAL PROCESS)

"Chance, Love, and Incompatibility" (Presidential Address read before the meeting of the Western Division of the American Philosophical Association at Columbus, Ohio, April 29, 1949). Published in THE PHILOSOPHICAL REVIEW, LVIII, No. 5 (September, 1949), 429-450. (*see* chapter 5, REALITY AS SOCIAL PROCESS)

"Whitehead's Metaphysics" in WHITEHEAD AND THE MODERN WORLD: SCIENCE, METAPHYSICS, AND CIVILIZATION, THREE ESSAYS ON THE THOUGHT OF ALFRED NORTH WHITEHEAD, by Victor Lowe, Charles Hartshorne, and A. H. Johnson, Boston: The Beacon Press, pp. 25-41.

"Panpsychism," Chapter thirty-five, A HISTORY OF PHILOSOPHICAL SYSTEMS, ed. by Vergilius Ferm, New York: The Philosophical Library, 1950, pp. 442-453.

"Le Principe de relativité philosophique chez Whitehead," REVUE DE MÉTAPHYSIQUE ET DE MORALE, 55° Année, No. 1 (Janvier-Mars, 1950), 16-29.

"The Divine Relativity and Absoluteness: A Reply," THE REVIEW OF METAPHYSICS, IV, No. 1 (September, 1950), 31-60.

"God in General Philosophical Thought," in THE ENCYCLOPEDIA HEBRAICA, III, Jerusalem: Encyclopedia Publishing Company, 1951 (in the Jewish Calendar 5711), 467-478.

"Strict and Genetic Identity: An Illustration of the Relations of Logic to Metaphysics," in STRUCTURE, METHOD AND MEANING: ESSAYS IN HONOR OF HENRY M. SHEFFER, New York: The Liberal Arts Press, 1951, pp. 242-254.

"Philosophy of Religion in the United States," PHILOSOPHY AND PHENOMENOLOGICAL RESEARCH, XI, No. 3 (March, 1951), 406-410.

Discussion: "Arthur Berndtson on Mystical Experience," THE PERSONALIST, XXXII, No. 2 (Spring, 1951), 191-193.

"The Relativity of Nonrelativity: Some Reflections on Firstness," in STUDIES IN THE PHILOSOPHY OF CHARLES SANDERS PEIRCE, ed. by Philip P. Wiener and Frederic H. Young, Cambridge: Harvard University Press, 1952, pp. 215-224.

"Radhakrishnan on Mind, Matter, and God," in THE PHILOSOPHY OF SARVEPALLI RADHAKRISHNAN: The Library of Living Philosophers, VIII, New York: Tudor Publishing Company, 1952, 313-322.

"Tillich's Doctrine of God," No. 7 in THE THEOLOGY OF PAUL TILLICH: The Library of Living Theology, I, ed. by Charles W. Kegley and Robert W. Bretall, New York: The Macmillan Company, 1952, 164-195.

"La Philosophie de la religion aux Etats-Unis," LES ETUDES PHILOSO-PHIQUES, Septième Année, N° 1-2 (Janvier-Juin, 1952), 50-56.

"Time, Death, and Eternal Life," THE JOURNAL OF RELIGION, XXXII, No. 2 (April, 1952), 97-107. (see chapter 10, THE LOGIC OF

PERFECTION AND OTHER ESSAYS IN NEOCLASSICAL METAPHYSICS)
"Politics and the Metaphysics of Freedom," in ENQUÊTE SUR LA LIBERTÉ, Fédération internationale des sociétés de philosophie. Publié avec le concours de l'u.n.e.s.c.o., Hermann & Cie, Editeurs, Paris, 1953, pp. 79-85.

"Noch einmal, das Wissen Gottes," PHILOSOPHISCHES JAHRBUCH, 62, Jahrgang/2, Halbband, Verlag Karl Alber, Freiburg-München (1953), pp. 409-411.

"Spirit as Life Freely Participating in Life," THE BIOSOPHICAL REVIEW, X, No. 2 (1953), 31-32.

"The Monistic Theory of Expression," THE JOURNAL OF PHILOSOPHY, I, No. 14 (July 2, 1953), 425-434.

"The Immortality of the Past: Critique of a Prevalent Misinterpretation," THE REVIEW OF METAPHYSICS, VII, No. 1 (September, 1953), pp. 98-112.

Symposium: "Are Religious Dogmas Cognitive and Meaningful?", THE JOURNAL OF PHILOSOPHY, LI, No. 5 (March 4, 1954), 148-150.

"The Kinds of Theism: A Reply," THE JOURNAL OF RELIGION, XXXIV, No. 2 (April, 1954), 127-131.

"Mind, Matter and Freedom," THE SCIENTIFIC MONTHLY, LXXVIII, No. 5 (May, 1954), 314-320. (see chapter 8, THE LOGIC OF PERFECTION AND OTHER ESSAYS IN NEOCLASSICAL METAPHYSICS)

Review Article: "Whitehead's Philosophy of Reality as Socially-Structured Process." CHICAGO REVIEW, Spring-Summer, 1954. viii, no. 2, pp. 60-77.

"Biology and the Spiritual View of the World: A Comment on Dr. Birch's Paper." THE CHRISTIAN SCHOLAR, September, 1954. xxxvii, no. 3, pp. 408-409.

"Russian Metaphysics: Some Reactions to Zenkovsky's History." THE REVIEW OF METAPHYSICS, September, 1954. viii, no. 1, pp. 61-78.

"Causal Necessities: An Alternative to Hume," THE PHILOSOPHICAL REVIEW, LXIII, No. 4 (October, 1954), 479-499.

"Process as Inclusive Category: A Reply," THE JOURNAL OF PHILOSOPHY, LII, No. 4 (February 17, 1955), 94-102.

Panel Discussion: 1955 Edward Gallahue Seminar in Religion and Psychology at The Menninger Foundation, passim.

"Some Empty Though Important Truths," THE REVIEW OF METAPHYSICS, VIII, No. 4 (June, 1955) 553-568. (see chapter 12, THE LOGIC OF PERFECTION AND OTHER ESSAYS IN NEOCLASSICAL METAPHYSICS)

"The Unity of Man and the Unity of Nature," THE EMORY UNIVERSITY QUARTERLY, XI, No. 3 (October, 1955), 129-141. (*see* chapter 13, THE LOGIC OF PERFECTION AND OTHER ESSAYS IN NEOCLASSICAL METAPHYSICS)

"Some Empty Though Important Truths: A Preface to Metaphysics," in AMERICAN PHILOSOPHERS AT WORK: THE PHILOSOPHIC SCENE IN THE UNITED STATES, ed. by Sidney Hook, New York: Criterion Books, 1956, pp. 225-235. (*see* chapter 12, THE LOGIC OF PERFECTION AND OTHER ESSAYS IN NEOCLASSICAL METAPHYSICS)

"Royce's Mistake—and Achievement," THE JOURNAL OF PHILOSOPHY, LIII, No. 3 (February 2, 1956), 123-130.

Panel Discussion: 1956 Edward Gallahue Seminar in Religion and Psychology at The Menninger Foundation, *passim.*

Colloquium No. 8: "The Idea of Creation," THE REVIEW OF METAPHYSICS, IX, No. 3 (March, 1956), 464-465.

"The Idea of God—Literal or Analogical?" THE CHRISTIAN SCHOLAR, XXIX, No. 2 (June, 1956), 131-136. (*see* chapter 3, THE LOGIC OF PERFECTION AND OTHER ESSAYS IN NEOCLASSICAL METAPHYSICS)

Discussion: "New Propositions and New Truths," THE REVIEW OF METAPHYSICS, IX, No. 4 (June, 1956), 656-661.

"Two Strata of Meaning in Religious Discourse," in Symposium on Philosophy of Religion, THE SOUTHERN PHILOSOPHER, V, No. 3 (October, 1956), 4-7.

"Some Reflections Suggested by H. Wolfson's PHILOSOPHY OF THE CHURCH FATHERS, I, FAITH, TRINITY, INCARNATION," in COLLECTION OF REVIEWS, Southern Society for Philosophy of Religion, J. R. Cresswell, bibliographer, March 9, 1957, pp. 1-10.

"Whitehead and Berdyaev: Is There Tragedy in God?" THE JOURNAL OF RELIGION, XXXVII, No. 2 (April, 1957), 71-84.

"Charles Peirce, Philosopher-Scientist," No. 1 in Charles Sanders Peirce—A Symposium, JOURNAL OF PUBLIC LAW, 7, No. 1 (Spring, 1958), pp. 2-12.

"Discussion: Whitehead on Process: A Reply to Professor Eslick," PHILOSOPHY AND PHENOMENOLOGICAL RESEARCH, XVIII, No. 4 (June, 1958), 514-520.

"Science, Insecurity, and the Abiding Treasure," THE JOURNAL OF RELIGION, XXXVIII, No. 3 (July, 1958), 168-174. (*see* chapter 9, THE LOGIC OF PERFECTION AND OTHER ESSAYS IN NEOCLASSICAL METAPHYSICS)

"Outlines of a Philosophy of Nature," Part I, THE PERSONALIST, XXXIX, No. 3 (Summer, 1958), 329-348.

"Outlines of a Philosophy of Nature," Part II, THE PERSONALIST, XXIX, No. 4 (Autumn, October, 1958), 380-391.

"Freedom Requires Indeterminism and Universal Causality," THE JOURNAL OF PHILOSOPHY, LV, No. 19 (September 11, 1958), 793-811. (see chapter 9, THE LOGIC OF PERFECTION AND OTHER ESSAYS IN NEOCLASSICAL METAPHYSICS)

"Metaphysical Statements as Nonrestrictive and Existential," THE REVIEW OF METAPHYSICS, XII, No. 1 (1958), 35-47.

"The Logical Structure of Givenness," THE PHILOSOPHICAL QUARTERLY, VIII, No. 33 (October, 1958), 307-316.

"The Philosophy of Creative Synthesis," I, in Symposium: Creativity as a Philosophical Category, THE JOURNAL OF PHILOSOPHY, LV, No. 22 (October 23, 1958), 944-953.

"Discussion: The Structure of Metaphysics: A Criticism of Lazerowitz's Theory," PHILOSOPHY AND PHENOMENOLOGICAL RESEARCH, XIX, No. 2 (December, 1958), 226-240.

"Four Unrefuted Forms of the Ontological Argument," THE JOURNAL OF PHILOSOPHICAL STUDIES, XL, No. 1 (January, 1959) (Japanese text, 1-15; English Summary, 1-2 of the Outlines), Published Monthly by the Kyoto Philosophical Society (The Kyoto Tetsugaku-Kai), Kyoto University, Kyoto, Japan.

"A Philosopher's Assessment of Christianity," in RELIGION AND CULTURE: ESSAYS IN HONOR OF PAUL TILLICH, ed. by Walter Leibrecht, New York: Harper, 1959, pp. 167-180.

"John Wisdom on 'Gods': Two Views of the Logic of Theism," DOWNSIDE REVIEW (Bath, England) (Winter, 1958-59), pp. 5-17.

"The Principle of Shared Creativity," Unitarian Symposia No. 6, WHAT CAN RELIGION OFFER MODERN MAN? (April, 1959), pp. 1-8.

"The Philosophy of Creative Synthesis" (reprinted from THE JOURNAL OF PHILOSOPHY, supra.), AMERICANA: A MONTHLY JOURNAL OF HUMANITIES, SOCIAL SCIENCES, AND NATURAL SCIENCES, V, No. 8 (August, 1959), 80-90. (In Japanese)

"Freedom, Individuality, and Beauty in Nature," SNOWY EGRET, XXIV, No. 2 (Autumn, 1960), 5-14.

"Equalitarianism and the Great Inequalities," THE EMORY ALUMNUS, 36, No. 7 (November, 1960), 24-25, 49.

"The Buddhist-Whiteheadian View of the Self and the Religious Traditions," PROCEEDINGS OF THE IXth INTERNATIONAL CON-

GRESS FOR THE HISTORY OF RELIGIONS. Tokyo and Kyoto, 1958, Tokyo, Maruzen, pp. 298-302.

"Whitehead and Contemporary Philosophy," in THE RELEVANCE OF WHITEHEAD: PHILOSOPHICAL ESSAYS IN COMMEMORATION OF THE CENTENARY OF THE BIRTH OF ALFRED NORTH WHITEHEAD, ed. by Ivor Leclerc, London: Allen and Unwin, 1961, pp. 21-43.

"Metaphysics and the Modality of Existential Judgments," *ibid.*, pp. 107-121.

"Hume's Metaphysics and Its Present-Day Influence," THE NEW SCHOLASTICISM, XXXV, No. 2 (April, 1961), 152-171.

"The Social Structure of Experience," PHILOSOPHY, XXXVI, No. 137 (April and July, 1961), 97-111.

"The Structure of Givenness," THE PHILOSOPHICAL FORUM, XVIII (1960-61), 22-39.

"God's Existence: A Conceptual Problem," No. 26 in RELIGIOUS EXPERIENCE AND TRUTH: A SYMPOSIUM, ed. by Sidney Hook, New York: New York University Press, 1961, pp. 211-219.

Discussion: "Professor Hall on Perception," PHILOSOPHY AND PHENOMENOLOGICAL RESEARCH, XXI, No. 4 (June, 1961), 563-571.

"Tillich and the Other Great Tradition," ANGLICAN THEOLOGICAL REVIEW, XLIII, No. 3 (July, 1961), 245-259.

"The Logic of the Ontological Argument," THE JOURNAL OF PHILOSOPHY, LVIII, No. 17 (August 17, 1961), 471-473.

Discussion: "Absolute Objects and Relative Subjects: A Reply," THE REVIEW OF METAPHYSICS, XV, No. 1 (September, 1961), 174-188.

"Man in Nature," No. 6 in EXPERIENCE, EXISTENCE, AND THE GOOD: ESSAYS IN HONOR OF PAUL WEISS, ed. by Irwin C. Lieb, Carbondale: Southern Illinois University Press, 1961, pp. 89-99.

"Whitehead, the Anglo-American Philosopher-Scientist," PROCEEDINGS OF THE AMERICAN CATHOLIC PHILOSOPHICAL ASSOCIATION. The Catholic University of America, 1961, pp. 163-171.

SAINT ANSELM, BASIC WRITINGS: PROSLOGIUM, MONOLOGIUM, GAUNILON'S ON BEHALF OF THE FOOL, CUR DEUS HOMO, translated by S. W. Deane, with an introduction by Charles Hartshorne, Second Edition, Open Court Publishing Company, LaSalle, Illinois, 1962, pp. 1-19.

"The Modern World and a Modern View of God," THE CRANE REVIEW, IV, No. 2 (Winter, 1962), 73-85.

"Religion and Creative Experience," DARSHANA, AN INTERNATIONAL QUARTERLY OF PHILOSOPHY, PSYCHOLOGY, PSYCHICAL RESEARCH,

RELIGION, MYSTICISM AND SOCIOLOGY, II, No. 1 (January, 1962), 47-52.

"What Did Anselm Discover?", UNION SEMINARY QUARTERLY REVIEW, XVII, No. 3 (March, 1962), 213-222.

"La Creatividad Participada" (translated by Sira Jaén), REVISTA DE FILOSOFIA DE LA UNIVERSIDAD DE COSTA RICA, III, No. 11 (January-June, 1962), 237-244.

"Religion and Creative Experience," THE UNITARIAN REGISTER AND THE UNIVERSALIST LEADER, 141, No. 6 (June, 1962), 9-11.

"Mind as Memory and Creative Love," in THEORIES OF THE MIND, ed. by Jordan M. Scher, New York: The Free Press of Glencoe, 1962, pp. 440-463.

Discussion: "How Some Speak and Yet Do Not Speak of God," PHILOSOPHY AND PHENOMENOLOGICAL RESEARCH, XXIII, No. 2 (December, 1962), 274-276.

"Present Prospects for Metaphysics," THE MONIST (Winter, 1963), 188-210.

"Individual Differences and the Ideal of Equality," NEW SOUTH, 18, No. 2 (February, 1963), 3-8.

"Martin Bubers Metaphysik," in MARTIN BUBER, herausgegeben von Schilpp und Friedman, Stuttgart: Kohlammer Verlag, 1963, pp. 42-61.

"Further Fascination of the Ontological Argument: Replies to Richardson," I, UNION SEMINARY QUARTERLY REVIEW, XVIII, No. 3, Part I (March, 1963), 244-245.

"Whitehead's Novel Intuition," in ALFRED NORTH WHITEHEAD: ESSAYS ON HIS PHILOSOPHY, edited by George L. Kline. Englewood Cliffs, New Jersey, Prentice-Hall, 1963, pp. 18-26.

"Sensation in Psychology and Philosophy," THE SOUTHERN JOURNAL OF PHILOSOPHY, I, No. 2 (Summer, 1963), 3-14.

"Rationale of the Ontological Proof," THEOLOGY TODAY, XX, No. 2 (July, 1963), 278-283.

"Whitehead's Conception of God" and "Whitehead's Theory of Prehension," ACTAS—SEGUNDA CONGRESO EXTRAORDINARIO INTERAMERICANO DE FILOSOFIA, 22-26 Julio, 1961. August 1963 (dated 1962), Imprenta Nacional, San Jose, Costa Rica, pp. 163-170.

Communication: "Finite or Finite-Infinite?", PHILOSOPHY AND PHENOMENOLOGICAL RESEARCH, XXIV, No. 1 (September, 1963), 149.

"Real Possibility," JOURNAL OF PHILOSOPHY, LX, No. 21 (October 19, 1963), 593-605.

"Man's Fragmentariness," WESLEYAN STUDIES IN RELIGION, 1963–1964, 56, No. 6, 17-28.

"Abstract and Concrete in God: A Reply," THE REVIEW OF METAPHYSICS, XVII, No. 2 (December, 1963), 289-295.

"Santayana's Defiant Eclecticism," THE JOURNAL OF PHILOSOPHY, LXI, No. 1 (January 2, 1964), 35-44.

Discussion: "What the Ontological Proof Does Not Do," THE REVIEW OF METAPHYSICS, XVII, No. 4 (June, 1964), 608-609.

"From Colonial Beginnings to Philosophical Greatness," THE MONIST, XLVIII, No. 3 (July, 1964), 317-331.

Comments and Criticism: "Deliberation and Excluded Middle," THE JOURNAL OF PHILOSOPHY, LXI, No. 16 (September 3, 1964), 476-477.

"Thinking about Thinking Machines," THE TEXAS QUARTERLY, VII, No. 1 (Spring, 1964), 131-140.

Replies to "Interrogation of Charles Hartshorne, conducted by William Alston: I. PROCESS, II. FEELING, III. MORALITY, IV. GOD, V. METHOD," pp. 321-354. Also questions to John Wild, 158-160; Brand Blanshard, 205; Paul Tillich, 374-375. PHILOSOPHICAL INTERROGATIONS: INTERROGATIONS OF MARTIN BUBER, JOHN WILD, JEAN WAHL, BRAND BLANSHARD, PAUL WEISS, CHARLES HARTSHORNE, PAUL TILLICH, edited, with an introduction, by Sydney and Beatrice Rome, New York, Holt, Rinehart and Winston, 1964.

"Is God's Existence a State of Affairs?" In FAITH AND THE PHILOSOPHERS, edited by John Hick. New York, St. Martin's Press, Inc., 1964, pp. 26-33.

"El valor como disfrute del contraste y la teoria acumulativa del proceso." DIANOIA, ANUARIO DE FILOSOFIA, 1964, 10, pp. 182-194.

"Charles Peirce's 'One Contribution to Philosophy' and His Most Serious Mistake." No. 26 in STUDIES IN THE PHILOSOPHY OF CHARLES SANDERS PEIRCE. Second Series. Edited by Edward G. Moore and Richard S. Robin. Amherst, The University of Massachusetts Press, 1964. Pp. 455-474.

"Negative Facts and the Analogical Inference to 'Other Mind'," No. 21 in DR. S. RADHAKRISHNAN SOUVENIR VOLUME. Edited by Prof. J. P. Atreya et al. Moradabad (India), DARSHANA INTERNATIONAL, 1964. Pp. 147-152.

"The Necessarily Existent." (From MAN'S VISION OF GOD.) No. 11 in THE ONTOLOGICAL ARGUMENT. Edited by Alvin Plantinga. New York, Anchor Books, Doubleday, 1965. Pp. 123-135.

"The Idea of a Worshipful Being." THE SOUTHERN JOURNAL OF

PHILOSOPHY, 1965. [dated Winter, 1964], 2, 4, pp. 165-167.
"The Meaning of 'Is Going To Be,'" MIND: A QUARTERLY REVIEW
OF PSYCHOLOGY AND PHILOSOPHY, LXXIV, No. 293 (January,
1965), 46-58.
"The Theistic Proofs." UNION SEMINARY QUARTERLY REVIEW, Jan-
uary, 1965, XX, no. 2, pp. 115-129.
"Abstract and Concrete Approaches to Deity." UNION SEMINARY
QUARTERLY REVIEW, March, 1965, XX, no. 3, pp. 265-270.
"A Metaphysics of Individualism." In INNOCENCE AND POWER.
Edited by Gordon Mills. Austin, University of Texas Press,
1965. Pp. 131-146.
"Determinism, Memory, and the Metaphysics of Becoming." THE
PACIFIC PHILOSOPHY FORUM, May, 1966 [sic], iv. no. 4, pp. 81-85.
"God as the Supreme Relativity." JAPANESE RELIGIONS, December
1964 [appeared May, 1965], iv, no. 1, pp. 30-33.
"The Social Theory of Feelings," THE SOUTHERN JOURNAL OF PHI-
LOSOPHY, III, No. 2 (Summer, 1965), 87-93.
"The Development of Process Philosophy." Introduction to PHI-
LOSOPHERS OF PROGRESS, edited by Douglas Browning, New
York, Random House, 1965. Pp. v-xii.
"Religious Aspects of Necessity and Contingency." In GREAT ISSUES
CONCERNING THEISM, edited by Charles H. Monson, Jr., Salt
Lake City, University of Utah Press, 1965. Pp. 147-164.
"Criteria for Ideas of God." In INSIGHT AND VISION: ESSAYS IN
PHILOSOPHY IN HONOR OF RADOSLAV ANDREA TSANOFF, edited
by Konstantin Kolenda. Rice University Studies, vol. 51, no.
4, Fall, 1965. Pp. 85-95. Also in INSIGHT AND VISION: ESSAYS IN
PHILOSOPHY IN HONOR OF RADOSLAV ANDREA TSANOFF, edited
by Konstantin Kolenda. San Antonio, Principia Press of Trinity
University, 1966. Pp. 85-95.
"A New Look at the Problem of Evil." In CURRENT PHILOSOPHICAL
ISSUES: ESSAYS IN HONOR OF CURT JOHN DUCASSE, compiled and
edited by Frederick C. Dommeyer, Ph.D., Springfield, Illinois,
Charles C. Thomas, 1966. Pp. 201-212.
"Idealism and Our Experience of Nature." In PHILOSOPHY, RELIGION
AND THE COMING WORLD CIVILIZATION, edited by Leroy S.
Rouner. The Hague, Martinus Nijhoff, 1966. Pp. 70-80.
"Tillich and the Nontheological Meaning of Theological Terms,"
RELIGION IN LIFE, XXXV, No. 5 (Winter, 1966), 674-685.
"Some Reflections on Metaphysics and Language." FOUNDATIONS
OF LANGUAGE: INTERNATIONAL JOURNAL OF LANGUAGE AND
PHILOSOPHY, February, 1966. 2, no. 1, pp. 20-32.

"Is the Denial of Existence Ever Contradictory?" THE JOURNAL OF PHILOSOPHY, February 17, 1966. LXIII, no. 4, pp. 85-93.

"The Idea of Creativity in American Philosophy." THE JOURNAL OF KARNATAK UNIVERSITY [India]: SOCIAL SCIENCES, 1966. II, pp. 1-13.

"Religion in Process Philosophy." In RELIGION IN PHILOSOPHICAL AND CULTURAL PERSPECTIVE, edited by J. Clayton Feaver and William Horosz. Princeton, D. Van Nostrand, 1967. Pp. 246-268.

"Royce and the Collapse of Idealism," REVUE INTERNATIONALE DE PHILOSOPHIE, 23, No. 79-80 (1967, Fasc. 1-2), 46-59.

"Science, Art, and Religion as Sources of Happiness." JAPAN-AMERICAN FORUM, March, 1967. XIII, no. 3, pp. 47-66. [In Japanese. Tr. M. Noda.]

"Pantheism." THE ENCYCLOPAEDIA BRITANNICA (1967), pp. 233-234.

3. Book Reviews

Martin Heidegger, *Sein und Zeit* and Oskar Becker, *Mathematische Existenz*, from *Jahrbuch für Philosophie und phänomenologische Forschung*. Max Niemeyer, Halle, 1927; THE PHILOSOPHICAL REVIEW 38, No. 3 (May, 1929), 284-293.

Etienne Souriau, *L'Avenir de l'esthétique: Essay sur l'objet d'une science naissante*. Félix Alcan, Paris, 1929; INTERNATIONAL JOURNAL OF ETHICS 40, No. 1 (Oct., 1929), 132-133.

André Lalande, *Les Illusions Evolutionnistes*. Félix Alcan, Paris, 1930; THE INTERNATIONAL JOURNAL OF ETHICS 43, No. 1 (Oct., 1932), 94-97.

G. Watts Cunningham, *The Idealistic Argument in Recent British and American Philosophy*. Century, N.Y., 1933; THE INTERNATIONAL JOURNAL OF ETHICS 43, No. 4 (July, 1933), 447-449.

R. G. Collingwood, *An Essay on Philosophical Method*. Clarendon, Oxford, 1933; THE INTERNATIONAL JOURNAL OF ETHICS 44, No. 3 (Apr., 1934), 357-358.

Ernest W. Barnes, *Scientific Theory and Religion*. Macmillan, N.Y., 1933, J. E. Turner, *Essentials in the Development of Religion, A Philosophic and Psychological Study*. Macmillan, N. Y., 1934, T. V. Seshagiro Row, *New Light on Fundamental Problems*. University of Madras, India, 1932; THE INTERNATIONAL JOURNAL OF ETHICS 44, No. 4 (July, 1934), 465-471.

Gerhard Kraenzlin, *Max Schelers Phaenomenologische Systematik: mit einer Monographischen Bibliographie Max Scheler*. S. Hirzel, Leipzig, 1934, Adolph Sternberger, *Der verstandene*

Tod: eine Untersuchung zu Martin Heideggers Existenzial-ontologie. S. Hirzel, Leipzig, 1934; THE INTERNATIONAL JOURNAL OF ETHICS 44, No. 4 (July, 1934), 478-480.

Louis Vialle, *Le Désir du Néant: Contribution à la psychologie du divertissement*. Félix Alcan, Paris, 1933; THE INTERNATIONAL JOURNAL OF ETHICS 45, No. 1 (Oct., 1934), 116-117.

William Pepperell Montague, *The Chances of Surviving Death*. Harvard University Press, Cambridge, 1934; THE INTERNATIONAL JOURNAL OF ETHICS 45, No. 1 (Oct., 1934), 120-121.

John Nibb, *Christianity and Internationalism*. Elliot Stock, London, 1934, Georges Lakhovsky, *Le Racisme et l'orchestre universelle*. Félix Alcan, Paris; THE INTERNATIONAL JOURNAL OF ETHICS 45, No. 1 (Oct., 1934), 121-122.

D. Draghicesco, *Vérité et révélation*, Vol. I. Félix Alcan, Paris, 1934; THE INTERNATIONAL JOURNAL OF ETHICS 45, No. 2 (Jan., 1935), 248-249.

Adolphe Ferrière, *Der Primat des Geistes als Grundlage einer aufbauenden Erziehung*, tr. Emmi Hirschberg. Julius Beltz, Berlin, n.d.; THE INTERNATIONAL JOURNAL OF ETHICS 45, No. 2 (Jan., 1935), 250.

Henry C. Simons, *A Positive Program for Laissez Faire: Some Proposals for a Liberal Economic Policy*. University of Chicago Press, Chicago, 1935; THE CHRISTIAN CENTURY 52, No. 23 (June 5, 1935), 761-762.

John Wisdom, *Problems of Mind and Matter*. University Press, Cambridge, 1934, Thomas Whittaker, *Reason: A Philosophical Essay with Historical Illustrations: Comte, Mill, Schopenhauer, Vico, Spinoza*. University Press, Cambridge, 1934, Julius W. Friend and James Feibleman, *Science and the Spirit of Man: A New Ordering of Experience*. London, Allen and Unwin, 1933; THE INTERNATIONAL JOURNAL OF ETHICS 45, No. 4 (July, 1935), 461-465.

Gajanan Wasudeo Kaveeshwar, *The Metaphysics of Berkeley Critically Examined in the Light of Modern Philosophy*. A. Kaveeshwar, Mandleshwar, India, 1933; THE INTERNATIONAL JOURNAL OF ETHICS 45, No. 4 (July, 1935), 494.

D. Draghicesco, *Vérité et révélation*, Vol. II: *Vers une nouvelle idée de Dieu*. Félix Alcan, Paris, 1934; *The International Journal of Ethics* 47, No. 1 (Oct., 1936), 133-135.

André Cresson, *La Représentation: essai philosophique*. Boivin et cie., Paris, 1936; THE PHILOSOPHICAL REVIEW 47, No. 1 (Jan., 1938), 90-91.

Wilhelm Keller, *Der Sinnbegriff als Kategorie der Geisteswissen-schaften.* Ernst Reinhardt, Munich, 1937; THE PHILOSOPHICAL REVIEW 48, No. 1 (Jan., 1939), 95.

G. P. Adams, W. R. Dennes, J. Loewenberg, D. S. Mackay, P. Marhenke, S. C. Pepper, E. W. Strong, *Knowledge and Society: A Philosophical Approach to Modern Civilization.* Appleton-Century, N. Y., 1938; THE CHRISTIAN CENTURY 55, No. 30 (July 27, 1938), 917.

Rasvihari Das, *The Philosophy of Whitehead.* James Clarke, London, n.d.; THE PHILOSOPHICAL REVIEW 48, No. 2 (Mar., 1939), 230-231.

Alfred North Whitehead, *Modes of Thought.* Macmillan, New York, 1938; THE REVIEW OF RELIGION 3, No. 4 (May, 1939), 494-496.

James Bissett Pratt, *Naturalism.* Yale University Press, New Haven, 1939; THE JOURNAL OF RELIGION 19, No. 3 (July, 1939), 234-235.

Ralph Barton Perry, *In the Spirit of William James.* Yale University Press, New Haven, 1938; THE JOURNAL OF RELIGION 19, No. 3 (July, 1939), 247-248.

Jacques Maritain, *The Degrees of Knowledge.* Scribner's, New York, 1938; THE JOURNAL OF RELIGION 19, No. 3 (July, 1939), 267-269.

A. Campbell Garnett, *Reality and Value: An Introduction to Metaphysics and an Essay on the Theory of Value.* Yale University Press, New Haven, 1937; THE SCROLL 37, No. 3 (Nov., 1939), 93-95.

Justus Buchler, *Charles Peirce's Empiricism.* Harcourt Brace, New York, 1939; ETHICS 50, No. 2 (Jan., 1940), 248.

Josef Maier, *On Hegel's Critique of Kant.* Columbia University Press, New York, 1939; THE JOURNAL OF RELIGION 20, No. 1 (Jan., 1940), 106.

Paul Arthur Schilpp, ed., *The Philosophy of John Dewey.* Northwestern University, Evanston, 1939; THE CHRISTIAN CENTURY 42, No. 10 (Mar. 6, 1940), 313-315.

Irwin Edman, *Arts and the Man.* Norton, N. Y., 1939; ETHICS 50, No. 3 (Apr., 1940), 369-370.

Arthur Hazard Dakin, *Man the Measure: An Essay on Humanism as Religion.* Princeton University Press, Princeton, 1939, Archibald Allan Bowman, *A Sacramental Universe: Being a Study in the Metaphysics of Experience*, Princeton University Press, Princeton, 1939; ETHICS 50, No. 3 (April, 1940), 363-366.

Milton Karl Munitz, *The Moral Philosophy of Santayana.* Columbia University Press, New York, 1939; THE JOURNAL OF RELIGION 20, No. 2 (Apr., 1940), 196-198.

Charles M. Perry, *Toward a Dimensional Realism*. University of Oklahoma Press, Norman, 1939; THE JOURNAL OF RELIGION 20, No. 2 (Apr., 1940), 214.

Theodore Meyer Greene, *The Arts and the Art of Criticism*. Princeton University Press, Princeton, 1940; ETHICS 51, No. 1 (Oct., 1940), 116-117.

Frederick J. E. Woodbridge, *An Essay on Nature*. Columbia University Press, New York, 1940; ETHICS 51, No. 4 (July, 1941), 488-490.

DeWitt H. Parker, *Experience and Substance*. University of Michigan Press, Ann Arbor, 1941; THE CHRISTIAN CENTURY 48, No. 27 (July 2, 1941), 864.

Ledger Wood, *The Analysis of Knowledge*. Princeton University Press, Princeton, 1941; PHILOSOPHY AND PHENOMENOLOGICAL RESEARCH 2, No. 1 (Sept., 1941), 104-108.

Justus Buchler, ed., *The Philosophy of Peirce: Selected Writings*. Harcourt Brace, New York, 1940; THE PHILOSOPHICAL REVIEW 51, No. 1 (Jan., 1942), 92.

Etienne Gilson, *God and Philosophy*. Yale University Press, New Haven, 1941; THE JOURNAL OF RELIGION 22, No. 2 (April, 1942), 221-224.

Paul Arthur Schilpp, ed., *The Philosophy of Alfred North Whitehead*. Northwestern University, Evanston, 1941; RELIGION IN LIFE 11 No. 3 (Summer, 1942), 469-470.

Paul Arthur Schilpp, ed., *The Philosophy of Alfred North Whitehead*. Northwestern University, Evanston, 1941; THOUGHT: FORDHAM UNIVERSITY QUARTERLY 17, No. 66 (Sept., 1942), 545-547.

DeWitt H. Parker, *Experience and Substance*. The University of Michigan Press, Ann Arbor, 1941; THE PHILOSOPHICAL REVIEW 51, No. 5 (Sept., 1942), 523-526.

Stephen C. Pepper, *World Hypotheses: A Study in Evidence*. University of California Press, Berkeley, 1942; ETHICS 53, No. 1 (Oct., 1942), 73-75.

John Blyth, *Whitehead's Theory of Knowledge*. Brown University, Providence, 1941; PHILOSOPHY AND PHENOMENOLOGICAL RESEARCH 3, No. 3 (Mar., 1943), 372-375.

Lewis Edwin Hahn, *A Contextualist Theory of Perception*. University of California Press, Berkeley, 1942; ETHICS 53, No. 4 (Apr., 1943), 233.

Stephen Lee Ely, *The Religious Availability of Whitehead's God: A Critical Analysis.* The University of Wisconsin Press, Madison, 1942; THE JOURNAL OF LIBERAL RELIGION 5, No. 1 (Summer, 1943), 55.

A. Campbell Garnett, *A Realistic Philosophy of Religion.* Willett, Clark, Chicago, 1942; THE JOURNAL OF RELIGION 23, No. 3 (July, 1943), 70-71.

Jacques Maritain, *Saint Thomas and the Problem of Evil.* Marquette University Press, Milwaukee, 1942, *The Maritain Volume of the Thomist,* Sheed & Ward, New York, 1943; ETHICS 54, No. 1 (Oct., 1943), 53-57.

A. Campbell Garnett, *A Realistic Philosophy of Religion.* Willett, Clark, Chicago, 1942; ETHICS 54, No. 1 (Oct., 1943), 62-63.

K. R. Sreenivasa Iyengar, *The Metaphysics of Value, Vol. I: General Principles and the Kingdom of Values.* University of Mysore, Mysore, 1942; ETHICS 54, No. 3 (Apr., 1944), 230-231.

John Elof Boodin, *Religion of Tomorrow.* Philosophical Library, New York, 1943; ETHICS 54, No. 3 (Apr., 1944), 233-234.

Werner Jaeger, *Humanism and Theology.* Marquette University Press, Milwaukee, 1943; THE JOURNAL OF RELIGION 24, No. 5 (July, 1944), 230.

Henry Alonzo Myers, *The Spinoza-Hegel Paradox: A Study of the Choice between Traditional Idealism and Systematic Pluralism.* Cornell University Press, Ithaca, 1944; ETHICS 55, No. 1 (Oct., 1944), 71-72.

Adhar Chandra Das, *Negative Fact, Negation, and Truth.* Calcutta University Press, Calcutta, 1942; ETHICS 55, No. 1 (Oct., 1944), 77.

Francis X. Meehan, *Efficient Causality in Aristotle and St. Thomas.* Catholic University Press, Washington, 1940; THE JOURNAL OF RELIGION 25, No. 1 (Jan., 1945), 25-32.

Rudolf Jordan, *Homo Sapiens Socialis:* Principles of the Philosophy of Responsibility. Central News Agency, South Africa, 1944; ETHICS 55, No. 4 (July, 1945), 312-313.

Jacques Maritain, *The Dream of Descartes.* Philosophical Library, New York, 1944; ETHICS 55, No. 4 (July, 1945), 321.

Vladimir Soloviev's Lectures on Godmanhood. Intro. by Peter Zouboff. International University Press, New York, 1944; ETHICS 55, No. 4 (July, 1945), 322.

K. F. Reinhardt, *A Realistic Philosophy: The Perennial Principles of Thought and Action in a Changing World.* Bruce, Milwaukee, 1944; THE PHILOSOPHICAL REVIEW 54, No. 5 (Sept., 1945), 521-522.

Paul Arthur Schilpp, ed., *The Philosophy of Bertrand Russell.* Northwestern University, Evanston, 1944; THE JOURNAL OF RELIGION 25, No. 4 (Oct., 1945), 280-284.

Erich Frank, *Philosophical Understanding and Religious Truth.* Oxford University Press, London, 1945; THE REVIEW OF RELIGION 10, No. 2 (Jan., 1946), 182-189.

William Ernest Hocking, *Science and the Idea of God.* The University of Carolina Press, Chapel Hill, 1944; PHILOSOPHY AND PHENOMENOLOGICAL RESEARCH 6, No. 3 (March, 1946), 453-457.

Henri Bergson, *The Creative Mind,* tr. Mabelle L. Andison. Philosophical Library, New York, 1946; THE JOURNAL OF RELIGION 27, No. 1 (Jan., 1947), 64-65.

José Ortega y Gasset, *Concord and Liberty.* Norton, New York, 1946; THE CHRISTIAN CENTURY 64, No. 7 (Feb. 12, 1947), 207.

Walter Lowrie, ed. and trans., *Religion of a Scientist: Selections from Gustav Theodor Fechner.* Pantheon, New York, 1946; THE JOURNAL OF RELIGION 27, No. 2 (Apr., 1947), 126-128.

Nels F. S. Ferré, *Faith and Reason.* Harper, New York, 1946; THE REVIEW OF RELIGION 11, No. 4 (May, 1947), 409-413.

Martin Foss, *The Idea of Perfection in the Western World.* Princeton University Press, Princeton, 1946; THE JOURNAL OF MODERN HISTORY 19, No. 2 (June, 1947), 15.

Henry N. Wieman, Arthur E. Murphy, Gardner Williams, Jay William Hudson, M. C. Otto, James Bissett Pratt, Roy Wood Sellars, *Religious Liberals Reply.* The Beacon Press, Boston, 1947; THE CHRISTIAN REGISTER 126, No. 9 (Oct., 1947), 412-413.

A. H. Johnson, compiler, *The Wit and Wisdom of Whitehead.* The Beacon Press, Boston, 1947; THE CHRISTIAN REGISTER 126, No. 10 (Nov., 1947), 446.

Paul Weiss, *Nature and Man.* Henry Holt, New York, 1947; ETHICS 58, No. 2 (Jan., 1948), 143-144.

A. Campbell Garnett, *God in Us: A Liberal Christian Philosophy of Religion for the General Reader.* Willett, Clark, Chicago, 1945; ETHICS 58, No. 2 (Jan., 1948), 151.

Jean Wahl, *The Philosopher's Way.* Oxford University Press, New York, 1948; THE PHILOSOPHICAL REVIEW 57, No. 5 (Sept., 1948), 509-511.

Otis Lee, *Existence and Inquiry.* The University of Chicago Press,

Chicago, 1949; THE REVIEW OF METAPHYSICS 3, No. 1 (Sept., 1949), 107-114.

Kelvin van Nuys, *Science and Cosmic Purpose.* Harper, New York, 1949; THE REVIEW OF RELIGION 16, Nos. 1-2 (Nov., 1951), 79-84.

Georg Siegmund, *Naturordnung als Quelle der Gotteserkenntnis: Neubegründung des teologischen Gottesbeweises.* Herder, Freiburg, 1950; PHILOSOPHY AND PHENOMENOLOGICAL RESEARCH 12, No. 4 (June, 1952), 584-585.

John Wisdom, *Philosophy and Psycho-Analysis.* Philosophical Library, New York, 1953; ETHICS 63, No. 4 (July, 1953), 317-318.

Risieri Frondizi, *The Nature of the Self: A Functional Interpretation.* Yale University Press, New Haven, 1953; PHILOSOPHY AND PHENOMENOLOGICAL RESEARCH 14, No. 3 (March, 1954), 419-420.

Alfred North Whitehead: *An Anthology.* Selected by F. S. C. Northrop and Mason Gross. Macmillan, New York, 1953; CHICAGO REVIEW 8, No. 2 (Spring-Summer, 1954), 60-77.

F. W. Eggleston, *Reflections of an Australian Liberal.* F. W. Cheshire, Melbourne, 1953; ETHICS 64, No. 4 (July, 1954), 332.

J. Defever, S. J., *La Preuve réelle de Dieu: étude critique.* Desclée de Brouwer, Paris, 1953; PHILOSOPHY AND PHENOMENOLOGICAL RESEARCH 15, No. 2 (Dec., 1954), 285-286.

Brand Blanshard, *The Nature of Thought.* Allen & Unwin, London, 1948; PHILOSOPHISCHE RUNDSCHAU 3, ½ (1955), 119-120.

Eranos (Various Authors), *Spirit and Nature. Papers from the Eranos Yearbooks,* Vol. I. Pantheon, New York, 1954; *The Journal of Religion* 35, No. 2 (Apr., 1955), 106-107.

Wilmon Henry Sheldon, *God and Polarity: A Synthesis of Philosophies.* Yale University Press, New Haven, 1954; THE PHILOSOPHICAL REVIEW 64, No. 2 (Apr., 1955), 312-316.

Robert Leet Patterson, *Irrationalism and Rationalism in Religion.* Duke University Press, Durham, 1954; THE REVIEW OF RELIGION 20, Nos. 3-4 (March, 1956), 211-213.

Harry Austryn Wolfson, *The Philosophy of the Church Fathers, Vol. I, Faith, Trinity, Incarnation.* Harvard University Press, Cambridge, 1956; *Collection of Reviews,* Southern Society for Philosophy of Religion, March 9, 1957, 1-10.

William Ernest Hocking, *The Coming World Civilization.* Harper,

New York, 1956; THE CHICAGO THEOLOGICAL SEMINARY REGISTER
47, No. 5 (May, 1957), 21-22.

William Ernest Hocking, *The Coming World Civilization*. Harper,
New York, 1956; PHILOSOPHY AND PHENOMENOLOGICAL RE-
SEARCH 17, No. 4 (June, 1957), 562-563.

Gerda Walter, *Phänomenologie der Mystik*. Walter-Verlag, Olten
und Freiburg im Breisgau, 1955; PHILOSOPHY AND PHENOME-
NOLOGICAL RESEARCH 18, No. 1 (Sept., 1957), 140-141.

R. S. Srivastava, *Contemporary Indian Philosophy*. M. R. M. Lal,
Delhi, 1965; RESEARCH JOURNAL OF PHILOSOPHY, Ranchi University, India 1, No. 1 (Sept., 1966), 110-111.

B. Ornithology

"First Encounter with Hawaiian Songbirds," ELEPAIO (Hawaii),
XII, No. 12 (June, 1952), 76-78.

"A Foreigner's Impression of the Lyrebird's Singing," THE VIC-
TORIAN NATURALIST (Australia), LXIX, No. 5 (September,
1952), 73-74.

"Musical Values in Australian Bird Songs," THE EMU (Australia),
LIII, Part 2 (June, 1953), 109-128.

"The Monotony Threshold in Singing Birds," THE AUK (U.S.A.),
LXXIII (April, 1956), 176-192.

"The Phenomenon of Bird Song," THE EMORY UNIVERSITY QUAR-
TERLY (U.S.A.), XII, No. 3 (October, 1956), 139-147.

"Some Biological Principles Applicable to Song-Behavior," THE
WILSON BULLETIN (U.S.A.), LXX, No. 1 (March, 1958), 41-56.

"The Relation of Bird Song to Music," IBIS (Great Britain), C,
No. 3 (1958), 421-445.

"Freedom, Individuality, and Beauty in Nature," SNOWY EGRET
(Shorter Apts., Rome, Ga.), XXIV, No. 2 (Autumn, 1960).

Review of A TREASURY OF NEW ZEALAND BIRD SONG: AN ALBUM OF
THREE RECORDS, THE WILSON BULLETIN, 72 No. 4 (December
14, 1960), 421-422.

"Sketch of a Theory of Imitative Singing," THE ORIOLE, XXVI, No. 2
(June, 1961), 23-27.

2—Recently Published Works Treating Hartshorne's Thought

A. Book

Díaz Blaitry, Tobias, LA IDEA DE DIOS EN CHARLES HARTSHORNE.
Panama: University of Panama, 1967.

B. Chapters in Books

Peters, Eugene H., THE CREATIVE ADVANCE, AN INTRODUCTION TO PROCESS PHILOSOPHY AS A CONTEXT FOR CHRISTIAN FAITH. With a comment by Charles Hartshorne, St. Louis: The Bethany Press, 1966. (*See* especially Chapters VI and VII.)

Reese, William L. and Eugene Freeman, editors, PROCESS AND DIVINITY, THE HARTSHORNE FESTSCHRIFT, Philosophical Essays presented to Charles Hartshorne. LaSalle, Illinois: Open Court Publishing Co., 1964. (*See especially* No. 25. A. Boyce Gibson: "The Two Strands in Natural Theology," pp. 471-492; No. 26. Schubert M. Ogden: "Bultmann's Demythologizing and Hartshorne's 'Dipolar Theism,' " pp. 493-513; No. 27. J. N. Findlay: "Reflections on Necessary Existence," pp. 515-527; Howard L. Parsons: "Religious Naturalism and the Philosophy of Charles Hartshorne," pp. 533-560.

Rome, Sydney and Beatrice, editors, PHILOSOPHICAL INTERROGATIONS. New York: Holt, Rinehart and Winston, 1963. (*See* "Interrogation of Charles Hartshorne Conducted by William Alston," pp. 319-354.)

C. Articles

Brown, Delwin, "Recent Process Theology," THE JOURNAL OF THE AMERICAN ACADEMY OF RELIGION, XXXV, No. 1 (March, 1967), 28-41.

Nelson, John O., "Modal Logic and the Ontological Proof of God's Existence," THE REVIEW OF METAPHYSICS, XVII, 2 (December, 1963), 235-242.

Ogden, Schubert M., "Theology and Philosophy: A New Phase of the Discussion," THE JOURNAL OF RELIGION, XLIV, 1 (January, 1964), 1-16.

Ogletree, Thomas W., "A Christological Assessment of Dipolar Theism," THE JOURNAL OF RELIGION, LXVII, 2 (April, 1967), 87-99.

Purtill, R. L., "Hartshorne's Modal Proof," THE JOURNAL OF PHILOSOPHY, LXIII, No. 13 (June 23, 1966).

Rhodes, O. Thompson, "Your God Is Too Big," JOURNAL OF THE AMERICAN ACADEMY OF RELIGION, XXXV, No. 1 (March, 1967), 42-49.

3—General Bibliography

Books

Altizer, Thomas J. J. THE GOSPEL OF CHRISTIAN ATHEISM. Philadelphia: Westminster Press, 1966.

———, ORIENTAL MYSTICISM AND BIBLICAL ESCHATOLOGY. Philadelphia: Westminster Press, 1961.

Anselm, St. BASIC WRITINGS: PROSLOGIUM, MONOLOGIUM, GAUNILON'S ON BEHALF OF THE FOOL, CUR DEUS HOMO. Translated by S. W. Deane, with an introduction by Charles Hartshorne, 2nd edition, LaSalle, Illinois: Open Court Publishing Company, 1962.

Aristotle, WORKS. Edited and translated by W. D. Ross and J. M. Smith, Oxford, Clarendon Press, 11 volumes.

Baldwin, James Mark (ed.). DICTIONARY OF PHILOSOPHY AND PSYCHOLOGY. Gloucester, Massachusetts: Peter Smith, II, 1960.

Barth, Karl. ANSELM: FIDES QUAERENS INTELLECTUM (FAITH IN SEARCH OF UNDERSTANDING). Translated by Ira W. Robertson, Richmond, Virginia, John Knox Press, 1962.

Berdyaev, Nicolas. THE DESTINY OF MAN. New York: Harper and Brothers, 1960.

Berkeley, George. THE WORKS OF GEORGE BERKELEY. Edited by Alexander Campbell Fraser, Oxford, England: Clarendon Press, 4 volumes, 1901.

Boler, John F. CHARLES PEIRCE AND SCHOLASTIC REALISM: A STUDY OF PEIRCE'S RELATION TO JOHN DUNS SCOTUS. Seattle: University of Washington Press, 1963.

Bonhoeffer, Dietrich. THE COMMUNION OF THE SAINTS: A DOGMATIC INQUIRY INTO THE SOCIOLOGY OF THE CHURCH. Translated by R. Gregor Smith, New York: Harper & Row, 1964.

Brunner, Rudolf. PHILOSOPHY OF RELIGION. Translated by A. J. D. Farrer and Bertram Lee Woolf, London: James Clarke and Company, 1958.

Buren, Paul van. THE SECULAR MEANING OF THE GOSPEL. New York: The Macmillan Company, 1963.

Buri, Fritz. CHRISTIAN FAITH IN OUR TIME. Translated by Edward Allen Kent, New York: The Macmillan Company, 1966.

Carnap, R. MEANING AND NECESSITY. Chicago: University of Chicago Press, 1947.

Church, A. "A Formulation of the Logic of Sense and Denotation," in STRUCTURE, METHOD, AND MEANING: ESSAYS IN HONOR OF

HENRY M. SHEFFER. Edited by P. Henle, New York: Liberal Arts Press, 1951.

Cobb, John B., Jr. A CHRISTIAN NATURAL THEOLOGY, BASED ON THE THOUGHT OF ALFRED NORTH WHITEHEAD. Philadelphia: Westminster Press, 1965.

Copleston, Frederick. A HISTORY OF PHILOSOPHY. Westminster, Maryland: The Newman Press, 7 volumes, 1946-1963.

Cusa, Nicolai de. DE VENATIONE SAPIENTIAE. Edited by Paulus Wilpert, Verlag von Felix Meiner, Hamburg, 1964.

Descartes, René. OEUVRES. Edited by C. Adam and P. Tannery, Paris, 13 volumes, 1897-1913.

Dostoevski, Fyodor. THE BROTHERS KARAMAZOV. Translated by David Magarshack, Baltimore, Maryland: Penguin Books, 2 volumes, 1958.

Emmet, Dorothy M. WHITEHEAD'S PHILOSOPHY OF ORGANISM. London: Macmillan and Company, 1932.

Farber, Marvin (ed.). PHILOSOPHICAL ESSAYS IN MEMORY OF EDMUND HUSSERL. Cambridge, Massachusetts: Harvard University Press, 1940.

Farley, Edward, THE TRANSCENDENCE OF GOD, A STUDY IN CONTEMPORARY PHILOSOPHICAL THEOLOGY. Philadelphia: The Westminster Press, 1960.

Ferm, Vergilius (ed.). AN ENCYCLOPEDIA OF RELIGION. New York: The Philosophical Library, 1945.

Fjellmann, Carl. PROCESS THEOLOGY. Doctoral Dissertation, Madison, New Jersey: Drew University, 1955.

Fletcher, Joseph. SITUATION ETHICS: THE NEW MORALITY. Philadelphia: Westminster Press, 1966.

Gilson, Étienne. HISTORY OF CHRISTIAN PHILOSOPHY IN THE MIDDLE AGES. New York: Mary S. Rosenburg, 1945.

Gollwitzer, Helmut. THE EXISTENCE OF GOD AS CONFESSED BY FAITH. Translated by James W. Leitch, Philadelphia: Westminster Press, 1965.

Hamilton, William, and Thomas J. J. Altizer. RADICAL THEOLOGY AND THE DEATH OF GOD. New York and Indianapolis: The Bobbs-Merrill Company, 1966.

Harvey, Van A. THE HISTORIAN AND THE BELIEVER: THE MORALITY OF HISTORICAL KNOWLEDGE AND CHRISTIAN BELIEF. New York: The Macmillan Company, 1966.

Heidegger, Martin. BEING AND TIME. Translated by John Macquarrie and Edward Robinson, New York: Harper and Brothers, 1962.

———. DISCOURSE ON THINKING. Translated by John M. Anderson and E. Hans Freund with an introduction by John M. Anderson, New York: Harper & Row, 1966.

———. HOLZWEGE. 2nd edition, Frankfurt: Klostermann, 1952.

———. THE QUESTION OF BEING. Translated and introduced by William Kluback and Jean T. Wilde, New York: Twayne Publishers, Inc., 1958.

Husserl, Edmund. CARTESIAN MEDITATIONS: AN INTRODUCTION TO PHENOMENOLOGY. Translated by Dorion Cairns, The Hague: Martinus Nijhoff, 1960.

———. IDEAS, GENERAL INTRODUCTION TO PURE PHENOMENOLOGY. Translated by W. R. Boyce Gibson, New York: Collier Books, 1962.

———. THE PHENOMENOLOGY OF INTERNAL TIME CONSCIOUSNESS. Edited by M. Heidegger and translated by James S. Churchill with introduction by Calvin O. Schrag, Bloomington: Indiana University Press, 1964.

James, William. PRAGMATISM, A NEW NAME FOR SOME OLD WAYS OF THINKING, FOUR RELATED ESSAYS FROM THE MEANING OF TRUTH. London: Longmans, Green and Company, 1946.

Jonas, Hans. THE GNOSTIC RELIGION. Boston: Beacon Press, 1963.

———. THE PHENOMENON OF LIFE. New York: Harper & Row, Publishers, 1966.

Jüngel, Eberhard. GOTTES SEIN IST IM WERDEN, VERANTWORTLICHE REDE VON SEIN GOTTES BEI KARL BARTH. Tübingen: J. C. B. Mohr, Paul Siebeck, 1965.

Kegley, Charles W. and Robert W. Bretall (eds.). THE THEOLOGY OF PAUL TILLICH. New York: The Macmillan Company, 1952.

Kierkegaard, Søren. CONCLUDING UNSCIENTIFIC POSTSCRIPT TO THE "PHILOSOPHICAL FRAGMENTS." Translated by David F. Swenson, completed and edited by Walter Lowrie, Princeton: Princeton University Press, 1941.

———. FOR SELF-EXAMINATION AND JUDGE FOR YOURSELVES! Translated by Walter Lowrie, Princeton: Princeton University Press, 1944.

———. THREE DISCOURSES. Translated by Walter Lowrie, except the final discourse, "God's Unchangeableness," translated by David F. Swenson, Princeton: Princeton University Press, 1941.

Leonard, Henry S. "Two-Valued Truth Tables for Modal Functions," STRUCTURE, METHOD, AND MEANING: ESSAYS IN HONOR OF HENRY M. SHEFFER. Edited by P. Henle, New York: Liberal Arts Press, 1951.

Lossky, N. O. HISTORY OF RUSSIAN PHILOSOPHY. New York: International Universities Press, Inc., 1951.

McLuhan, Marshall. UNDERSTANDING MEDIA. New York: McGraw Hill Book Company, 1964.

Ogden, Schubert M. THE REALITY OF GOD. New York: Harper & Row, 1966.

Otto, Rudolf. IDEA OF THE HOLY. Translated by John W. Harvey, New York: Oxford University Press, 1958.

Pollard, William. CHANCE AND PROVIDENCE. New York: Charles Scribner's Sons, 1958.

Rauschenbusch, Walter. CHRISTIANIZING THE SOCIAL ORDER. New York: The Macmillan Company, 1962.

Richardson, William J. HEIDEGGER THROUGH PHENOMENOLOGY TO THOUGHT. The Hague: Martinus Nijhoff, 1963.

Rome, Sydney and Beatrice (eds.). "Interrogation of Jean Wahl Conducted by Newton P. Stallknecht," PHILOSOPHICAL INTERROGATIONS. New York: Holt, Rinehart and Winston, 1964.

Rubenstein, Richard L. AFTER AUSCHWITZ: RADICAL THEOLOGY AND CONTEMPORARY JUDAISM. New York and Indianapolis: Bobbs-Merrill Company, 1966.

Sartre, Jean-Paul. BEING AND NOTHINGNESS. New York: Philosophical Library, 1956.

Schleiermacher, Friedrich. THE CHRISTIAN FAITH. Edited by H. R. Mackintosh and J. S. Stewart, Edinburg; T. and T. Clark, 1960.

Schmidt, Heinrich. PHILOSOPHISCHES WÖRTERBUCH. New York: Mary S. Rosenburg, 1945.

Schütz, Alfred. COLLECTED PAPERS; I, THE PROBLEM OF SOCIAL REALITY. Edited and introduced by Maurice Natanson, The Hague: Martinus Nijhoff, 1962.

Schweitzer, Albert. THE QUEST OF THE HISTORICAL JESUS. Translated by W. Montgomery, New York: The Macmillan Company, 1961.

Tillich, Paul. SYSTEMATIC THEOLOGY. Chicago: The University of Chicago Press, I-III, 1950-1963.

Vycinas, Vincent. EARTH AND GODS. The Hague: Martinus Nijhoff, 1961.

Welch, E. Paul. THE PHILOSOPHY OF EDMUND HUSSERL: THE ORIGIN AND DEVELOPMENT OF HIS PHENOMENOLOGY. New York: Columbia University Press, 1941.

Wells, Rulon. "Peirce as an American," PERSPECTIVES ON PEIRCE.

Edited by Richard J. Bernstein, New Haven: Yale University Press, 1965.

Whitehead, Alfred North. PROCESS AND REALITY: AN ESSAY IN COSMOLOGY. New York: Harper and Brothers, 1960.

————. THE CONCEPT OF NATURE. Ann Arbor: The University of Michigan Press, 1959.

Wolfson, Harry Austryn. THE PHILOSOPHY OF THE CHURCH FATHERS: FAITH, TRINITY, INCARNATION. Cambridge, Massachusetts: Harvard University Press, Volume I, 1956.

Articles and Essays

Brentano, Franz. "The Distinction Between Mental and Physical Phenomena," translated by D. B. Terrell, REALISM AND THE BACKGROUND OF PHENOMENOLOGY. Edited by Roderick M. Chisholm, Glencoe, Illinois: The Free Press, 1960.

Bultmann, Rudolf. "New Testament and Mythology," KERYGMA AND MYTH. Edited by H. W. Bartsch, translated by Reginald H. Fuller, New York: Harper and Brothers, 1961.

Cairns, Dorion. "Phenomenology," in A HISTORY OF PHILOSOPHICAL SYSTEMS. Edited by Vergilius Ferm, New York: The Philosophical Library, 1950.

Cobb, John B., Jr. " 'Perfection Exists': A Critique of Charles Hartshorne," RELIGION IN LIFE, Spring, 1963.

Hartt, Julian. "The Logic of Perfection," REVIEW OF METAPHYSICS, XVI, No. 4 (June, 1963).

Hopper, Stanley Romaine. "On the Naming of the Gods in Hölderlin and Rilke," CHRISTIANITY AND THE EXISTENTIALISTS. Edited by Carl Michalson, New York: Charles Scribner's Sons, 1956.

Michalson, Carl. "Theology as Ontology and History," NEW FRONTIERS IN THEOLOGY, Volume I, THE LATER HEIDEGGER AND THEOLOGY. Edited by James M. Robinson and John B. Cobb, Jr., New York: Harper & Row Publishers, 1963.

Ogden, Schubert M. "Bultmann's Demythologizing and Hartshorne's Dipolar Theism," ESSAYS IN HONOR OF CHARLES HARTSHORNE. Edited by William L. Reese and Eugene Freeman, LaSalle, Illinois: The Open Court Publishing Company, 1962.

————. "What Sense Does It Make to Say, 'God Acts in History'?" THE JOURNAL OF RELIGION, XLIII (1963).

Peirce, Charles Sanders. "How to Make Our Ideas Clear," POPULAR SCIENCE MONTHLY, January, 1878.

————. "The Fixation of Belief," POPULAR SCIENCE MONTHLY, November, 1877.

Platt, David. "Some Perplexities Concerning God's Existence,"
    JOURNAL OF BIBLE AND RELIGION, XXXIV, No. 3 (July, 1966).
Wieman, Henry Nelson. "Reply to My Critics," RELIGION IN LIFE,
    Summer, 1963.
Wild, John. "An English Version of Martin Heidegger's BEING AND
    TIME," THE REVIEW OF METAPHYSICS, XVI, No. 2, Issue No. 62
    (December, 1962).

Index

INDEX

Four Related Essays from the Meaning of Truth (James), 32n
"Freedom, Individuality, and Beauty in Nature" (Hartshorne), 164n
Freiburg University, xvi
Fulbright Lectures, xvi

Garnett, A. Campbell, 162n
Geist, xxv, 4, 7, 8, 13, 19, 95n, 173
Gelassenheit, see Discourses on Thinking
Gilson, Etienne, 91n
Gnosticism, 184-185
Gnostic Religion, The (Jonas), 184n
God, ontological argument for the existence of, 20, 48n, 83, 84, 97, 99, 103-106, 124, 144-145, 148, 167, 173, 184; *see also* Death-of-God theology
"God and Man Not Rivals" (Hartshorne), 184
"God's Unchangeableness" (Kierkegaard), xxiin
Goethe University, xvi
Gogarten, Friedrich, 174
Gollwitzer, Helmut, 94, 95, 96, 111
Gospel of Christian Atheism, The (Altizer), xxiin
Gottes Sein ist im Werden, Verantwortliche Rede von Sein Gottes bei Karl Barth (Jüngel), 95n

Hamilton, William, xix-xxi, 84-86, 174, 185
"Harmony in Life and Nature" (Hartshorne), 47
Hartshorne, Charles: and brotherhood, 179-180; and classical theism, 83-106, 107-126 *passim*, 173, 185; and confessional witness, 178-179; and consub-

Hartshorne, Charles—Cont.
stantiality, 158; and divine relativity, 115, 121, 177; and the Gospels, 100, 162; and humanism, 25, 29; and the Old Testament, 100; and the ontological argument, *see* God, ontological argument for the existence of; and philosophy, 34, 36, 42, 57, 59, 171-191; and prayer, 134, 138-139, 141, 148; and rationalism, 98; *see also* Christology; Death-of-God theology
"Hartshorne to Ebbinghaus on the Ontological Argument" (Hartshorne), 102n
Hartshorne Festschrift, Process and Divinity, The (ed. Reese and Freeman), xxviiin, 50n
Hartt, Julian, 103-104
"Harvard Law of Indeterminacy," 53
Harvard Theological Review, 187n
Harvard University, xvi, 31
Harvey, Van A., 137n
Haverford College, xvi
Hegel, Georg Wilhelm Friedrich, xxii, xxiv-xxvii, 4, 19, 48, 89, 95
Hegel's Phenomenology: Dialogues on the Life of Mind (Loewenberg), xxv
Heidegger, Martin, 7, 7n, 17-29, 41, 44, 47n, 54, 57, 78, 115, 116, 128-129, 146, 186, 188, 189
Heidegger Through Phenomenology to Thought (Richardson), 24n, 27
Herberg, Will, 190
Hermeneutical circle, 139, 139n
Hibbert Journal, The, 65n
Historian and the Believer: The Morality of Historical Knowledge and Christian Belief, The (Harvey), 137n

Lossky, N.O., 157, 158
Lovell, Sir Bernard, xv
Luijpen, William A., 4n

McLuhan, Marshall, xvi, xxiii, 15, 172, 175, 176
Macquarrie, John, 21n
Malebranche, Nicolas, 99
"Man's Fragmentariness" (Hartshorne), 165n
Man's Vision of God and the Logic of Theism (Hartshorne), 62, 63, 66, 66n, 87, 88, 120, 122, 132, 133, 136, 140, 141, 160
Marburg University, xvi
Marcuse, Herbert, 172
Martin Buber (ed. Schilpp and Friedman), 114n
"Martin Buber's Metaphysics" (Hartshorne), 114n
Marxism, xxvi
Mathematische Existenz (Becker), 17n
Meaning and Necessity (Carnap), 100n
"Meonic freedom," 183
"Metaphysical Statements as Non-restrictive and Existential" (Hartshorne), 71, 119n
"Metaphysics for Positivists" (Hartshorne), 182n
Metaphysik als strenge Wissenschaft (Scholz), 61
"Method of Imaginative Variation, The" (Hartshorne), 9, 9n, 10n
Michalson, Carl, 139n
Modes of Thought (Whitehead), 120n
Monist, The, 34n, 75n
"Monistic Theory of Expression, The" (Hartshorne), 185
"Monotony Threshold in Singing Birds, The" (Hartshorne), 164n
Moore, George Edward, 39

Müller, Max, 25, 26
"Musical Values in Australian Bird Songs" (Hartshorne), 164n

Nature of Thought, The (Blanshard), 78n
New Frontiers in Theology: The Later Heidegger and Theology (ed. Robinson and Cobb), 139n
New Frontiers in Theology: The New Hermeneutic (ed. Robinson and Cobb), 138n
New Scholasticism, The, 66n
New School for Social Research, xvi
"New Testament and Mythology" (Bultmann), 118n
Nicaea, Council of, 96
Niebuhr, Reinhold, 162, 162n
Nietzsche, Friedrich, xix
"Notes Concerning Husserl" (Hartshorne), 9n

Oeuvres de Descartes (ed. Adam and Tannery), 74n
Ogden, Schubert M., 85, 96, 127-129, 133n, 146, 153n, 174, 181
"On the Naming of the Gods in Hölderlin and Rilke" (Hopper), 26n
Ontological argument (for the existence of God), see God, ontological argument . . .
Oriental Mysticism and Biblical Eschatology (Altizer), xxvii
Oriole, The, 164n
Ornithological writings of Hartshorne, 164, 164n, 165
Otto, Rudolf, 190

Panentheism (surrelativism), 85, 85n-86n, 90, 103, 134, 138, 150, 169, 175
Panpsychism, 39